WAR WOUNDS

WAR WOUNDS

Korea 1952

ZAKARY SCOTT

To order additional copies of this book, contact:
Xlibris
1-888-795-4274
www.Xlibris.com
Orders@Xlibris.com
619736

ACKNOWLEDGEMENTS

I want to thank my wife for her untiring efforts for over more than thirty years it has taken us to dredge out the events, compose, write, and edit. I am not a good writer and have needed a lot of help.

Also my heart felt thanks go out to family members and many friends who listened to the stories and for their encouragement. There have been many who have helped with my writing efforts.

I sincerely thank you all.

Zak

ABOUT THE TIME AND PLACE

In order to stop World War Two President Truman authorized the use of the Atomic Bomb on Japan which may have caused him to be somewhat reluctant to aid South Korea in a continuing all out manner. North Korea was Communist so Russia was on their side and expressed their displeasure of our actions to support the South Koreans. General MacArthur had us up on the Yalu River and in the western mountains. That is when the Chinese crossed the Yalu River with full force. Also being Communist they had the full aid of Russia who provided ample aircraft, advisors and supplies. The Cold War was created due to the massive bombs and their worldwide delivery capabilities.

Russia threatened our homeland with their intercontinental missiles. Congress and the press reacted to that threat by creating a frenzy causing many US citizens to build bomb shelters under their homes and creating a counter missile defense system along the northern border and other places. That ICBM system remains in operation.

Truman fired McArthur and made us defend the 38 parallel's general boundary. Also he ordered the news to hush our involvement and called it a "mere police action."

Korea 1952-53 was a lot like World War One. We were in a trench and holding a line. The air was full of bursting shells and flying debris. It was a test of determination and resolve on both sides.

We Americans are still there to protect South Korea. Occasionally fighting still occurs, but we don't hear about that.

PREFACE

———◈———

This book is written to answer my wife's question, "What happened over there?" It is for people who have never been close to war or war like circumstances, or the military. For that reason acronyms are avoided and the time is in civilian hours. It is to provide some idea of what one unimportant person experienced.

All names and descriptions have been made up so not to resemble anyone living or dead, that I know of. It has to be fictionalized because most all conversation has been made up to fit my memories.

Zak

A NAVY CORPSMAN'S PRAYER

Grant me, oh Lord, for the coming events,
enough knowledge to cope and some plain common sense.
Be at our side on those nightly patrols,
and be merciful when judging our souls.
Make my hands be steady, and sure like a rock
when others go down with a wound or fall in shock.
With courage and purpose I tend to my flock.
Here with the enemy near,
there is no comfort around, no lightness nor cheer.
Just help me, oh Lord, save lives when I can,
If it's Your will, make casualties light,
and don't take me with you this murderous night.
Lord, I'm no hero. - - My job is to heal.
Vulnerable and nervous, I need focus to heal.
Divinely You see just how helpless I feel.
Lord protect us, hopefully we are part of your plan.
We must carry on.
Amen!

Author Unknown
Edit by Zakary Scott

CONTENTS

Chapter One

<hr>

BOARDING SHIP

A huge seagoing tug had towed our disabled troop ship for three days into our first Japanese port. The water was boiling and churning aft as it made a sharp turn to approach our port side to push us into a berthing. As its bow fender pressed into our ship, black smoke billowed out of its stack swirling into howling wind and driving snow.

I was standing by a port railing watching. A loud speaker near by crackled, snapped, and popped, then blared, "Seaman Zakary Scott, report to the Quarter Deck immediately."

That's me! That's just on the other side of this ship. I threaded my way through the crowd.

The Officer of the Day asked, "Are you Scott?"

"Yes sir."

"Good. You are in charge of getting all Navy personnel to the Naval Base." He presented several bags of papers saying, "Here are all their orders."

I stepped back off the passageway and took a quick look. They were not in any order! I had joined the Navy Reserve well over a year before entering Boot Camp where I was class Adjutant. I had to take charge of my boot camp class because our appointed Chief had a heart attack on our third day. That gave me seniority and leadership ahead of the other recruits on board. *Perhaps that was the reason for this honor.*

While the troop ship was being moored I went down to the mess hall out of the blowing snow to sort the orders out. A few sailors standing by came forward to help. We made piles on several tables according to destination, alphabetized and then counted them. After we finished I asked for the ship's loudspeaker to make an announcement, "All Navy personnel now hear this. This is Seaman Scott. I have just been put in charge of getting us to the Naval Base. Your orders are now available in the mess hall."

We sailors remained in the galley while the Army troops disembarked. The Army troops had buses and personnel waiting and promptly departed.

Earlier today an announcement had been made that buses would be at dockside for all disembarking personnel. We shouldered our sea bags and disembarked. We found that there were no buses waiting for us. Another snow squall had just started. It was very cold and blustery. I went to speak to the Officer of the Deck; "There are no buses for us. What has happened to our transportation?"

"A messenger has been sent to the base to get your buses. They should be here in a few hours."

I became quite agitated, "In a few hours! You expect us to stand out there in this snow and wind for two or more hours?"

"You have disembarked and you all have pea coats"

Earnestly I said, "Sir! That order needs to be countermanded. We need to be out of the cold in the mess hall, pea coats or not! There is no telling how long it will take to get our transportation!"

"I'll ask the Captain." He rang the bridge.

The Officer of the Deck told me, "The Captain said that you may use the mess hall and restrooms, and that is all." Japanese workmen were boarding and were scurrying about.

"Thank you sir."

From across the bay an aircraft carrier sounded one long blast of her horn. *Does that signal mean she was in reverse and departing?* A signal light was flashing a message in Morse code in our direction. One of the guys from my boot camp class said, "Skipper, that ship is leaving in ninety minutes."

I had a great feeling of uncertainty. We had been warned about missing a ship's movement and of its dire consequences. *Was that message directed at us or not? I better act on it.*

"Mate, stand by one minute."

I again went back to the Officer of the Deck and asked, "Was that message directed at us? Was that from one of our ships? One of our guys said a message flash indicated we had ninety minutes."

He rang the troopship bridge. The Officer of the Deck said, "Yes we just got a flash message and that carrier is a destination for some of you and it leaves in ninety minutes."

Maybe we can march there?

I asked the Officer of the Deck, "How far is it to the base?"

"I don't really know. It's on the other side of the bay, at least eight or ten miles, maybe more. See that carrier way over there? That's the one that flashed us a message. The bay goes about three miles to the other side of her and the road goes around further."

We are not marching!

"Mate, that was our ship. Can you send a message telling them who we are, and that we have no transportation? Ask what should we do."

"Aye." He went up to the bridge to use their signaling light, "There is no juice, nothing's working!"

Okay, the ships electricity has not yet been fixed or attached, along with the water and the engines problems that have been going on for weeks. Now this could make us later yet! I looked at my watch. *It is one thirty.*

"Mate, do they have a flashlight?"

"Yeah, they have one!" He used it to send the message in Morse code.

While he was doing that I saw four Japanese trucks off loading a variety of equipment and lines used to supply the troop ship with electricity, telephone, water and sewerage. *They look like they are and were having problems with the fittings and the hookups.*

I went over to a truck driver, "Can you good fellows take some of us to the base gate when you are finished unloading?"

"Ah. No speakee."

I said, "Navy Base." and pointed in that direction. That still did not communicate. I pointed to my group of about a hundred men, to their truck and then toward the base. "Over there." I held up the orders and pointed out the words that said Navy Depot. Almost, but they did not quite understand what I was trying to tell them.

"Ah, - so sorry."

Just then I saw a jeep with two Military Policemen driving by with its radio antenna waving in the wind. I hollered, "Mates we need a loud whistle! We need those military policemen!"

One of our guys put fingers in his mouth and let out a good strong whistle. A second guy did the same thing sounding a higher shriller, louder, longer note.

"Thank you." Then I got in the open and started waving my arms overhead with my orders in hand. Some of our other guys waved too.

They drove over to us. They were US Marines, a sergeant and a corporal.

I blurted out, "Our ship is leaving in ninety minutes and the promised buses are not here. We'll surely miss the ship. Can we get those trucks to take us to base? They don't speak any English."

The Sergeant had a radio in the Jeep and called the base to get advice about our situation.

The base said that it would take well over an hour for the buses to get over to us. Drivers would have to be summoned to pick us up and bring us back to the ship. It would take too long and we would miss the ship and they confirmed that our ship was departing in an hour and a half.

The Corporal who was driving knew of a shore patrolman who spoke Japanese. He used his radio to call him. He was not far away and agreed to translate for us.

One of the Japanese trucks was leaving. I stepped out in front of it and held my hands up. Some of the sailors came over and did the same. The truck drivers nodded and said something to each other. We continued to stand in front of the trucks. Each truck could hold ten or twelve of us with our bags. We needed all four.

The shore patrolman arrived in a few minutes, got the facts, and then he spoke to the truck drivers. He was able to convince them to take us over to the Navy Base for a fee. The driver's heads were nodding up and down and they were smiling. The Marines were talking to the Base on their radio.

I asked two guys from Boot Camp who had also been Adjutants to form up the guys who were going aboard the carrier into alphabetical order and to count them off into groups of ten. They had done that often in boot camp.

I had to shout over the wind to the sailors who were not going aboard the departing ship, "The Base Command knows of this situation and transportation will be here as soon as possible, probably in an hour or so. Go back aboard and stay in the mess hall. You can use the head but do not go any further."

I told the guys going to the carrier, "We need to get all the remaining supplies off those trucks to keep that stuff from sliding around and injuring us." After that was done forty-three sailors clambered aboard the four trucks with their sea bags. A Navy Shore Patrol jeep was in the lead and a second followed so none of us would be driven off to some other place or held for ransom. *We have a convoy!*

We arrived at the Base several minutes before three, which was the departure time. We were promptly passed through the main gate then escorted up to the ship's aft gangway. While boarding each sailor saluted the flag and then requested permission to board from the Officer of the Deck. Each arriving sailor had both his sea bag and orders in hand. I called out to our guys, "Form up!"

There was a Lieutenant pacing the deck nearby. I approached, saluted and said, "Sir, forty-three recruits have boarded and are in alphabetical order."

"Very good. The processing tables are right there. You are first." He pointed to three tables with Yeomen from personnel, each with a bunch of forms and two chairs.

A Yeoman took my orders and asked in an interestingly way, "Would you like to sign up for some parties?"

Parties sounded very enjoyable to me. "Why, yes I would."

"We have a landing party."

Hmm, a party ashore that would be nice. "That sounds like fun."

He promptly pushed the form in front of me and gave me an ink pen saying, "Sign right here." I signed the paper.

The Yeoman continued, "We have a painting party."

"What kind of painting? Is it oil or water?" There was some giggling from some sailors standing a few yards aft of the tables.

The Lieutenant standing nearby asked, "Sailor, what do you know about these parties?"

Looking puzzled I answered, "They are social?"

"No, they are working parties." I turned red. I had been duped!

To the Yeoman the Lieutenant said, "Easy Boxer. They can volunteer for parties after they are assigned a division. Let's get this line moving."

I was stuck with the Landing Party as I had signed the chit. When I turned to talk to the Lieutenant that Yeoman wrote a few more words on that chit which he promptly turned over. He had a smirk in his face. He told me, "Scott, your assignment is to Aviation Gas. Go over to that guy wearing a yellow cloth deck helmet." Five of us were assigned to that division. Later we would be given purple cotton cloth deck helmets. That guy with the yellow cloth helmet led us to our berthing place, assigned us a rack and a shiny metal locker nearby. There were other guys in the berthing compartment. They gave us quite a good looking over. Feeling self-conscious I looked at my uniform to see if there was something on it. There was nothing on it, nor was there anything wrong with it.

I put my sea bag on my bunk. I could stow it later. It would only take minutes as everything was in a certain order and could easily be placed in its proper place. I climbed up to the hanger deck and over to the port side. Our ship was moving away from the mooring place. The gangway was swinging from a crane as it moved back from the boarding platform.

I was having a 'de ja vu,' a premonition. I felt that I had been here, heard this, and seen all this before. It had started to snow again. I was wondering how the other groups of sailors had fared. I saw two gray navy buses going down a road.

A Commander came up behind me, surprising me. He had a kindly deportment, his cap cocked slightly to the left. We saluted. He said,

"Are you Scott?"

"Yes sir."

"I'm Commander Baker, ship's Executive Officer."

"Aye sir." We briefly shook hands.

"Are you looking after your shipmates?"

"Yes sir." I felt embarrassed and may have turned red or something.

"Your shipmates are in those gray buses en route to barracks located behind the Base Hospital which is that large white building over there." He pointed it out.

"Thank you, sir."

We each turned to go on our way.

The sun was setting. It shone on several layers of clouds with holes of various sizes and shapes. They were churning in the cloud cover creating various hues, most with a golden glow. The evening air was cold. Large flakes of snow were starting to float down.

I returned to my berthing quarters. A little later another petty officer took all five of us new guys on a short tour of the ship pointing out the off limit places, the ship's store, and the evening chow line which was now being served. We were early to get in that line.

Chapter Two

---❖---

TRAINING AT SEA

The next morning promptly at eight o'clock there was a daylong training session for all new flight deck crewmen. We were introduced to the handling of several kinds of aircraft and instructed in every detail on what was going on and how it was done. That way every possible event could be adequately and safely handled. Also we would be better able to help other divisions when needed. We were guaranteed that there would be a wide variety of emergencies. It also included a discussion about what would happen when the controls were moved.

The following day in my division we learned about the many details of fueling aircraft, stow the gas hoses and the location of both pump rooms. Also we learned how to make napalm bombs. We were told that we would be trained in emergency drain and purge procedures at a later time, one trainee at a time as there was little additional space in those rooms.

Our ship plied up and down the Eastern Korean coastline occasionally firing its cannons at targets ashore up north. A few days later the ship was firing well up the North Korean coast. One forward outboard cannon was holding a misfired shell. As the ship started a turn into the wind, I failed to hear an announcement to secure operations forward on the flight deck. I was on the edge of the flight deck working just a little forward of that turret, bent over coiling a fuel hose into a flip open locker just under the catwalk. Not hearing anything I continued to coil the hose line. The turret moved into its standard position pointing forward. As the forward turret jerked to a stop the round fired.

The tilt of the ship and the gun's concussion ring picked me up off the deck. I was being forced overboard. I held onto the gas hose as I flew overboard. The hose drew out of its storage well, greatly slowing my descent. I hung tightly onto the hose and was able to shinny up the gas hose. The nozzle jerked backward as it hit a swell. I had climbed well above the waves. I could become totally immersed in a wave and swept away. I heard a yell, "Hang on! We're hauling you up!"

Once back aboard I was taken to sickbay where they made me lay with my head blocked between two large pillows. I had a concussion.

Commander Baker paid me a visit. This time I got a good scolding for not securing as ordered in the announcement. He growled, "Didn't you hear the command over the loudspeaker to secure forward?"

Meekly I said, "No Sir. I did not hear any announcement."

He ordered someone standing at his elbow, "Check those speakers, right now." He continued, "Don't you know a large swell could have swept you off and pulled you right under the ship and into the props? They would have chopped you into little pieces!" Louder, and sharply "I could have you court marshaled for disobeying orders! You endangered the ship!"

"Yes Sir. That is why I was climbing up the hose."

"You will be hearing more about this!" He turned abruptly and stalked out.

Later Commander Baker returned in a more congenial manner, "I want to thank you for informing me about those speakers forward on the starboard side. We checked them and found that they were corroded and none were operative. They are being replaced." With that he departed.

Chapter Three

❖

INTERVIEW

A new volunteer personnel program for those who had served less than a year was launched aboard ship. The Navy was interested in its personnel being in a place of their interest and thus being more willing and able to be of a service to the Navy. First we all took a vocational interest test and stated our career wish. They took us in alphabetical order. So, by being interviewed later I had some time to hear what the others had to say about their interviews. Most were rather long. The interviewers seemed not to be in any hurry. They encouraged us to talk about ourselves.

This was a very good idea. I wondered if I could get into flight training. I would spend hours thinking of how I would tell them of my life long dream and desire to fly. *Surely they would understand such a sincere and burning desire!*

My turn came on a cool blustery morning. I was refueling a replacement Panther jet for one that was grounded. This plane was due to depart in a few minutes. Panther jets have their main tanks on both wing tips. Someone came up to the plane and shouted that personnel wanted to talk to me. I was to go to a certain room. He wanted me to come down right then. There were no other gas guys around to relieve me. The guy had promptly departed saying something about how cold and windy it was. I waved my agreement and continued refueling the jet. I was wondering what it was all about, probably something concerning that inquiry about our interests.

I went down to the room he mentioned. It didn't seem like I was in the correct place. It was in officers' country and was off limits to the crew. I decided to go to personnel to check on my information. Sure enough I had the correct room. It was not far away. There were four men in the room waiting. One was the ship's Executive Officer Commander Baker, the one I had spoken to before.

"Is this the correct room?"

Chief Dryer, who had two crossed pens on his sleeve's rank patch growled, "It is. Why didn't you follow the page we sent up to tell you that we are waiting for you?"

"I was ordered to refuel that jet as quickly as possible as it was a stand in. I was halfway finished when he hollered up to me. The page could have waited for me inside the hatch. He walked off complaining about the cold and the wind. I think refueling that replacement jet should come first."

Commander Baker replied, "It certainly does. Have a seat Scott."

He introduced me to the other panel members consisting of Dr. Gold and Marine Captain Mower who promptly asked; "We see that you were admonished for swimming and diving at a closed pool in Honolulu in your records. Can you tell us about that?"

"They have a huge ocean fed pool in Honolulu, Hawaii. There were no signs, ropes or any other indication that it was closed. In fact there was a table with towels, so I swam a few laps and did some high platform diving practice. Two officers of the Honolulu Police watched my diving for about ten minutes. They gave me applause but took me for a ride to their station where I was questioned. Then they took me back to my troop ship where I was told that this would appear in my personnel record.

"When did you start to swim?"

"I can't remember when I didn't swim."

"Have you done any competitive swimming?"

"I entered a Fourth of July swim every year."

"How far was that?"

"Five miles. We had to swim a mile out around a buoy, then down around a boat anchored half a mile off the beach.

"How old were you when you started that?"

"Thirteen." He nodded and seemed to be satisfied.

Dr. Gold asked, "I see that you have a reference about First Aid training in your record. Tell me about that."

"I had three merit badges to earn for my Eagle Scout badge. I had to do first aid, public service and public speaking. A neighbor, a Red Cross nurse, helped me with those projects. She used me to demonstrate artificial respiration and to assist teaching several of the classes."

"Was there any intimacy between you two?"

"The relationship was very platonic to start with because I was under age. That changed a while after I turned sixteen." He nodded that he was satisfied.

Captain Mower asked, "What academic grades did you earn and on what point scale?"

"My average was three on a four point scale."

"Were you active in any extra school activities?"

"I played a Sousaphone in the band and in the spring I ran middle distance in track. I always had an after school job and on week ends so I missed many events."

Chief Dryer asked, "How are you getting along with your shipmates in your division?"

"They seem to be an odd lot. I become quite uncomfortable when they stare at me in the shower."

"What do you do when they stare you?"

"Turn my back, and then remove myself as soon as possible."

"Would you like a transfer?"

"Yes I would!"

"Where to?"

I beamed and said, "The Navy Flight School in Pensacola!" *Yeah! I did it! I got a chance to ask and I did.* I was glowing with interest and enthusiasm.

Commander Baker was smiling as he asked, "Have you ever flown?"

"No Sir."

"Well, perhaps we can get you in the air. You may be interested in a volunteer program for swimmers. We send volunteers out on helicopters and lower them to the water to get downed airmen into slings. The pilots are then hoisted up into the helicopter for transport back to ship or to shore if they are wounded. The swimmer then paddles a life raft to shore or swims and we pick them up and bring them back. Would you be interested?"

"Yes Sir! That sounds like something I can do. I also trained as a life guard with the Red Cross."

"Excellent!" Chief Dryer had the form. He filled it out and I signed it.

Commander Baker then asked, "Are there any further questions? Hearing none, we stand adjourned." Commander Baker was smiling. He held out his hand, as did the others.

Wow, I will get to fly and swim!

Chapter Four

LANDING PARTY

The fleet was preparing to turn into the wind to launch and receive aircraft. We were standing outside our sea crew room portside in a former anti-aircraft gun tub just below the flight deck. A stocky Chief Petty Officer stomped up the short ladder, his cap pulled rather low over his forehead. He held a paper in his hand. Loudly he announced, "I need to speak to Scott!"

"I'm over here." I raised my hand.

He took a few stomps toward me and without lowering his voice, "I'm Cutter from X division, Captain Mower, our Marine Corps Officer needs to speak to you."

"What's this about?"

He held out the paper and said. "You volunteered for the Landing Party when you came aboard. Your service is needed now. Follow me, and that is an order!" He turned and tramped up the ladder to the flight deck where he stopped and waited for me.

I was wearing a foul weather jacket and a purple cloth helmet, which I removed and gave to a friend to put in our sea cabin. I then scrambled up the short ladder to the Flight Deck to follow. My gas crewmates in the gun tub were laughing about my being called for the 'Landing Party.'

The interview with Marine Captain Mower was rather brief. They needed a temporary medic as theirs had transferred to the school for Frogmen, our Underwater Demolition Team. I was still attached to the gas crew but would be called for when needed. They had a training exercise starting in an hour. The main reason was to determine if I could perform adequately in the field. They feared a fumbler. Chief Hospital Corpsman Smith from another ship would do the testing of my performance.

I was the same size as their former medic. The Marines quickly fitted me with full gear including a gray metal helmet with four large white patches, each with bright red crosses connected by a thin white line to mark the wearer as a navy noncombatant. As such the person wearing it was protected under the Geneva Convention. No one was supposed to shoot at the wearer. They also had given me their former corpsman's locker for my gear and his med bag. I was ushered back up to the flight deck to where the Marines had assembled.

Captain Mower started our briefing, "This morning we are holding a practice drill for the whole landing party in full gear." He went on to outline details of this exercise. The Marines were all in good spirits, as they liked to be doing this sort of thing. To me it seemed to be a bit on the serious side.

Our ship was close to land. From the flight deck we could make out some people on the beach, where the exercise was to start and it should not take over two hours to execute.

Sergeant Butcher led me into a chopper. Inside was a radioman, Paul. We promptly lifted off. The ship's Dragonfly made a lot of noise and was rather shaky.

Butcher put his big heavy arm around my neck and held me bent over below the window. We each had one knee on the deck football style. He had to speak loud over the noise and into my ear. He said, "Medics are first out, that way you are the least likely to be shot. Spring straight out, keep your arms out and head up when the door opens. Expect soft wet grass or mud, it has been raining."

"Aye."

The chopper's crewman announced, "Stand by to land." The chopper landed with a thump. Butcher jerked the door open and bellowed, "Go!"

I sprang straight out. I landed as instructed, arms out, face forward, and head up. My landing was not on a soft wet grassy or a muddy field.

It was on the wood of our flight deck! Marines and flight deck crew surrounded me. The starboard tower was filled with observers. Captain Mower was the first to greet me with a wide grin, a handshake and a pat on the back. It took a few minutes for the flight deck to clear so we could fly off to the practice. This time my head was up and I could see out the window.

Chief Smith was ashore waiting for our helicopter to land. "This exercise will take a few hours. You will have a dozen or more guys to patch up. It depends on how well you do. We don't need a screw up."

The first guy looked like a burned person. Chief Smith said, "This is water. We will pretend it is morphine. Inject it."

"Do you really want me to give him an injection?"

"Do you want to pass? I need to see and know what you can do."

"I don't have any alcohol to wipe his arm with."

"I know that and you won't on the line either. We are not walking hospitals."

I gave the guy the shot like Nancy had taught me, as if I were giving a diabetic an emergency insulin shot. Chief told me, "Put lipstick on his forehead to note the injection with an M and the time it was administered on his forehead." I did that. Then I put him into a basket and onto the evacuation chopper. *That was a first.* Next I applied an improvised splint on a made-up broken leg. He was taken off on a stretcher. Then there was a pretend eye wound. On my elbows, I crawled to him, taped a wet 4×4 over the eye and evacuated him by getting a Marine to help him walk off. I did everything he wanted me to handle in this exercise and that was a great variety. My treatments were adequate, but the evacuation process was new to me. Chief Smith briefed me on those procedures. "We need to move all eye, nose and mouth injuries back to a hospital as soon as possible because the blood drains back close to the spinal column and there is a high risk of meningitis. They need immediate hospital care. Use choppers if possible, but they can't be everywhere."

"Aye."

Chapter Five

◆◇◆

ADRIFT

A seagoing tug was working its way into a South Korean harbor in heavy seas. A sailor on deck was at work winching a trailing barge up into a side tow so it could be maneuvered in the harbor. He was bashed by a swamping wave, forced off balance and unable to promptly push the emergency stop button. His leg was caught up in the winch as line was being taken up and his leg was severely cut before he was able to stop it.

Our carrier was within pickup and recovery distance for our helicopter to make the rescue. Aircraft carriers are like floating cities of more than three thousand men. It had complete facilities of every kind in every field. The Medical Department had a fully equipped operating room with surgeons and many other highly skilled medical personnel.

Our helicopter, a Dragonfly had four seats with two behind the pilot. They had to off load the swimmer in order to carry a corpsman and a patient in a wire stretcher to and from the accident. The trip there and back would likely take about an hour or a little longer.

The duty swimmer went into their sea cabin to wait for them. He had some time so he told another person in the cabin area, "I'm going to chow."

Our helicopter made a faster than expected round trip, as the patient was ready to transport. Our carrier was between launches and off loading the injured sailor went very fast. A messenger was sent to

31

the chow hall for the on duty swimmer. He was not found. A crew wide announcement was made but he failed to answer.

Commander Baker saw me refueling the helicopter. I could get one of the rides he had promised. He sent an officer to tell me to board the chopper and take the swimmer's place for a little while. I could do a standby flight and become acquainted with the equipment on board. After all I did sign up as a volunteer swimmer and this was a good time for an introduction. My crew boss was told where I was and what I was doing.

The copter crewman checked me out on the operation of the winch and harness. He pointed out the raft and told me how it would be used and that there was a patch kit inside in case it got a leak. There were signaling items tied up inside the now folded and stowed raft. We were instructed in boot camp on the use of all that equipment. The crewman put the swimmer's helmet on my head so I could hear the communications. I sat back and enjoyed the flight. *Wow, this is wonderful!*

The copter took its place between two carriers as several flights were approaching. They would be punching through a very thick dark overcast at about two thousand feet above the sea. It was delightful to watch them fly out of the clouds trailing some water vapor for a moment.

The headset came alive, a clear voice saying, "This is Fleet Command Mayday Relay, taxi five, take a heading of two, zero, eight at max."

The pilot replied on the radio, "This is taxi five, on two, zero, eight, at max."

The copter slanted hard forward and picked up speed rapidly to its maximum forward speed. Then he told me, "A plane is in trouble and that was an emergency message. We are on the way at maximum flying speed on a heading of two, zero, eight. Now you will get to use your newly acquired knowledge." The chopper pilot, Lt Gardner, was able to hone in on a radio bearing and fly in that direction. He pointed to an instrument on his panel then moved off center for a momentary demonstration, then back on it. I was able to see what he was doing.

"Thanks for that info and demo!"

The plane was going down a few miles from land. The pilot had held his mike open so the chopper pilot and others could get a direction bearing from it. Other ships in the convoy also picked up on the distress radio bearing. From those bearings the disabled plane's position was determined. Radar reflections were also noted and put on a chart and would guide us to that position. The crewman told me what I was to do as wet pilots weigh much more being heavily dressed and very cold and wet. The copter would not be able to carry me. I would get in the raft.

It took about nine or ten minutes for us to fly there. The pilot had stood up in the plane for the minute it was afloat. When it started to sink he jumped in the water, inflated his vest and paddled off far enough so not to be pulled under by its structure or sinking suction. Navy Pilots wore special foul weather gear to increase their cold-water survivability and had a light on their inflatable life vest.

I hit the water close by. He was conscious but getting rather cool and stiff when I helped him put the copter's harness on. I waved for the crewman to pull him up.

A life raft was pushed out of the chopper. It was being fully inflated as it floated down. We exchanged hand signals. The crewman pointed towards land, his hand waved that way several times. I pointed my hand understanding that way and waved good-bye.

My instructions were to paddle aggressively that direction and when ashore get to an open place on the beach for my pickup. My marker was to be the raft's yellow bottom. It was comforting to know that I would soon be picked up. Now all I had to do was get in the raft and paddle to shore. Survival time is about four or five minutes dressed in the lightweight working dungarees we wore on the flight deck in the early spring of the year.

I soon discovered it was no small task boarding that raft! There were no ladders or lines around the thing. The sides were round, hard, smooth and clear of any encumbrances except for a few small-attached line eyes that were empty of any line. I had to lift myself up and over its wet, fat and slippery side. The lowest end was about a foot or more out of the water!

I splashed and pulled up trying to get into the raft several times. I pulled hard on a line tied to a ring on the bow. I managed to flip it up and on top of me. It thumped me on the noggin.

Wow! I needed that!

I turned it over as quickly as possible by flipping the bowline over the bottom and pulling the bowline across one side. I planted my feet on one side and pulled on the line. Even by tugging on the wet slippery bowline I was not able to get far enough in. I did get my elbow up on the raft's side. I wished that the line around the raft had been there and threaded properly through their loops. That would have helped a lot. I had tried getting aboard from the front end. That didn't work at all. It was much too high. I turned the raft around and put a stopper knot about a third of the way up on the bowline. The aft end of the raft was a little lower. I sunk underwater. It was very cold down under the water. I kicked vigorously and with two arms over the end heaved hard on the slightly smaller end while still kicking. I shoved my head up and into the raft and pushed harder and got my chest up almost on top of it, still kicking my feet very fast. I was starting to panic. Franticly I pushed the raft down very hard, wiggled from side to side and pushed the raft down harder again and again and again. Finally I was more in than out and was barely able to wiggle over its edge and pull my legs in. I was gasping for air, cold, tired and shivering hard. That was very likely to have been my last effort. I was very afraid, but in the raft!

I forced myself to shut my mouth and breathe through my nose to prevent over ventilation. In a long minute I looked for any supply packages like a flashlight, a mirror, or a smoke flair. I found nothing. *Where was all that emergency stuff?* There was one paddle tied in it.

A quick look at the raft I wondered where the second person would fit in it. Considerable water had been shipped aboard. I bailed water out by splashing it out by hand, as it was making me colder sloshing around. I continued looking around. I had moved in circles while trying to get in. There was a small amount of foam from my kicking all around on the water to show that. *Now which way was I supposed to go?* From the chopper some twenty or thirty feet or so above the water land was barely visible. Here and now from the water land was hidden by very thick fog. There were very thick clouds above and there was only calm water, not even a few small ripples. There was absolutely no sound. As I looked around I felt doom flow through my shivering body. The clouds looked to be quite smooth, very dark and thick. A few minutes passed. I was shivering hard. I took off my shirt and wrung it out, then wiped myself off including my head and wrung it a second time. I wiped again only harder and wrung the shirt out. Then I sopped up the water in the raft and I wrung it out again, snapped it hard in the still air, and then put it on. I worked my arms and legs, wiggled my feet and rubbed my hands together to stir up circulation for a few minutes. It was a little help. I would do that constantly during the next hour. With intensity I looked around and listened while breathing through my mouth so not to interfere with my hearing, for whatever there was to hear. Perhaps a helicopter - - There was - - Nothing. - - Nothing at all. - - Silence. - - Total silence!

I sat shivering on the bottom of the raft. *I am getting wetter from the fog!*

It would be close to half an hour before the chopper would be back to look for me. It seemed like an hour had already passed, but it was probably only a few minutes.

I heard something. Water was softly lapping at its side. There was another faint sound. The sounds from the helicopter's rotor blades have a very distinct sound. I could scarcely hear that sound. The sound faded. In this fog visibility was very limited. I did not see the helicopter. *Hopefully they are looking for me. They may start an expanding square from the pickup point. Maybe they would first do a route search but then perhaps they are looking along the coast. Under perfect conditions, maybe I could have paddled that far. Will this thing go five knots? No! Perhaps two.*

The main current flow was known to generally be out of the northeast at an average of two knots and the breeze should be from the northeast. No breeze here.

I'm not enjoying this much!

Wet and cold out here alone I'm adrift, sitting on the soft flexible bottom of a raft. - - No provisions. - - No equipment. - - A feeling of dread crept all over me. - - I shook hard for several moments. *I'm so damn cold! - - Cold to the bone. No! My bones are also cold! Be accurate man, I am cold through the bone!*

"Okay!"

In civilian life I had worked for a while in an ice making plant. *That was a lot warmer than it is here and now!* I started to move in spite of my shivering. My panic was increasing.

Dying from cold was said to be pleasant and peaceful. *I am not. I am shivering cold! This is worse! Hey! Maybe I'm not dying! Not yet!*

I called out at the top of my voice, "Good Lord, please some - - some sun! I would hope you would want me to survive to do something that may please you. I should be able to be of some service, somehow, someplace, someday! I will try to do something. I need some help! I need it now. - Amen!"

The realization that I was about to die was fearsome. I prayed again, this time for forgiveness of my sins. "I'm so sorry that I am such a wretched incompetent person. You say fear not. I'm sorry, but I am very afraid. I have never been this afraid. I know I need to have faith." *Am I now too far gone? How much time do I have? Do I have only a minute, maybe two?* "I am so sorry that I have done so little. I do need to be better at everything! More energy is needed in everything I do!"

Minutes passed. The raft was drifting. I heard lapping at its side.

Get a grip! You are losing it. If you are going to talk to yourself you must first tell the world that you are talking to yourself! So now, I need to recognize that I am talking to myself by answering myself, as self. First I must start by saying self to myself.

"Hello self."

"Okay, self! I am now talking to myself and answering myself, acknowledging myself, as self."

"Hey self. There is too much of all this I, I, and I, stuff! There is also a me!"

"Okay, self. It's we. There is a me, myself, and I."

"Yeah. That is better."

I realized that I had survived another full minute, maybe two or three. Again I shook hard all over. It took a few minutes to calm down.

I moved my body more briskly. In a while my shivering slowed. *Is that good or bad? Don't you quit shivering just before you die?*

"Hey self, get your head in gear! Make do with what you have. Study the swells and the sky."

While fueling the helicopter I had looked at the clouds. The clouds were showing strong wind from the northeast. Darker clouds were north having a longer fetch of light filtration, if all other things such as drop size and temperature are equal. This is the northern hemisphere above the thirty eighth parallel so both wind and clouds should be moving from west to east with the general flow of wind which directs the flow of surface water and swells.

"Okay, self! So, let's face the lightest clouds. It is morning so then I will have my body facing north. Land will be left and ahead of the swell's motion." The sea is flat and clouds are also very flat and dark, where is there any difference? I can't tell any difference!

"Hey Self! I saw a second paddle falling out of this raft as it came out of the chopper."

"Yeah, I saw it too! It hit the water first."

"There was a second paddle! Thank you Lord! Thank you for the reminder!"

"So, where is that other paddle?" *It should be nearby if it floats. Try this one and see if it floats.*

"Place a hand under to grab if it doesn't."

"Okay."

"Okay." That paddle went in the water. "It floats!" I quickly grabbed it up. *The other paddle must be near by. I could have kicked it off in any direction during my boarding efforts.*

"Aye self, ya kicked the hell out of the water."

"Your first task is to start a paddle search."

"Aye. An expanding square."

"Aye." First look about!"

"Okay! I'm rubbing and moving all great body parts. Moving is not death." *So, paddle one stroke on that side, turn ninety degrees then another paddle stroke on the other side.*

"First look!"

"Okay!" I was shivering hard.

Now face ninety degrees by turning the head. Make one stroke. We are going to use the swell as a base of direction. Now, isn't that just so lovely. The swell is barely detectable.

"Hey self!" Hit the water with that paddle.

"Yeah!" That makes a ring in the water and some froth."

"That's good for a minute!" This is the second leg. I made two strokes. *Coast. - Look. - Nothing to be seen, but calm water. With the paddle stroke there is some movement aft of the raft showing on the water. Also the paddle makes a swirling motion that is good for a reference point.*

"Okay self! Let's go! Hang in there! We can do this!" Take two strokes on this leg with a ninety-degree turn. After those I need a ninety-degree turn to port. I need to paddle one additional stroke on this leg on the starboard side. "Hey, did we do that?" *I'm so numb I can't remember.*

"Look around. - - Nothing."

"Hey self! Did you actually see when you looked?" - - "Look again. Try to see while moving your various body parts. Hey, self are you confused?"

"So what if I am! I am doing something."

Now again turn to port ninety degrees, turn the head full left. Then do another leg by using the swirl of the water's motion as a turning point. Paddle again on the port side, do a second paddle on the other side to keep a straight line. Now do that again.

"Look!" - - Nothing but calm water.

"Okay. Turn this vessel to port ninety degrees." *This will start a longer leg.*

"Hey self! We are looking for a paddle." I made the strokes and coasted.

"Ahoy! Cast an eye three points off our starboard."

"Aye self, thar she be. - YAY!"

"Fish her out!"

"Aye! Now there are two paddles aboard this vessel!"

As loud as possible I hollered, "Thank you Lord! - - Thank you! I have done one thing! I can do more." I weep for joy. I prayed for a clear head, a small amount of wind from the northeast, His guidance, and patience, and a bit of sun. His lovely sun would feel so very good! Sun would stir the air and get rid of this fog.

Some time later, "Hello! I faintly hear a chopper's sound again. - It is - very faint." I was not able to determine a direction. Sound should carry well in this thick haze. It disappeared. - Silence.

It must have been from very far. I sat there for a few moments, and then realized that may have been the second search. Again I felt dread flow through my body. I needed to count on myself now.

"Well self, do something."

"Sure self. What?"

"What do we have? There is no equipment in this emergency vessel." *Make do!*

Sitting on the soft bottom I took off my shirt then ran the paddle poles through each of the sleeves. I removed my bootlaces and used one lace to tie the paddles together at the cross with grip up, paddle down. A bare foot could be placed against the paddle. The other paddle head I could use to steer with. My shirt was now a sail placed against the presently very soft breeze. Any air movement would dry both my skin and the shirt. I will be cold but not as cold as being in the water. I would be dead by now if I were in the water.

At this time there was a tiny amount of current flow around the raft because the water was flowing around the raft like a rock in a stream. *I am in a current.*

"Hey self that looks good! It's pretty strong to show any sign of movement."

One more thing I can do is to catch all that I can. I need a sea anchor, a drogue. What if I put a boot over the side and tie a shoelace to the painter line? That will put them a few feet under the water. The deeper current could be a little stronger than on the surface. I made a square knot and used two half hitches on both sides of the square knot. One boot went overboard. Slowly the stronger current turned the raft around and it was pulling the raft faster. A tiny wake movement was being made behind the raft.

"Ahoy self. Three points off to starboard, there is a kelp bulb floating."

"Aye."

It too has a very small wake downstream from it. The water is moving us past the kelp. We are being pulled faster than the surface is moving. We have a good sea drogue.

"Aye! I see."

"Yeah! Tough man, tough."

"Remember self, we are enjoying this!"

Maybe I'm making about three to four knots south and perhaps one west. Oh boy, this trip could take days, a week or longer! I can be a hundred or more miles above any friendly civilization.

The sun slowly came out. "Thank you Lord!" *From my shadow I could tell that I was traveling close to a heading of southwest. Yeah! I'm on course to the peninsula!*

I said thanks to God for the warmth of the sun, the direction assurance, and the natural help.

"Yo self, paddle over to those ripples two points to port."

"Aye."

After putting on my partly dried shirt my paddling shortened my travel time. It took some four or five minutes to reach those ripples. There the breeze did increase. *I am thankful for that, as it would press the raft further west towards land, and hopefully the comforts of a warm place.*

"Hello self, we are in enemy country." I put the shirt sail up again.

The clouds were getting thicker, lumping up and mashing together more. The sea had risen and looked to be almost a foot.

"Really?"

"Try a half a foot?"

"Really?"

"Okay, less than a half-foot? Hey, they are visible now, earlier they were not!"

"Yeah, that is a better guess self. The wind and drift are pressing towards shore!"

"Aye, but by very small amounts!"

"Okay self, how far can we see with the haze dissipating a little?"

"It might be up to half a mile by now."

"Hey self! You can't see a third that far in all this haze. We are on the water, not in a chopper at five hundred feet."

"Okay self. Enjoy what self has. I'm alive, paddling and talking. Also we have two paddles, a drogue and my shirt sail. So, get one's self to sit down, relax and enjoy the sunlight and the ride!"

"Aye self. - - One more thing self."

"What now?"

"Send a thank you message up to the thank you desk in the sky for not being dead in the water. That could have been where this oneself would find himself. Dead!"

"Aye self." I bent my head and sent the prayer up.

Meanwhile, back aboard ship our helicopter landed with a very wet cold pilot who was rushed to sickbay. Chopper pilot and crewman went to a debriefing room and provided details of the pickup and did mention that it was foggy.

A helicopter from another aircraft carrier had been dispatched and would look for a swimmer by circling the pick up area and flying directly to the coast, then down the coast eight miles. A second chopper was later dispatched from a third carrier to search the pick up area. Precise radar vectors were radioed to both copters with a drift value of two knots. They used half-mile passes using radar vectors sent by radio from our ship covering the most likely areas. Returning flights were asked to fly over that area upon completion of their return mission, circumstances allowing.

Returning aircraft had flown along the shore looking for signs of the swimmer or the raft. There were no sightings. Later a returning photo jet was sent to photo the shoreline ten miles south of the pickup point. Those photos were carefully looked at for any evidence of the swimmer, the raft and other evidence. Not a trace was found. Helicopter reconnaissance was suspended. A photo search would continue for two days along the shore in conjunction with the search for fishing entrapments to a point fifty miles south of the demilitarized line.

In the afternoon it was determined that a diligent search had been conducted over the probable area. A missing in action form was filed and a copy of that and the orders would go in my file

Chapter Six

MAKING IT TO SHORE

Quite sometime later that day I heard a faint sound of the drone of large engines. There were several planes, probably a returning squadron hopefully looking for me on their return. The sound was far to the north. It soon faded.

The air movement had picked up to maybe three or four knots. Some swells were rising up a little. A few could possibly be a foot from crest to trough. Some had small ripples on their crest. The swells were providing a small but definite forward movement. The swells had to be from stronger wind far out to sea, as they seemed to be moving faster than the air. I readjusted my shirt so it was nearly filled with air and could dry. Its sleeves were moving a little. The air motion had cleared the heavy wet fog and the mountains faintly started to emerge. What a relief! "Lord, thank you SO MUCH for the sight of land!" *Now I have a definite place to paddle toward!*

The remaining boot was used to hold the shirt paddle's stem. This provided a small balloon type of sail from my shirt and visibility to port. The sail was not all that effective but it was pulling in the right direction. A paddle was held on the starboard side to act as both a tiller and keel. This arrangement was good for a little forward motion and direction. A turn to the port and south near the bottom of a swell provided a little longer face contact with each swell and a wee bit higher forward speed. If nothing else it kept me occupied and a little calmer. I was trying to make the most of what I had. The results of my efforts were not clearly visible, but I would keep doing it. *Better than nothing. I had better take advantage of what is given.*

An hour or so later the haze was dissipating more and the mountains were now more visible. The mountains I was looking at were much closer to the shore, higher and more rugged. On several occasions our ship had been close to land both north and south of the demilitarized line. The southern mountains were further back and appeared to be smoother. I was fairly sure that I was a very long way above the demilitarized line.

I'm hoping that this raft is faster than walking. The drift was from the north. This is spring and there is runoff from tens of thousands of square miles of melting snow flowing from as far away as upper Mongolia into the Sea of Okhotsk straight down a long thin island with the force of a fierce fire hose. It was adding to the drift I'm riding on. Little wonder I'm drifting away and the water is so cold!

I'm as thirsty as a five-day camel in the Sahara on its seventh day. I could drink a ton of seawater. Perhaps I could tap one of those cold-water fingers of flow. Cold water didn't appeal to me, but hot yes. Nancy had warned me about drinking seawater. It had too much salt for the human body to handle. She gave me ten reasons.

"Okay self. This is a mental test. You need to try to use the head! How many can you remember?"

"Okay here we go: First, you just think you're quenching thirst but it dehydrates. Second, the kidneys will go to hell from an overload trying to get rid of the salt, and the last thing is death.

"Hey, self. That last one is the cincher. No other reasons are needed. We are not seeking death."

"Aye."

I could see the cliffs now and guessed I was a mile or two off shore. The surf and shoreline were not visible. There were about four or five hours of daylight left and I was feeling better after seeing the cliffs. I was still cold but not constantly shivering hard, just an occasional quiver. *I will be ashore in an hour or two.* I thanked God for the continued sun, the wind and being able to get this far.

A light drizzle had started well behind and north of where I was. I could faintly smell it. I was getting impatient. Forget the surfing efforts. I put my shirt on, extended the handle and paddled.

In awhile the land came into clear view. Well ahead there was a small island or an arm jetty with a sizable hill toward the windward side and sloping terrain on the leeward side. Those made me feel much better. The windward side of the island had high steep rocky cliffs. *I'm sure that I have an in-flowing tide. I am moving.*

When I got closer there was a cove. On the leeward side of the cove were sand hills that were entirely pocked by shell and bomb holes. In the cove the water was flat. I paddled up to a sandy strip where I beached and struggled to get out of the raft. My legs were cold and very stiff. The earth felt so very good! I put my wet boots on, then picked up the raft and struggled up a slope.

I selected a double bomb hole on a rise. There was some slope away from these bomb holes in all directions. It had drainage and it was surrounded with hand size rocks. I put a few medium sized rocks on the raft's bottom, and then pulled the raft over the hole so I could crawl under it. In that bomb hole I was out of the wind and the raft bottom was a shield from the expected rain. It would be warmer and I had an air hole at the small end.

Nearby there was another fairly deep hole. I would use that as a fire pit. I did not want the enemy to find me. In a hole the light from a fire would not be seen at night except from overhead and neither would the smoke. *Now I should look for some wood.* I wanted a soft dry piece of wood to use as a starter piece and a harder round branch that would create heat by quickly twisting a stick back and forth between my hands. I also had shoelaces to use and there are a few willows to make a bow out of if I needed more friction.

I wanted to look around before it was dark. The area was very rocky and had many bomb and shell holes. I discovered a damaged well. There was some water dripping out of a break in a bent pipe. I moved the bend back and forth a few times to develop a dribbling run of water. That worked. It took about a minute to get a handful. I smelled it. It seemed to be good so I drank several handfuls. What a feeling of relief that was and it tasted so good! I sent a message of thanks up to the Big Guy in the sky and then I continued to explore the island.

I walked quite some distance and heard a light tapping sound coming from behind a rise piled high with large dark rocks. I climbed up over that mound. By gosh it was a halyard tapping against a wooden mast! I couldn't believe my eyes. I rubbed them and went for a closer look. It was a mast of a beached sailboat. My spirits soared! That looked so very good! I was overwhelmed! It became difficult to see through the tears of joy running down my cheeks!

The sailboat had been there for quite a long time as grass was growing under the hull. The mast line was weathered some, but it seemed to be sound. The hull paint was dull and deteriorating.

The boat was made of wood planking and there was a carved Dolphin figure mounted on its bow.

It had a locked cuddy cabin. I was able to pound it open with rocks. There were slip windows on both sides. I had to work at it, but was able to open them. I took a quick look around the cabin. In a locker I found waterproof matches with candle wax over their striking end. The wax was to keep the match head dry. Also I found some fishing line and hooks. I would use those very soon. There was a glass container I cleaned by scrubbing it with wet sand. I went back and put it under the dripping water.

The boat was hard to dislodge as it was held tightly in place by the sand. I started digging with the raft's oar and removed enough sand to allow some movement. While digging I found a very large nail spike. I laid it to one side on a flat rock. I dug more and faster. I pushed and pulled on the boat to get it looser. While doing this I tapped the hull. The tapping caused a resonating sound indicating that the hull was sound. Visual inspection revealed that the hull was intact and had no apparent injuries.

This place looked like there had been a few small buildings that were bombed or shelled here. I looked all around and found a timber and wedged it under the hull. I placed a rock under the timber close to the vessel's side. My weight was applied to the timber's far end. The hull rose. *That is leverage!* I placed flat rocks where I was standing to hold the hull up, then carefully slid a few rocks under the boat to hold the grain. I would do that all around the vessel to free the bottom. I felt like I was moving a piano or a house.

I was delighted it had a dagger board rather than a solid keel and it was up! This process was done at several intervals until the bottom was lined with rocks holding it. I did the other side too.

It was time to look for firewood and some round pieces to use as rollers to move the sailboat into the water easier than a gut wrenching drag. There was considerable wood on the seaside of this island. I gathered an armful of wood. I found three rollers for each side of the boat and plenty for a fire. Most of it was well aged and would burn rather quickly.

I found that the rollers didn't work very well due to the soft soil. I found a few flat boards to place under and behind the transom. I splashed water on them so the boat would slide easier. Then I used the timber and a fairly large rock as leverage to raise the hull and move the timber down and forward to move the boat up and back into the water. That leverage enabled me to lift it and to move it further than trying to push or drag it a few inches at a time. I stopped when the transom was well in the water. The tide will come in. I tied the boat's bowline to a large ring that was cemented into a huge chunk of concrete at water's edge. I didn't want this gift to drift away!

The tide was coming in as evidenced by growth along rocks at water's edge. In about twelve hours the tide would be entirely in and starting its move out. By then I should be ready to take it out to sea.

I wanted to dangle a fish line out and gather some more wood for a fire before dark. There were too many holes and jagged rocks to be stomping around in the dark. I went looking for a fishing hole and while setting it up I saw some clams. They had their shell open and their foot out. Food! I picked one up in each hand and bit their protruding foot as they were retracting quickly. I then put them back in the water. Their foot would grow back.

I spotted a part of a gum wrapper foil, washed the dirt off and pressed the fishhook through it. I found a willow-like branch and wrapped fish line around its small end to get the hook further out in the water. I used some rocks to hold it in place. There was just enough water movement to move the gum wrapper a little. That may create some interest for a fish.

I found some harder wood and quite a bit of softer half rotted. I used the nail spike to dig into the wood for a dry place to ignite. I went back to my camp where I placed a few rocks on the bottom to provide a little more heat, and then dumped the wood into that deep hole close to my raft camp.

I returned to the fishing hole. A medium fish had hooked its self! Did that ever look good! I used the nail spike to clean the fish. Then I could put the branch through the fish for cooking. I retrieved the blanket from the sailboat. My pants were still quite damp, so I hung them on a bush to dry and wrapped the blanket around me. Later I would hold my pants over the fire to dry more.

I went to check the sailboat out to see if I would be able to sleep there. It was too musty for sleeping. Also there was less than five feet of bench. When in doubt, don't! I decided to sleep in the bomb hole.

The wind was blowing harder now and the clouds were much thicker. The smell of rain was definitely in the air. A rainsquall was about a mile or two to sea heading south. There was movement from the cloud to show its direction. Shadows from a still standing small grove of pine trees stretched across the small bay which were reflecting the setting sun's rays and sky, creating a beautiful sunset with a mix of yellow, red, orange and gold interspersed with blue. What a gorgeous place, mostly blown to smithereens by war! I wished for my camera. There was great contrast in the light and foliage! I said thanks to God for all the remaining natural beauty to gaze upon.

"Hello self. Those pine trees have dry needles!" I went over to the grove of pine trees and gathered up a big armful of pine needles and returned to the shell holes. I dumped most of the pine needles in the bed hole to make it softer and warmer for me to sleep on and held on to some as starter fuel in the hole where my fire would be made.

In the boat I found sails in a locker forward of the cockpit. They were neatly folded. I pulled them out for an inspection and found some mildew on the main sail as it was on top. Also it had a patch. I didn't like that. It was a little slimy and stinky. I pulled the jib sail out. It had less mildew on it and was a light brown and mostly grey with a few darker spots.

A salt-water soak may kill the mildew and clean them. It's worth a try. I flared the main and jib out and placed them both into the water and draped them over rocks so the seawater would get to both sides. I knew of a guy who said he did that to clean sails and to condition them. I had no idea of the details. Their stink was reason enough for the dunking, if it would do any good. I laid a line over a rock and under a larger rock to anchor the sails. That would keep them secured, wet and spread out overnight. The storm sail was stretched out over a few low bushes and I put a few rocks on it to hold it down. It too had a little grey and rust coloring evidence of mildew.

I looked around the cabin some more and found a faded red jacket that had three golden dragons embossed on it. Two small dragons were in front and one large on its back. It was too dirty to put on, so I held it up to my chest to see if it would fit. It would be a snug fit, but I could get it on. The jacket was very dirty so into nature's washer it went, that being the waves. I ran a stick through the jacket's arms, then and placed it into the surf that was moving enough to do a fair job of scrubbing. I laid a few large rocks on top of the stick at both ends, and then I left it in the surf while I continued to look about. After awhile I went back and spread the jacket on a bush to dry. It was not very well washed, but it was much better.

On my knees, I thanked the Lord for his bountiful provisions and my successful day's venture. Then I boldly asked for His care and a good day for sailing tomorrow. *If you don't ask, you don't get.*

When it was dark I made a small fire so I could get close and become warmer, also I could cook the fish. Later I would hang my boots and pants over the fire. I laced them to a long stick that more than spanned the hole. So, I'm in my skivvies.

The sky was clouding up. A few very bright stars appeared through holes in the clouds. In the black darkness the stars seemed to be so very close. I crawled under the raft with the blanket on top of the pine needles and wrapped it around me.

WAR WOUNDS

I heard the sound of a few large drops of rain hitting the bottom of the raft. I thought of my pants and that the rain could sop them worse than they were now. I got up and put them and my boots in the small hole at the end of the raft and pulled the raft over both holes and lay down.

That hole should be plugged up better. I got up again and tossed the storm sail over a shrub and the hole and held it down with a few rocks. Now I could sleep.

Chapter Seven

SAILING SOUTH

I got up a little after sunrise, stretched off some stiffness then went to the spring and drank the now over flowing bottle of water and placed it to refill. The sailboat was less stinky. I found small items in several lockers including several charts in Korean and a wide brimmed hat. Unfortunately I did not find a compass.

I pulled the sails out of the water and hauled them up the mast. Drying would take hours. The main sail failed to provide much confidence due to its patch. I have not dealt with that. The jib would be useful even being a little chafed and having several stains on its top. It was longer at its base than any jib I had used. I looked at the storm sail. I was confident it would withstand a storm where the others could fail.

I noted the growth in the water was still flowing in so I paddled the raft across the small bay to look over that area and trudged up a sand dune. There I saw an area about the size of a village with some larger buildings that obviously had been the subject of very intense shelling and bombing. Bomb and shell holes were everywhere. Everything was pulverized, including the roads. One place looked to have been blown apart much cleaner than the others around it and was probably the main target. I don't think a person could step any place that had not been bombed or shelled. Holes were side by side, even one on top of the other, some with several very large depressions. Some fields close by had bomb holes that were evenly spaced apart in precise order. The scene was total carnage with tons of trashed building debris. I saw no pieces of anything much larger than my foot. The quiet was death-like. The place had a forbidding odor.

The north end of the island was barely touched by the bombardment. I paddled back to the island where I walked around. I went to the clam cove and found some more clams with their foot out. I bit off several more clam feet and returned them, and then drank more water. That was breakfast and lunch.

I looked at the growth in pools for several minutes and saw that the plants were not moving. A slack tide is when there is little or no water movement. The tide would be flowing out soon because it was flowing in when I came through this channel yesterday. There are two tides a day in the Pacific and all waters around it. Maybe in about half an hour it should start flowing out enough so I can be clear of the beach. In an hour or so it should be stronger. *That would be better.*

My watch had quit yesterday while I was in the water. How do I tell the time without a working watch? Each hour the earth moves fifteen degrees. Hold your arms straight out, make a fist and hold your thumb out. Then put one hand over the other until you reach the sun. Each fist and thumb is fairly close to an hour. It is noon when the sun is directly overhead.

I carried the raft to the boat to use as my emergency vehicle. Some air had to be let out to cram it into the cabin and out of sight. Then I strung lines through the boom pulleys and tied the boom amidships to the port aft cleat. I tossed my shirt and pants in the boat, and picked up the jacket from its bush and tried it on. It was still damp so I tied it to a mast cleat.

I went over to look at the clams. All had receded into their shells that were closed up tight. Next I went to the water well and drank all that I could hold and refilled the bottle. I saw that the growth in the pools was now showing an outflow. *Soon it will be time to move out to sea. There are some marks on the charts, better look at them.* The charts indicated this place and many shallow and rocky areas to the south a few miles. They had some crosses and circled dotted markings and some of the print was larger. *I need to avoid this area. A southeast heading should carry me out to sea beyond the danger markings on the chart and out of sight.*

I picked up the water bottle, placed both paddle handles together for a longer reach, untied the mooring line and pushed off into the bay. *I will start with as much sail as possible. Perhaps the stains will be some camouflage.* I paddled the boat towards the open sea and soon picked up the ebb tide. That didn't last long but it carried me off the shoreline.

A few minutes later I caught a draft of air. The wet sail's weight was very evident. The boat rolled quite a bit from a small draft of air. That raised my level of concern. I continued to paddle for some time before there was enough air to slowly move the boat. I did not like the main being up to the top. It healed over too much. I lowered it to half and let its bottom hang loose on the upwind side. There were no sail ties. I held the boom amid ship to lessen the tilt angle. The boom was extra long too. After a few minutes that light air faded.

It was tempting to stay close to the shore, but if drifting I would not have steerage and if sailing I would not be able to see far enough ahead to see and react to a rock. Also, if close to shore I could easily be seen by a patrol and shot. Better to be far out to sea.

The swells were light, calm and far apart. Further out I could see where the air was moving the water. Its hue was different, a darker color. *That is where I want to be. It's safe and I will be moving.* With determination I paddled out to sea. It took quite some time to paddle that far out. Once there the sail filled a bit, the boat rolled quite a bit then it started to move slowly. I sat on the upwind gunwale.

How smart was it to soak them all night? I'm not moving forward all that much. The shore is looking the same. I may be drifting south faster than I'm sailing east. I may not avoid that danger area. I am out from the very shallow and it is only a little past high tide. I prayed for more wind.

I tied a line with a fishing hook and wrapped a small piece of that shiny gum wrapper as a lure and attached it to the starboard cleat in the water. I might catch something. I needed to try.

I got the idea that perhaps I should be flying an ensign. I looked in the lockers aft and found two flags. The North Korean Flag was in good condition. It's red and has blue stripes top and bottom with two thin white stripes between the blue and red. A white circle with a red star was in its center about a third from the staff. There was a second flag for

South Korea. It was all white with a central round symbol representing the opposing principles of nature, also four other bar markings. I was told that they represent family, seasons, nature and elements. It was quite faded and worn. For a vessel this far north, that was puzzling. The red flag went into a holder on the stern.

Then I put on a black cap with the neck cover to prevent more sunburn. I was in the sun a lot yesterday. The cap had two eyelets and a string for adjusting size. *Clever.*

It was awhile later when I saw a boat cruising about half a mile further out. In a few moments it turned towards me, increased its speed and turned on its lights and siren. I promptly turned port into irons, which is directly into the wind. I quickly hauled the main sail to the top and secured it to its cleat, then put on the still damp jacket open in front. Its sleeves were up over my wrist a bit. *Maybe I will look more like a Korean with a coat and hat on.*

The sails were luffing slightly when the police patrol boat pulled up less than ten yards on my starboard quarter. They wore light blue police like uniforms and had police shield like badges.

They were giving me a wave off. They pointed to the water shouting excitedly. I was being told to move further north. *Sure, as if I could just jam the power lever up and move off.* I looked to the place they pointed to and saw a monstrous dark object just under the water, now just some twenty yards south. The hair raised on the back of my neck. I calmly raised my hand. The breeze had increased a tad.

A Navy Panther jet was flying high right overhead. The man on the boat aft deck ducked undercover as the plane passed overhead. It was silver, so it probably was a navy photo plane.

Quickly I held the boom out to port for a back sail. At the same time I pushed the rudder handle with my foot pointing to starboard to get the stern to move to port. The boat moved back and turned. I was now pointing out to sea parallel to the danger spot and continued the turn a little more to port. I hauled the boom close to amidships. The tiller had a holding hole. I put a line through it and a stopper knot and then laid it over the gunwale. My boat was now moving. Quickly I secured a line with a clove hitch as high as I could reach up the mast. On the other end wrapped around my waist I tied a bowline knot. While holding the tiller line I hung my body out over the boat's port side while standing on the port gunwale. I'm hiked out, but not much. Then I hauled the boom inboard quite a bit. The boat heeled a lot and its speed increased several knots. *I'm leaving a wake.* Still the drift looked to be greater than my forward movement. I was holding what I had. I was getting very close to that dark object. I could see the water rising and flowing rapidly up and over it. I could feel some turbulence from the increased current flow. *I don't like this!*

The man at the back of the boat was holding his hands over his ears as if expecting to hear a great grinding sound from my steady forward movement. In a few minutes that dark underwater object started to recede. Downwind I could see a few rocks that could have been big problems.

I continued my standout position and turned and waved. I got a high hand of approval. The man swiped his forehead. I waved. The North Koreans had their patrol boats engine turned up fairly fast just to keep on station off the darkest place. They were scanning for other traffic.

I was sure that they had been able to see the boat's painted name and homeport in Korean. One of them had held up binoculars and then only for a short time. That red flag may have been some help. This being a tacky boat possibly was a help, and a tacky me. I was glad to have had that hat on my head, which covered my neck and my crew cut. They didn't seem to be overly concerned except for my being in too close to the danger area. My being rather nervous had developed an urgent need to pee.

The outer buoy was a red cylinder ringed with two black stripes. That is a seaward sign of a danger zone. *I am not seeing dark objects below.* Once passed the buoy I looked back to locate the patrol boat. It was about fifty yards away. The man on the stern waved and pointed south. I waved back, pointed south, put my hands together pointing up and bowed. He bowed back. I continued sailing out-to-sea a bit then turned south. In a few minutes, I looked back and saw the patrol boat was moving more towards land. Several minutes later the silver Navy Panther jet again flew right overhead. I had pulled my hat and coat off. I held my hand up by the main sail gave it a wag, and thumbs up. The plane continued flying north and was soon out of sight.

I was sailing a quarter downwind and was moving along now. The boat seemed to want to heel over too much as the main sail was still wet and very heavy. I was not at all comfortable with the weight of the sails and the increasing wind. I didn't need a tip over accident. That would attract unwanted attention and perhaps even give me another raft exercise. *I wonder how much out of rig this altered boat actually has with its longer cockpit and boom? I've wrestled with this vessel more than any other sailboat, but then, I'm not a sailor with a lot of experience either.*

The fog bank was fairly close by. I turned towards it. I hauled the main in and the boat picked up several knots. I needed a break and to get to a safe haven. Also I was getting a clear message about another internal physical condition which needed attention fairly soon.

In a few minutes I entered the fog. It engulfed the boat. I was coasting deep into the fog bank. There the breeze lessened some. I dropped and removed the main sail, then stuffed it loosely into its locker. If folded it would not dry much in the locker. Stuffing it in would allow air to get around it and dry better. It may be needed later. I left the jib up, as it would provide some movement south.

I got rid of the natural urgency somewhat like the sailors of antiquity. On square-riggers they used the forecastle rigging. They would say, "Going to the head." Their ships had headpieces on their bow. They were usually of women, so that is one reason the feminine gender is used for the ships.

I removed all my lower clothing and hung them all out to dry on the boom close to the mast. I held a line from the aft port cleat and used the boom to lean against and to place my body over the starboard side. I dropped the waste and hauled myself back aboard. By tying to the opposite side I was able to pull back well into the boat. Then I stowed the lines, tied my still damp pants onto the halyard line at the top and hauled the storm sail up.

Slowly, I sailed out of the fog bank. I looked for the patrol boat upwind. It was barely visible. While drying myself in the sun, I put the coat back on a mast cleat and tied my shirt onto boom's end to dry. Again, I was in my skivvies.

I was underway. Now, I felt sure that I would not drag sailcloth in or under the water, or worse flip the boat completely over. Progress may be a bit slower, but it also had a lower smaller profile. This boat would appear to be further away. Its tan and bluish color may be of some camouflage value. I took a good swig of water.

I was able to haul the boom further up the mast to get a tad more air and gain more visibility under the boom and pulled it in for a mast angle of about fifteen degrees. The sail picked up a little more wind and the current seemed strong. I was making a fair speed and my boat was leaving a definite wake. I would stay in the firm breeze and run along just off the fog bank. Ah, this felt so much better!

About an hour later I was abeam a town that was situated back towards the mountains. I was able to see the tops of some buildings and the mountains behind the town around a point. Mountains behind were high, rugged and rather close to the sea. There was an arm of land jutting out. That was not comfortable. *I need to be further out and well over the horizon for a few hours.* I turned to a more easterly heading.

"Self, maybe we could do a little math on how far out we need to go. We don't want to become a gunnery target."

"Okay self what are the facts? This vessel is definitely a subject of visibility along with our earth's curvature."

I am six feet tall and the earth curvature is pretty even at 7.5 inches per mile.

"Are you sure?"

"Yeah. From my personal memory bank that was suppose to be funny.

"Such as?"

"A girl's shoe size."

"That is not funny."

"It's different and I was able to remember it. That is called a memory hook."

"Okay. Use the round numbers of 8 inches and 72 in inches. Divide 72 by 8 and get 9. Those numbers relate to miles. So, that means it takes nine miles to hide me. The sail is about 18 feet above the water, so that is 3 times higher than me. So now multiply 3 times 9 and get

27. Okay, it takes 27 miles for this vessel to be out of sight. That would be three hours to sea and a whole lot safer. I will become smaller as I move out. The peninsula runs generally in a southeast direction. I won't lose much time by heading east. Also if I can sail in a trough this vessel will be that much lower."

The breeze was getting stronger and steady, about eight to ten knots out of the northeast. The sea became a little higher.

A little later I saw a boat moving to sea at what looked like a high speed. I was running towards the fog bank. That put my back to them. That would make this boat a smaller target. After several long minutes the powerboat turned towards the north. It was good to see that it was not interested in me. It didn't make me feel easy seeing that boat coming my way. I turned to provide as low a profile as possible.

I decided to tie the main sail to the bottom of the boom to dry. It will add a few more square feet and not heal us over much. *I may want more speed from the larger sail later to find a port. I only know of a few ports on the east side of South Korea.*

I was now moving fast enough that I should be able to make the fog bank and have my wake subside before they got close to me. I would hold what I had as the breeze was stiffer and the sun was warmer off the fog bank a little way. *The fog just might dissipate in an hour or so.* Before long I had a little air on my face. That felt good. It meant that I was moving a little faster than the wind. *I wish I knew more about sailing and the use of sea energy. More speed would be good. I'm feeling rather anxious.* It is a little worrisome being out of sight of land and having no compass, just using the swells as a guide.

Hours later after I turned south and was running with the swells I saw the top of a pointed hill. From the chart I could now be south of the demilitarized line. *I may be about five or six miles south.*

In another hour or so I removed and stowed the North Korean flag and hoisted the now damp mainsail. Clouds were gathering well to the north. Now I'm sailing along rather well leaving a good wake and can see some bow water splashing. The mountains are a little higher above the horizon. *I'm doing it!*

"Thank you Lord for the good passage I am having."

Chapter Eight

A PORT TOWN

While I was sailing south, a Christian wedding was being set up in a South Korean harbor town. The maid of honor, Mi-Yun, was a Republic of Korea Army nurse who had been on the front lines for several months tending to their wounded. Her groomsman had told her that morning that he would not be able to perform his honored duty as he had been transferred and would be leaving today for another base far to the west. Mi-Yun and the bride were devastated.

Their uncle, Ha-kun had made arrangements for this huge building several months ago. It was a former hangar for several large amphibious aircraft. There was more than enough room inside for dancing, tables for food, and all the important wedding festivities. It had a raised platform for a musical group and loudspeakers for making the many announcements. There was a fully equipped kitchen with places to store and prepare food. The former quarters for crew were now used as guest rooms. There were showers and bathrooms on both of the two floors. It would be very suitable for the many people who were invited.

Ha-kun lamented, only one thing was missing, the family sailboat. It had been confiscated when the north occupied their city and took their boat up north. Ha-kun would miss what he considered a family tradition. Alas that was the one thing he could not control.

Mi-Yun had an apartment on the second floor from where she could see the all of the harbor and beach area. She gasped in surprise when she saw their family sailboat enter the harbor. It was unique, in that there was a dolphin figure standing out on the bow and its cockpit was longer than most others. She ran down to tell Ha-kun what she saw. He had helped build that boat. It belonged to a close family member who was now serving in the South Korean Army and would be attending this wedding.

Ha-kun hurried upstairs to the balcony to see it. The sailboat was now out of sight in a bay for merchant ships. He wondered why a sailboat would go in there. Perhaps they were strangers to this place. In a few minutes the boat sailed out and was heading down the channel towards them. "Perhaps it is coming here!" Ha-kun hastened down to the dock and inspected the berthing. He tied and hung fenders over the decking and made ready mooring lines.

Mi-Yun went inside and wound up the Victrola and selected some popular music. She made a few minor adjustments to her hair, and then anxiously waited by the door.

For hours I had been looking for a port of some size as I needed food and rest and the day was well spent. This was the first port with visible facilities and the sun was starting to set.

I sailed into the first bay where I was hailed by an old man who had a local chart in hand. He pointed and told me where to go and tie up. The place was a mile or two down a long channel all the way to its very end. He motioned with his hands and with body language. I could eat and sleep down there in that building with a domed roof. I did see a few cranes as I came inside the bay. They had been out of sight only a few moments before. He pointed the way to go. It was fun talking in sign language to him! After I pushed the boat off the dock he bowed to me. I bowed back.

Under sail I was making fair speed. I had a mounting personal need.

An elder on the sea wall beckoned to me and motioned where to tie the boat up. I dropped the sail too early and was at a stop a few yards out from the dock. He had a boat hook on deck and heaved me a casting line, which I caught. The wind blew the boat closer to the dock. Ha-Kun used the boat hook and we both pulled the boat in against the fenders and secured the lines. I put my hands together and bowed a bit and said, "Thank you," and then hurried along towards the domed building.

Ha-kun smiled. It was indeed their boat. He had helped carve the dolphin and had helped on many other things. It looked weathered and it was in need of much restoring. He could have that done. He knew that many of the family members who built it would enjoy fixing it up. They all would be coming here. He would have them come early for a painting party. He hastened to tell everyone his good news.

Mi-Yun spoke to her uncle in Korean, "I will take this stranger up to my room. We will be down as soon as I can get every piece of boat information from him in about an hour." Then she could then tell Ha-kun all about the boat.

Ha-kun held up his hand and said, "No, my dear niece. His shirt has his name and USN on it so he is an American. I think this person should first be fed and served American beer. That we have. Then we can all talk about the boat. I have a room downstairs with a shower and nice facilities. He can stay there as long as he wants to!"

"Yes, of course dear Uncle."

When I came out of the small room Mi-Yun gently took my arm and led me over to a table. "You now eat and drink. Later we all talk of boat and other things."

"Thank you!" *I was very relieved, as that was exactly what I wanted and desperately needed!*

Ha-kun came to this table with a tray loaded with a pitcher of beer and three tall glasses. Mi-Yun poured the beer. She had a fetching smile.

Mi-Yun told me her situation and about the wedding and I told her mine. "I may be of some use with this wedding by advising on a few procedures, but I am not an expert by any means. Would you be able to put me on some transportation to Pusan so I can catch an airplane to Japan in a few days?"

"I'll be happy to, yes! I have to go to Pusan for my new duty assignment in a few days. I will take you there, yes."

"Thank you, that would be very helpful."

American food was served. It consisted of boiled hot dogs, buns, mustard, and relish. Boy those really looked and tasted good! Then after a few quick bites, "It would be improper for me to be the groomsman. You need a Korean man for that honor." Mi-Yun translated to her uncle.

Ha-kun spoke up, "I have asked a cousin to help out. He said he would be honored to do that. He took me to the room he had mentioned to Mi-Yun. There he had a nice full-length black robe that had a large ring of gold embroidery around its neck and sleeves. So what if it was a tad short. It was good for formal occasions, and also it was warm.

I had been told the name of this place, but it went in one ear and out the other. I was too tired and there were so many Korean names ending with dong, song or a wong. They all seemed to sound alike.

Ha-kun wanted to know all about the boat. Mi-Yun translated. The Northern Army took this boat away last year. How did I come to bring it here?"

"It is your boat. I just had the good fortune to find it and to use it."

I told him the story in some detail. Ha-kun said, "It is the will of the Gods."

He was so very happy to have their boat returned and for me to help Mi-Yun during the wedding rehearsal. He wanted to get on with the sailboat reconditioning project and left to make arrangements to get it all done.

At the rehearsal I walked Mi-Yun down the isle with the traditional step together step. She just did not get the rhythm. I placed her in the front row. The others also had difficulty doing that step. The wedding planner was also having a very hard time with everyone else catching on to that step. I suggested, through Mi-Yun the use of short half steps. Everyone would look like they were floating. They were able to do that easily with much less swing and sway. That went over nicely and they all looked much more graceful, even elegant.

A photographer was having a lot of fun taking pictures of everybody and everything. He was shooting embarrassing moments and lots of laughter.

The rehearsal took several tries before they all understood their parts. It was all new and strange to them. The whole wedding party had a large dinner after the practice. Mi-Yun cared for me very well as she took the things that were too spicy for me from my plate. Uncle provided me with more beer than I should have drunk. We talked about his boat and boating techniques. I learned quite a bit. He would get the sails replaced by midday tomorrow. He was having the boat repainted as we were speaking. It was being done in a building just like this one next to theirs. We all went there to take a look. Fans were blowing and the paint was drying. The boat looked and smelled like new.

The storm had hit and was in full force. It would stay for a few days.

The wedding went off very well. Mi-Yun was beaming and she was talking nonstop to her partner. The bride and groom wore colorful traditional gowns and they posed for many photos.

Mi-Yun wanted to retire early so we could catch the train to Pusan. It left here rather early.

We arrived in Pusan and took a taxi to the base. The first plane departed to Japan in three hours. That flight arrived in Tokyo that afternoon. There I caught the fast train and then walked to the base. My ship would return in a few days.

I got a pay advance and bought a new set of uniforms, I had lost ten pounds. Then I went to town on liberty and was looking for things to send home. This task would likely take a long time because I don't like shopping and especially when I don't have any idea what I want. I bought a box of twelve cigarette lighters for a few American bucks. Some lighters had leather bands with attractive etchings. Those would do for the smokers like my much older half sister and brother. I took them back to the barracks and stowed them in my locker.

It had turned quite cold and blustery that evening. There was a definite need for a pea coat, so I borrowed one.

My remaining gift buying problem was what to buy my mother. I wandered through many town shops. There were plenty of shops that had nice silk scarves of various colors with oriental designs. Some things might work, but most were not quite right.

A squall came rushing down the street blowing dust, trash and snow. Shopkeepers rushed out in the street quickly picking up articles being blown away and placing covers in front of their fair weather open shops. Soon another gust hit so hard I turned my back to it and pulled the pea coat collar up. There was a china shop only a few steps away. The shopkeeper was wrestling against the wind with his storefront cover. I grabbed the quivering front frame covering. The shopkeeper and I placed two panel covers up, and then secured their tops and bottoms with sliding hasps and rods into established flooring and headboard holes. We placed and secured a door the same way. Two of us were able to proceed rapidly. These were heavy front coverings used for cold winter storms. He had just removed them a few days ago when the weather changed to nice. As the front was being secured some wares were dancing and rattling in their saucers. They looked to be very fragile and could break any second. Many shelves were lined with dishes and saucers. They were of greatly differing patterns and colors. I asked, "Should these be moved further back?"

"Aha so, - yes."

The shopkeeper and I each lifted an end of each bench and moved them further back in the shop. I looked at a few items as I moved into the depth of the now darkened shop to see some more displays. *Now this is interesting.*

In the back there was a small elegant area. There was a table with a candle inside an etched glass holder. Papa-San motioned to a stool. "Please honor us by having tea." Mama-San was at his side holding an elegant teapot and a dish with a piece of cake on a platter. It was a carrot cake unlike any I had before. It was absolutely delicious!

The type of bone china of the tea set they were using was explained. It was made only by special order once a year in late October. *My Mom would love this set. Maybe not this pattern but that one over there.* "Does it come in a pattern like that?" as I pointed out a pattern I was sure Mom would like. The shopkeeper said, "That would be possible. They are all special orders and I could not get it until early in November." *The time frame will fit too.*

"Then I should be able to ship it home in time for Christmas on December twenty fifth."

"That would be possible."

I paid in full, and then gave the proprietor my home address where I wanted it to be delivered. It would arrive in a well-packed wooden box. Now I was broke, but happy.

After boarding ship I was called to Personnel. They wanted me to attend a debriefing that afternoon. There Commander Baker, Executive Officer, Commander Barber from Air Operations and Chief Kelley from Personnel met me. They were happy that I had returned safely.

Commander Barber asked, "Why were you off station?"

"I got in the raft as soon as possible and drifted."

"Did you see or hear our search team?"

"Yes Sir. I faintly heard a chopper but it was impossible to see in the thick fog.

"Why didn't you signal?"

"Signal with what? There was nothing in that raft, just two oars and only one was tied in. The raft had loops for a hand line but was no line through them. I nearly failed to climb aboard it and then I was extremely cold."

He asked, "How did you get back?" I told them a short version and they were satisfied.

Chapter Nine

FORWARD OBSERVATION PARTY

Before daybreak about a week later a Marine Corporal came to our berthing area, shook me out of the sack and then took me to the Marine quarters for my field gear. Sargent Butcher briefed us on our mission. "We are forward spotters providing feedback on the effectiveness of a battleship and two cruisers that will be shelling a gook ammunition and a supply dump a few ranges inland from the coast of North Korea in the valley below our observation point. The area is located a few miles north of the front lines."

Six men from our ship's Marine detachment and I climbed into three bubble nosed S-52 Sikorsky helicopters along with radio gear. In formation the helicopters labored their way to the appointed hillside. The Korean mountains all looked rugged, brushy and brown. Many were burnt over. *They look just like southern California Mountains.*

We landed on a bleak hillside in the middle of a shale rockslide. The hill had been burned and heat was radiating off the rocks and the burnt debris. The choppers raised a ton of choking black dust upon landing and taking off. We were covered with black ash.

Our observation point would be at the top of this hill, about thirty feet up. Two men were sent up to the left to a high point. Two others were sent to a second point a little lower and to the right and close to a rock outcropping on a ridge. They were about thirty yards or so from each other. Each team had an observer with binoculars and a guy with a short-range walkie-talkie so they could talk to Sergeant Butcher who stayed close to the landing point, an open place where the radio signals were receivable. The long distance radio was energized by hand cranking. It could reach the ships at sea but not a whole lot further. He called the two observation teams on their handhelds and got their reply, and then he called the controlling ship on the crank radio that we were in position and ready. Then he pointed to a fair size rock about ten yards away and ordered, "Get down behind that rock and stay there. Come when I call."

Suddenly there was a blinding flash of light, an ear busting thunderous noise. The round had landed directly on top of the two men up at the left point. Debris and dust were flying all around us at extremely high speed for many yards. It blew in every direction. The sideways stuff hit first, then the stuff that went up came down. The ground shook and rolled violently. Our bodies were severely slammed by the concussion wave. Our fear factor was instant and extreme. I had not heard any incoming sound from the missile.

Sergeant Butcher and the radio guy, Paul, were tossed flat onto the ground. Paul was hysterical. Butcher erupted in a rage and bellowed, "Turn that fucking crank!" Quickly he bellowed an order to "Cease firing! You fucking bastards have just wiped two of us out!" He ordered the immediate return of our choppers for an instant med evacuation. His commentary involved frustration and exasperation well mixed with a full measure of his profanity. He jabbed his arm pointing for me to go up the hill.

Several rocks had hit all of us very hard. We would have bruises from many. Thank God for the metal helmet! I was protected some by that rock but one rock hit so hard it dented my helmet. It sounded like a gong. That hit hurt my neck and I would have a strained neck for several days. Maybe I didn't position myself correctly behind it to avoid being hit by the debris.

Our life foundation is a solid earth. Terra firma should not be shaking! Shaking earth causes a deep-seated terror in all mankind. Each of us had an instant involuntary expulsion of all body fluids from the fearful surprising light flash, noise, shock wave and the shaking ground. I was rather shaky but I ran as fast as I could up the hill to those guys on the right. I looked left and saw total obliteration. Flying rocks and debris had hit the men hard on the right. The observer was hit by a large flying rock. He had a bone protruding from his leg, a compound fracture, and had several other cuts. His leg had a spurting artery. I tied a tourniquet and taped some gauze on it. I turned to his teammate and examined his chest. He was gasping for breath and his rib cage was very tender to a light touch. He had several chest cuts. I was sure he had a few broken ribs. I pulled him to a reclining position, tore his shirt open, flushed his wounds out with my canteen water and taped bandages in place using as much pressure as he could stand. I tried to get him to breathe through his nose to prevent over ventilation and to ease up the pain caused by large rib cage movements.

I gave both of them a shot of morphine, and then used their blood to put an M on their forehead and the time. My broken watch had stopped at 8:15. I think they both would have a lot of contusions as they had been hit very hard with rocks. Morphine will ease pain, cause small blood vessels to contract and slow bleeding under their skin that would reduce bruising. I patched a few smaller cuts by applying gauze and tape on those injuries.

I ran down to Butcher and Paul the radioman. Both had small bleeding wounds. They got bandaged. Both got a special pill, aspirin. By thinning the blood it will get rid of bruises pretty quick. I did not tell them what they were getting. I just stuffed a pill in their mouth and forced water down. "It's a special pill for this kind of an occasion." I was sure that they would have bruises from flying rocks.

Sergeant Butcher had not stopped his curse binge. Paul continued to energetically crank power for the radio and was sweating profusely. He was exhausted from turning the crank. I took it over for a few minutes while he caught his breath. By then Butcher had calmed down some, and he was asking people at the other end of the radio contact how long until our pickup. He was told, "The choppers are refueling and it will be several more minutes. One chopper has a mechanical problem and is grounded."

In a few minutes I scrambled back up the hill a second time. The broken leg was leaking. I lit a cigarette, took a few puffs, sponged the wound then stuck the glowing tip on his bleeding artery twice for a cauterization. That stopped the serious bleeding. He got a new bandage. The morphine had taken effect. Still he howled in pain as I moved the bone more in line and next to his other leg. I wound tape to tie his feet and the legs together above and below the break to prevent the broken one from moving around. That would have to serve as a splint. Then a bandage was applied. Finally, I filled out the forms for the injured.

Two choppers approached. It seemed to have been an hour. Butcher waved one up closer to the injured. As the second chopper approached I covered the faces of my patients with their blankets in an effort to keep some dirt out. The chopper landed on the hillside near the wounded and shut down its engine. I helped the crewman place and secure our wounded into the basket litters. I watched how he did that. I thanked him for showing me how that was done. The two wounded on wire basket litters took all available room in the first chopper. It quickly departed again raising another huge cloud of black dust.

Butcher and Paul with their radio equipment filled up the other chopper, as it was now nearly full of fuel. With all the gear in it that chopper would not be able to carry my weight. There was no room for me anyway. Butcher shouted over the engine roar and the noise of the rotors winding up, "Doc, you pick up all the remains that you can find. Get every scrap of flesh! Then go down the hill to a road with all of it. I just ordered a truck to pick you up. It's on the way here now. It will take an hour or so to get here. See you back aboard ship!"

I yelled, "Okay!" I showed my understanding with a few nods and thumbs up while taking many steps back out from under the rotor blades, which were now standing straight out. It took off in another cloud of ash dust. My mouth had an awful taste it was so full of dirt, ash and soot. I spat as much out as I could as soon as possible after they had departed. I had to open my mouth to talk.

I felt itchy and very uncomfortable. After they departed I removed my clothes and shook them out. I found some clean dirt and used it to wipe my backside and rub clean my dirty clothing as well as possible. I spread them on a bush to air and dry out. I would put them on later.

I climbed up to the impact area. Everything had been totally incinerated. I carefully looked over a very wide area. There were some tissue strips to pick up here and there, a thumbnail, small bits of parts and pieces, part of a watchband, and a boot heel. Further off I found a shoe with a foot in it. They all went in one bag. I did not find much.

It was a long mile cross country down to the road. This hill had not been trampled upon. I had to press through brush, some waist high, and slide down several steep parts towards the road. I was very hot, dirty and tired when I finally got to the road. I drank all the rest of the water in my canteen and sat on the road with the bag of remains. Finally I heard a truck followed by a jeep with two guys and a mounted machine gun grinding along the road. They both came into view. I waved them down.

"Hi, you here to pick me and some body parts up?"

"Yeah. Put the bones in the back. You ride up here. Hey, I'm Mack, like the truck's name."

"Hi, Mack, I'm Zak. Ya got any water?"

"Yeah, right behind ya."

This truck was a WWII leftover. Stiff springs in these trucks made them able to go anywhere. The truck bounced and shook making it a very rough ride. I was very happy to be on our way back!

I drank all the water that Mack had. We chatted along the way. An hour or so later we entered a rear base. Mack was waved through the gate and he took me directly to the morgue. This base had many tents including several with red crosses and the morgue was further away. He stayed at the wheel while I took the bag and approached the morgue tent. No one was around. Everything was dead quiet.

"Any noise? Is anyone in there?"

"I don't hear anyone moving around." I left the bag outside the tent entrance on a metal chair.

At Mack's motor pool tent area he pointed out a tent and to a bunk where I could stay tonight, then departed. I took a cool shower with my clothes on, then took them off and washed them, wrung them out and gave them a good snap or two. There was an old razor and little bar of soap, so I didn't do a good shaving or bathing job. I wasn't all that steady doing that either. It was more of a rinse off of the black dust. It had started to rain so I hung my wet clothes on the bunk ends to dry, then I crashed on the bed and slept for about an hour.

One of the guys in the tent woke me up and loaned me some clean dry clothing, then we went to chow. On our return I gave his stuff back and put mine on and I thanked him for his help. My clothes were damp but it was raining. I walked over to the hospital tent to see if this was where our wounded men were brought.

"No new patients have been brought in this morning. That type of injury would go to a hospital several miles further behind the lines."

The morgue was many yards down wind from the main tent area and well off the runway. I walked on the taxiway. There was a dirt road around the field's perimeter, but it was muddy with lots of big puddles. It was still raining. I stood in front of the morgue and called out, "Knock, knock, anyone here?" I heard nothing.

The tent entry flap was open and moving in the breeze. I noticed that the bag I had put on a chair was gone as was the chair. I stuck my head inside and smelled the odor of formaldehyde. I called out another time, "Anyone here?" I pulled my head back outside and stood there a minute looking around wondering what to do next.

Suddenly the flap opened. In front of me was a stunning woman! She was pinning a cap on her head. She was of medium build with bright blue eyes and strawberry blond hair pulled back and tied.

Holding her hand out she introduced herself, "I am Lieutenant Medford, Mildred Medford a nurse serving with the British Army. I rarely get anyone to drop by. It is a morgue, don't you know. Come in now out of the rain." I stepped inside the tent.

I was totally flabbergasted! I had some difficulty in speaking and stammered, "Uh, an explanation should be given."

I introduced myself, "Scott, - Zakary Scott. U. S. Navy Hospital Corpsman Trainee off a carrier at sea." I stuck my hand out for her to grasp.

She shook my hand briefly and said, "Scott is a good English name."

"Yes. Mum came over to the states on a boat from Gilford in Surrey."

"Have you been there?"

"Yes, when I was six or so."

She smiled, "Gilford you say. Blimey! What a small world! I'm from Avenger Hammer in Surrey. Gilford is about ten miles from home!"

She had reviewed the bag's contents and said with her lovely Southern English accent, "I gave them to the cook while they were still fresh for lunch, don't you know."

I replied, "Well of course! I picked up only the best pieces from the field. Which would you prefer the heel or the boot?" We had a laugh.

I gave her the information for the forms to be filled out on the two guys that had been blown to bits. Aboard ship I had been given a list of everyone and their personal information before I boarded the chopper. The forms only took a short while to complete.

"I don't quite know what to do about getting back to the ship."

She stepped back, gave me the once-over. "Oh that. I can get you fixed up quite right, don't you know. It will take a day or two. You do need to get spruced up a bit better and get the local passes. I will want some reciprocation."

"You say it, I'll do it."

"I will get you all set up here if you buy me a drink and dance with me this evening."

"Why, I would be honored. Ah, first let me check my wallet." I saw that I had twenty dollars. *That might do here. In Korea booze is inexpensive.* "I have a twenty."

"That will do just fine! We don't have to be smashed out of our minds, don't you know. I will want some personal attention from you later."

She said, "You need a shave. I don't like stubble." She fingered a miniature Samurai Sword. She approached using a burlesque type of a walk saying, "You must do exactly what I say. I have a very sharp instrument in my hand."

"I will do exactly what you ask."

She assured me that was part of her job was to make the men as presentable as possible. "It's so nice to work on a man not constantly pounded by the artillery! No worries love, I'm an expert." She moved in very close to shave my face. She was rubbing against my legs, and bent over towards me. I could see down her blouse. A heartbeat or two of interest started showing.

"Now get out of those filthy and torn clothes and in that tub." She had a number two tub and a cup that she used to pour warm water over me. I soaped down and she poured more nice almost warm water all over my body.

She went to a locker and removed some items of clothing and handed them to me. Teasingly she said, "I can size a guy up quite quickly." They were scrubs. "They come in three sizes, large, medium and small." She pointed out her stash of uniforms for internment saying, "These are for later. This is for now." She presented a lab coat to put on over the scrubs. "Come along now. It may take a bit of time to get everything done. There will be queues, don't you know."

The rain had stopped and the sun was shining when we went to personnel where I gave them my facts and asked them to tell the ship where I was. I was given a temporary pass.

Operations arranged transportation back to my ship. I could fly there tomorrow in the back seat of a World War II Torpedo bomber, now used as a mail plane to service the carrier fleet. It was scheduled to land here shortly after noon.

I stopped by the Motor Pool and asked if I could stay another night. Permission was granted for tonight. They had replacements coming in the next day. If I had to stay longer then I would have to make other arrangements.

"That will work. I am scheduled to fly out tomorrow at noon on the mail plane."

Mildred had stopped by the hospital to see if she was likely to have any business coming her way later that day. "It will be slow because it is near a full moon."

Mildred was speaking to three of them. She waved me to come closer to her, "Zak and I are going on a date this evening." As they departed she told me, "Tis jolly good news for them to hear when someone scores. It is all too infrequent. Around here everyone has been beaten up or down. The women want it up and the guys can't get it up because they are too beaten down."

I asked, "What difference does the moon make?"

"It's getting to be too light at night for either side to do much of their stealthy maneuvering. Both sides prefer darker nights or overcast. More moonlight generally means less shooting which means fewer casualties, some of the time."

I tried to pick up new clothing at the quartermaster's. I found that they would not be able to issue any clothing without a chit from my unit commander. "You can purchase them."

I wonder if I have enough money for uniforms and tonight? I better wait and see if I can borrow some off Mildred's rack.

I called through the morgue tent flap, "Anyone at home?"

"Come in, I just got home."

"Is there any way I can improve my clothing? Perhaps a uniform off your rack?"

"Certainly, I will find you something. You are a tad untidy." Mildred had a long rack with a variety of uniforms for the deceased. Most bodies were a mess when they were brought in. They had to be made as presentable as possible in their correct uniform.

She made herself up nicely. "I will have some of the formaldehyde odors and you will have some odor too. It gets into everything and it bothers some and makes others ill."

"It doesn't seem to bother me."

"I'm sure you have some nasal congestion from all that helicopter dust. Still that's very good news for my ears!"

"Yeah, my nose is a bit stuffy."

We sat outside. After dinner we went to the place she mentioned. It had a jukebox loaded with hit tunes and popular music from around the world. She selected the close cheek-to-cheek variety of music. We drank and danced most of the early evening away.

At one point I went into the men's room where I found a nice selection of condoms. They would definitely help me to do a good job, particularly the French version with ticklers. A condom's ring would put some pressure at the base of my stem. That ring would hold back some blood causing this particular organ to become harder and a tiny bit larger. To a woman harder is better as the organ would provide more satisfaction. It would also increase my tension, all good reasons to use them, not to mention the advertised issues. *Hopefully, I will need a few extra condoms.* All my change went into that machine.

More patrons arrived as the sun sank in the west. Mildred and I would soon go 'home.' She knew of a place at the end of the runway where she could scream her head off and no one would hear. "Can you make me do that?"

"I think so. I'm okay now, so I should be pretty much up to par." I pulled several condoms out of my pocket. She also had a package. We laughed as we waved them gaily at each other.

We picked up a blanket and wandered arm in arm to the east end of the damp grass runway towards Mildred's secret place. It was dark now. With blanket spread over the grass and leaves we found each other.

Darkness was also cover for some enemy who had entered on the northeast end of this base. They squatted in the long grass beside the runway to watch a couple wander past and remained hidden. Then they planted explosives in soft places of the runway. Explosives would be timed to go off one at a time to render the runway useless and create as much fear in the base and town as possible. This group was able to string their devices, set timers, and exit the base without being heard or seen. They would wait nearby off the base for a few hours until most everyone would be asleep.

During that time Emma, Chief of Personnel, had seen the dim outline of the couple as they were walking towards the runway's end. She wondered what they were up to. It was unusual for anyone to be down there at this time of night. Emma returned to her tent where she would finish a glass of wine before she got up to investigate. She thought she would catch them in the act of doing something illegal. She took her flashlight. It had a sleeve to channel the light beam and she held the beam down towards the runway to avoid giving away her position to any possible viewers.

On the way Emma's foot caught a wire. She stumbled, bent over, picked it up and followed it. That wire was connected to something and then went to a stick of dynamite. She forgot about her nosy mission and went straight to the Operations' tent.

Operations' men went into action instantly. One person trained in explosives removed all the wires and timers. In a short time all hands present were giving Emma much praise for her acute observance and quick action.

During that time we were walking back along a sentry path on the north side of the field towards Mildred's tent. We were not observed.

Mildred had a cache of medicinal brandy which she thought would be a proper medication and would be enjoyable. We sat outside her tent, as it was cooler than inside and the almost full moon had risen above the hills.

Emma walked by and demanded, "What are you two up too?"

Mildred replied, "Just relaxing."

Emma said, "Didn't I see you two at the end of the runway?"

"Well, yes we did walk around the field."

Then Emma curtly asked, "Did you notice anything unusual? Did you see any enemy out there?"

Mildred answered, "No. We have been talking to each other about each other."

Pointing to the airfield I asked, "What was going on out there?"

"I found explosives. Damn enemy explosives!"

Pointing at me she said, "I haven't seen you. Who are you and what are you doing here?"

I stood at attention, "I am Scott; Zakary Scott, US Navy, a Corpsman Trainee off a carrier at sea. The Marines sent me here with remains for Mildred. I have been helping her out a little. I have a ride back to my ship tomorrow."

Emma snapped, "Well, you can't stay here with her all night!"

"We just finished the first part of a job." I replied. "Gee Whiz! I hadn't thought of staying all night! Good idea!" I waited for a reaction. Getting none, I said, "I have a bunk at the Motor Pool tonight." Turning toward Mildred, "What will we do about the body you had me working on?"

Mildred smiled. "We will have to start from the very beginning but we should have time to finish before you have to leave. You do want to continue the job don't you?"

"Sure do! I thought we were working very well together."

"My thoughts too."

I turned to Emma and boldly asked, "Would you like to see the body parts I brought in?"

"Heavens no!" She exclaimed. "Zakary! You come along with me right now!" She marched me up to the Motor Pool Tent. Once there she said, "I will be checking up on you later tonight."

"Yes, Ma'am!"

At the crack of dawn I was up and walked down to Mildred's tent. I saw sentry patrolling the field perimeter. He was walking away as I approached and entered her tent. I kissed her awake.

"That was a nice way to wake me up! - Get in this bed before you freeze!"

A bugler blew Reveille, and later the Call to Mess. I went to the Mess Hall and got two cups of coffee and brought them back to Mildred's tent. "My word, coffee in bed!" exclaimed Mildred. "Why I never. . . ." I stopped her with a kiss.

We nearly missed morning mess. After we returned to her tent and chatted as she packed. She was grateful for the attention I gave her. I had soothed her jitters.

Her counterpart was due today if the roads were passable. Generally traveling was very hard and slow. Locals used horses, donkeys and oxen pulled carts. The roads were mostly cart trails and paths between rice paddies. Travel time was given in how many hours it took to travel a mile, not how many miles in an hour.

I returned my lapel pins. We sadly said good-bye. I waited at the Motor Pool to take the mail plane back to my ship.

Chapter Ten

DECAPITATED

I was leaning against a doorpost of the Motor Pool's Quonset hut enjoying the warmth of the sun. I watched a windsock and noticed it was barely moving showing that a light breeze was blowing right down the runway, perfect for landing and a take off. The dirt strip was still damp from yesterday's rain with just a few small puddles here and there. The mail plane would stop close by to exchange bags of mail.

Suddenly a radio broke the quiet of the interior of this Quonset hut. There had been an accident up the road a few miles. They needed an ambulance and a medic. Mack pointed me out as he was running to an ambulance parked outside, "Sergeant, there is that Marine medic I picked up yesterday!"

The Motor Pool Sergeant bellowed at me, "Doc, get in that ambulance! I have one of my men out there and he is injured. Mack knows where the accident is."

"Aye!" I ran over to it and jumped in.

This may have been an ambulance but it bumped and jerked along the road like every other truck. Mack knew the fellow involved in the accident and he expressed his concern.

"I will do my best." *God help me!*

As we bounded down a road we heard the throaty sound of a large military aircraft engine. We looked up to see a former Navy dive-bomber droning along with wheels and flaps down. "That will be my ride."

"They don't stay long, five minutes max. They just sling a sack of mail out and take another one in, and then they are off. We won't get back in time. We're not even at the accident yet."

Shortly we arrived at the accident scene where several Koreans had gathered. They stepped aside when I walked up to the injured man. It was a quite shocking sight. He had been changing a tire. While filling it with air the ring that secured the tire onto the wheel had blown off and had struck him in the neck. It had torn his head completely off leaving ragged edges. His body was on a dirt road and his head in a ditch. Mack brought a stretcher out, saw the body and gagged.

"Mack, can you help me move the body onto the stretcher?"

Mack reached, and then puked. "Hell No! He's my buddy. I can't do that!" He shivered.

"Sit in the ambulance then."

I squatted at the side of the ditch. An elderly Korean couple came and squatted beside me. We exchanged looks. The man placed his hands together fingers pointing up. I did the same. I closed my eyes and asked for God's help with this situation. I needed His guidance and strength.

"Hey, Mack can you call base and tell them that this patient has suffered a mortal wound? We will need about another fifteen minutes or more. Also there is a need for a mounted tire to be brought out for this vehicle as this part is bent."

"Yeah, sure."

I heard the sound of the powerful engine of the World War Two Torpedo Bomber running at full take off power. It was quite a ways off. "Well, that sounds like my ride to the ship is taking off without me on board." I was not sure Mack heard. *Oh well.*

I pulled the body so the neck was down in the ditch and draining blood, then picked up the head and placed it neck down, also to drain. It took several long minutes for the blood to slow to a drip. Since the victim had been injured about twenty or thirty minutes before, I felt that some of the blood might have coagulated. I waited several more minutes until the draining had dribbled to a few drops, then I placed a stretcher at the bottom of the ditch where I could roll the body onto it with the neck stump just a bit off the end. As I started three young Korean men came over to help. We rolled and moved the body onto the stretcher chest up. I unbuttoned the man's outer shirt and pulled his under shirt up and over the neck stump, and then I placed the head stump up between his legs and secured it in place with tape. The same three Korean men helped pick up the stretcher and carry it to the ambulance. I thanked our Korean helpers by placing hands together and said "Thank you." They bowed back.

"Mack, are you okay to drive?"

"Yeah."

"The patient is secure in the back. I have to tidy this place up a bit. It will take a few more minutes."

"Okay."

I went back down to the ditch and scooped up dirt to cover the blood. Those same three Koreans also pitched in to help cover the bloody mess. They chattered happily as we did the cover up. Again, I put my hands together and bowed to each saying, "Thank you." They returned the motions saying something in Korean, probably about the same thing.

"Mack, - there is no hurry now."

Mack drove back slowly. He was very quiet and was drained of energy.

We drove directly to the morgue. I got five Korean laborers from a near by tent to help me unload the body and lay it on the wash table. I washed up, put on a clean scrub suit and a lab coat, and then went up to personnel. I told them about my duty call and missing my ride back to the ship. They knew all about it. They had sent a message to my ship. I was set to go on another mail plane in three days, weather permitting.

"Thanks a million."

I went back to the morgue. Now I was alone with this project before me. I really didn't know exactly what I should be doing but cleaning this guy up seemed to the first thing to get done. There didn't seem like any easy way to do this. I found a pair of heavy rubber gloves. I picked them up and waved them and my arms around as if that would do any good.

In the fifties there were no nice gloves for ordinary work. From what I had heard, sometimes gloves were being used in large hospitals for things like brain surgeries but most of the time they were not used. The gloves were hard to get on and off. Various powders were used to help slip them on and off. Here in Korea, there was little of either that I saw. On occasion there was a basin of water. Rarely was there a cloth towel around. Paper? Not in 1952. We just wiped our hands on the seat of our pants.

If there was something very stinky like burned flesh, we may be able to find a mask and put perfume or after shave lotion in it, but that was rare. Most of the time we used Vicks Vapor Rub under or in our nose because it wouldn't evaporate away or spill. It was a lot better than most stinky stuff. The Morgue used the heavy rubber gloves and an apron, then only for very dirty jobs like burns. There was cool water running here, but it was not approved for drinking. Also in morgues there was the smell of formaldehyde, which turned a lot of people off. Yeah, this was a rather warm afternoon. The tents seemed to attract and hold the heat very well. I opened a flap and more heat rolled in, then I went to the other side and opened that side up trying to vent it out. Really, I was just spinning around trying to avoid doing the job. I took a look around to see who might be around to help, but saw no one.

I got a flashback. It was close to our last week in Boot Camp. We were the last class to receive this special training in all forms of artillery provided by the United States Marines. Along the way to the Marine Base we had been detoured and delayed several times and were quite late arriving. We disembarked and promptly formed up. I delivered our credentials to Gunnery Sergeant Stout who seemed agitated as he begrudgingly accepted them. He demanded, "Why is this class so small and where is the Chief?"

"Our Chief had a heart attack on the third day and I was put in command. Four homosexuals were discharged and six class members are now in the hospital with pneumonia."

He loudly ordered us to hurry to a barracks across the muddy drill field. Our guys complied. A few had mentioned a personal need. They ran to the building and tipped over a nearly full bucket with a mop in it. They brought mud in too.

Stout bellowed, "ATTENTION! Get by a bunk, any bunk; NOW!" We each received face-to-face clear and understandable instruction. I was last. He bellowed in my face, "SEE IT! If you know what needs to be done. DO IT!" That was the first hour of the first day.

I found a rubber apron and put it on, then the heavy rubber gloves. I stood there wondering which end to start at. I decided to start at his boots. They had to be removed before his pants. I untied the boots and they came off normally. I started to cut his pants up the leg, through the belt and all the way up. That all went into the trash. I hosed his body. Well, that was the first squirt of water. A whole lot more needed to be done. I found some shampoo and started washing him all over. While washing the body a clot oozed out from his head. It was a long one. It slithered and shook as it slid down the table. I reached and then puked on the table. Some got on him. I turned the hose to wash it down the table, then took a mouth full of water, and spit my vomit out. Then I washed my puke and that blood clot down the drain.

I was looking for a swig of something to get that nasty bile taste out of my mouth. There was the brandy we had last night on a small table by the entrance. I gave my gloves a rinse and took a swig, gargled, and spit it onto the metal table. I washed it along the trough. I then took a swig for me. One gulp seemed to just help to get rid of a little of the nasty taste. Two would be better than one. I swirled that around and gargled. That just about got that nasty taste out. A third would do the trick. Just then Mildred came in and said in a teasing way, "Ah Ha! I caught you getting into the emergency medicine cache! I will report you to the highest authority in the land! - Emma will love this!"

Looking at me she exclaimed, "Good God Zak you are one filthy mess! How could you get so bloody dirty?" I took a few pretended tottering and staggering steps towards her and held the bottle out for her to grasp.

She sternly warned, "Don't get close to me! You are all bloody!"

I held the bottle towards her as I said again, "Here have a swig and be as guilty as me!" She stepped back. She found a towel and then took the bottle. She turned and took a look at the decapitated body.

She gasped! "Aren't you the big bad dog dragging the worst thing possible back home to gloat over. This is a royal bloody mess!" She went over to the body to examine it.

"You should have seen him a little earlier! He is mostly shampooed and rinsed off now." I explained what had happened.

Mildred had been in the 'O' bar waiting for her relief who had been delayed again by foul weather and mudslides. "He is taking a train the long way around." She had heard that I had ridden out on a pick-up and I had missed my plane. "We all thought it was just an injury."

"Such a pity that he will be a few days late!" We snuggled for a moment.

I asked, "How do you hook him up with his detached head?"

She said in a rather quiet voice, "I really have not worked on a body without a head. They are not accepting untreated bodies in Japan now. We will have to do something. This will be different." Pointing to the head she said, "There are several interconnections inside there." She paused. "Well. Let's see how it goes. We will have to do a few imaginative things here."

Mildred started a large bottle of fluid running through his right carotid and hooked up an exit on a vein on his left side. In a few minutes it was evident that would not work very well even with clamps. She slowed the flow by clamping the leaking arteries out of his neck. That worked fairly well, but it was still leaking quite a bit.

Now to do his head, she debated on what to do next, but only for a few moments. She would start another bottle on the right side through his carotid artery and just let it drain onto the table. That was ineffective and leaked a lot going in and was making a big mess.

"I can whip a line to hold the needle in place better."

"Can you do that?"

"I can do it on fishing hooks and poles." We briefly talked about the general idea.

"Give it a go! We will hook up the bottles later. Now Zak, you show me how you do that."

First she cut some tissue back so a whip knot could go around a needle shaft length inside the vein. I watched her cut.

"Your turn! Do your whip."

I did and explained the process. "The whip puts an even pressure along the needle which should prevent most leaking." We used that on all points of entry into the body and the head. There was much less leaking and less of a mess. Embalming fluid was flowing through the body and head, but not as fast as usual.

In the process of securing a needle inside a second vein a clot started oozing out of his neck. We cringed. It was a long stringy dark bloody glob running onto the table. That was the last whip. I reached for that bottle.

Mildred was also reaching for the bottle saying, "We need a break!"

"For sure." We sat on the edge of her bed for a few minutes.

I said, "Oh, I was thinking of screening him off by putting a wire from here to there." I pointed to the places.

"This is a ghastly sight. We have blankets, but where do we get wire?"

"Perhaps from the Motor Pool."

"Wash up and put some fresh scrubs on first!"

After washing and donning a clean scrub suit I went up to the Motor Pool. They gave me a roll of wire that I would call heavy bailing wire.

They asked if they could view the body, as he was one of their crew.

"Most likely, but Mildred is in charge. I will ask her. I know it will take some time for us to get him ready for viewing. These things are not easy on anyone."

Back at the morgue we strung the wire and folded blankets over it. I would return the wire at chow time. Five more bodies had arrived. Korean laborers had laid them on tables.

Mildred said, "I have set up the fluids and they seem to be doing fine. Is this hard work?"

"It sure is."

"You look like you need a break. This will take some time." She suggested the Officer's Bar. She went to her pin cash and picked up the warrant officer's pins again and fastened them on the lapel of a khaki shirt for me. Her reason was, "The blue matches your eyes." We would sit outside.

"The Motor Pool guys want to view the body."

"Well, either way; closed or open coffin we definitely need to attach the head. I can use a scarf to mask the sutures. Since this is a hard job and an unusual one, I will need your help." She thought I should be assigned to her until I was returned to my ship.

We went to personnel where she filed a request. We both smelled strongly of formaldehyde so the attendants quickly shrank away. We had dinner and drinks served to us on the patio on the downwind outside. *Hmm. How odd. They just didn't want us in there.*

After one drink we returned to the morgue. Emma tottered some thirty paces behind. She had consumed several glasses of wine with her dinner.

There was dampness in the air. Ground fog was rising up from the damp soil. There was a smell of wet grass. Our steps left imprints in the rather long grass that was all around.

Once inside I looked at the head and moved the curtain back as a light was casting a shadow. I could see how a connection could be made, much like fitting two pieces of wood that had frayed ends. I showed it to Mildred. She was able to see the fit.

Emma entered, she was instantly appalled. This tent had been closed during our absence, so the odor of formaldehyde was quite strong. The body had fluid oozing out of its head and it was dribbling out over the metal table. Emma saw that and the disconnected head and bottles with tubes. There were other bodies that had open wounds lying on cots. She turned gray, gasped and vomited on the floor. It was obvious what she had for dinner as it was mixed with wine. Emma's puke really stunk!

"Thank you so very much!" Mildred said. "Now we get to clean all that up."

I motioned Emma to come this way, "See up close what we were doing." I beckoned for her to come forward. "Come closer and see how my bright idea could solve an ugly problem."

Emma shook her head and backed out of the tent. We heard her retch again outside the tent but further away. She had taken a few more steps further along, as her retching was fainter. I put some Vicks under my nose and offered Mildred some. She took it.

There was still a trace of daylight. Earlier I had noticed the remains of a wood pile some ten or twenty yards down the path. There was a splitting wedge and a sledgehammer. I was hoping to find some sawdust to sop up the vomit. There was none. A shovel was lying to one side. I picked up some sandy soil and then took it to the morgue where I dumped some of it over Emma's vomit. Outside I did the same and scooped both up and carried all of it toward the chopping round. I dug a hole to put it in and covered it up.

Later that evening the wind blew and rain came down in sheets. The tent flap blew open and a puddle formed. We paid no attention.

After breakfast Emma summoned me to her office. She wanted to know for sure if I wanted to stay on at the morgue.

"Thank you for the consideration. I started a task, which I should finish, if only because it is hard to do. I have never seen or done anything like this before."

"All right, I will assign you to the morgue for two days. Where will you sleep?"

"There are lots of empty cots in there." *That's pure bull! I will be sleeping with Mildred!*

"That will be good. Mildred's relief will be along in two days. I will arrange your return to your ship on the mail plane."

"Thank you."

We matched the head to the body, put a towel behind the neck as a neck support and started suturing. She used deep wire sutures first to make the back and sides of the head fast, then smaller sutures for the front of the neck.

Mildred got a scarf that was part of his dress uniform and wrapped it and tied it using their special knot around the neck. His uniform was secured and we dressed him in that which was a lot more difficult than I had thought. A wooden coffin appeared along with four Korean laborers to place him in it. I cradled the head as they lifted the body into the casket. It was very carefully done. They carried it out to the roadside and gently placed it on two sawhorses. It was viewing time for an hour, after which an Army Chaplin held a service. There were quite a few attending. The casket was covered with the American flag. Later a helicopter came to take the body to one of the Transportation Corps shipping centers. Six men doing short steps carried him. It was a moving scene.

A little later Mildred's relief arrived on base. She left to go to her new assignment in Japan. Later, I got on the mail plane and flew out to my ship.

On board they asked about why I was delayed. "I went out on an emergency call and missed the flight." I did not go into details.

Later while in town on liberty I ran into some of the marines from the ship. Paul was telling his buddies an exaggerated story of our observation trek.

"I did patch the guys up but it was nothing out of the ordinary."

They all thought I should be wearing living proof that I was their corpsman and that being in the form of a tattoo. They volunteered to pay for it. They had tossed quite a bit of money on the table. There were several suggestions for the tattoo all including the Marine symbol. I was protesting saying, "I'm not a Corpsman and have no right to wear that symbol."

They thought that I was being modest. After the third beer I was completely blitzed. I had a story for my side of the argument. By this time I was speaking slower and with a little bit of a slur, "At home our preacher gave us a real Hell Fire and Damnation sermon because one member of the congregation had gotten a small heart tattoo on her ankle. We all would be damned to hell if we disobeyed His command. So, I should not get one. I'm not anxious to pave my way straight into Hell." They were quiet for a moment.

I got up to take a pee, turning right to get into the can. When I came out I turned right again. Oops, I'm in an alley. I became merged with the thick crowd of people passing by in the alley. I was forced to move with them. I staggered back to the ship. I had escaped the tattoo.

Chapter Eleven

---◆---

A SITUATION

I had been doing my flight deck job refueling aircraft and making napalm bombs for about a week or longer. During the last hour of my shift on this unusually warm day it was my turn to be checked out in the pump room in the belly of the ship. Everyone in this division had to know how to turn off the aviation gas and drain fuel lines in case of an emergency.

There were two pumping stations, one fore and another aft. They were both alike and were close to the bottom of the ship. If one fuel station was disabled the other could supply its lines. There was a watertight entry door with a chamber several decks below the hangar deck. When I arrived there was a working crew with various colored wires hanging out all over the place. The working crew moved a ladder so I could get through the door. They mentioned that cool air was not getting down there very well.

As soon as I had closed the door behind me the guys down below called up, "Get naked. It is hot as hell down here." I removed my shirt and boots, put them in a locker then descended a long brass ladder down to the pump room, "I see there is a line up here that has been cut."

Both men looked quite gaunt and wasted. *I'm sure something is very wrong with these guys. They look like walking dead.*

The first guy said, "Hi. That line is no longer used. You are the first guy to notice that in a very long time. It can't be removed until the ship is put in for restoration due to the high volatility of aviation gasoline. You Zak?"

"Yeah."

"Call me Jimmy it's not my real name, but I like it."

The second guy said, "Hi there Zak, call me Willy. It's not my real name; but if they say that, I answer."

They were both in skivvies, "Take your pants off. You will be more comfortable. It's always hot down here." *It was pretty warm and close.* I pulled them off and folded them over a wood chair. I was briefed on all the lines and valves. Each gas station had several colored valves. They told me what they all were for and why. This briefing was to learn how to shut the gas flow down and about draining the lines to lessen fire danger. There were three valves for each station on both the hangar and flight decks. They demonstrated a shut down operation and then I did that.

My guess was that there was enough room down there for four guys as they had four wooden chairs around a card size wood table. It had foreign magazines showing photos of nude or scantly dressed women in seductive poses. Several two-page centerfolds were taped to the bulkheads. I did feel a little moved just looking at them. Willy made lewd remarks about the photos. *Okay on that!* They were gorgeous women! Hugh Hefner would catch this wave of interest next year with *Play Boy*, but in a more flattering format.

Both of my trainers made comments about my body as I was spinning valves. They were similar to those we had made about the pin-up photos, but these were about me.

"He has nice legs and ass." The other said, "I like that bulge out front." That was only the start. I was being goggled. I kept my mouth shut and did the task. Those comments gave me an increasing sense of personal pressure. *I don't like this*! *Not at all!* My urge was to run out of there.

When the fuel shut down was finished and the line drain was started Jimmy said, "This is the safest place on ship for parties. Join us for some recreation. In the absence of a gal then a guy will do just fine."

Whoa!

Willy's comment was, "Isn't everything all about gratification?"
I'm not so sure about that!

I was offered a small paper water cup of their methyl alcohol mixed in orange juice.

"No thanks." *That stuff is poison.* They had removed their skivvies.

Jimmy said, "Take your skivvies off. I want to see how you're hung."

"We can do a fore and aft."

Those are parts of a ship. "What do you mean?" I was so naïve!

Jimmy provided a clear, but an unprintable explanation. He left nothing to the imagination.

They had started to fondle each other. "Watch us." They started a demonstration.

I felt pressured and slimed, but managed to say, "Yea, I get the picture! No thanks!" I grabbed my pants and scrambled up the ladder. Their sounds followed me.

A crewmate was waiting for me to clear the ladder so he could go down below. He pressed my shoulders down as I was stepping off the ladder.

"Why are you leaving? The party is just starting. Zak, I really want you to do this."

I jerked away, "I sure don't!" I grabbed all my stuff and leaped out of the chamber.

I was feeling panic like a trap had snapped shut all around me. There was no doubt that he wanted me for sex right then and there. He slammed the door and dog-eared it secured. The passageway was still full of workers. I muttered, "Some party!" I quickly pulled my clothes on.

I wanted to run away, but to where? The ship was one big cage. I ran up all the ladders to the flight deck where the air was refreshing. *I have had quite enough of this stuff!* It forced my decision to apply for another job or a school off ship. That was the best way to run away. *I'm too upset right now. I will do that tomorrow after my shift.*

The following morning the fleet was turning into the wind to launch aircraft. The crewmate who was one rank above me and was in the entry chamber yesterday, sharply commanded, "This plane is a replacement and it can't wait. Get your ass up there and fuel it!" It was the starboard tank of a Panther jet. It was positioned overboard. The ship was starting a turn to port and would tilt to starboard. The wing would be out further over the water.

I scrambled up the ladder, set the nozzle's catch and held on for dear life! I had not seen anyone do this before. This was downright dangerous! The ship's turning caused the plane and my ladder to lean well out over the water during the turn. I was being forced outboard and aft. I could clearly see the water directly below. One slip and I would be overboard and sucked under the ship and into those huge props. My shirtsleeves were rolled up above my elbows, so I pressed my forearms down hard onto the plane's wingtip fuel tank for traction. My left fingers squeezed into the fuel tanks open port with the nozzle pressing on them. I took another step up and pushed my butt up and out to put more pressure on the ladder like rock climbers do. By doing that I was able to stabilize myself somewhat but I was creeping aft while we were in that turn. I felt the ship slow down a little as it neared the halfway point of its turn. That stopped the creeping. *Thank God*!

In a few minutes the jets tank had filled and the ship was now nearly out of the turn. Cold aviation gas had started to pour out of the tank. I instantly elbowed the catch on the nozzle that turned it off, and then made a very quick movement of my left arm to remove the nozzle. I hollered, "Done!" and slowly pressed the gas nozzle and hose foreword with my left leg.

My deck boss was standing below not paying attention. He was giving someone hand signals forward of where he was leaning against the wing. Some of the gas in the nozzle flowed out and down onto him and was instantly very cold, by evaporation. Some may have got in his eyes as his hand quickly covered one. The nozzle slowly bent over and landed right on his face. It made a good gash on his nose and his cheek. Blood was dripping from his face. He loudly cursed me as a flight deck Corpsman standing nearby came to his aid and took him off the flight deck. When the turn was completed I descended, stowed the ladder and went to our sea cabin.

A crew member who was watching asked, "Hey, what happened?"

"He was not paying attention and the nozzle hit his head."

"Well seeing that gave me the jitters and forced me to have a smoke. Here want one?"

"Yeah thanks." *Maybe this will calm me down.* I was seeing the gun tub a little differently. It was a chilling realization of how easy it would be to fall over board. The deck was painted and damp from the ship's bow spray. It was slippery! That safety wire was more than a hand below one's belt. It does not look like it would stop a person in motion. When the ship was in a turn to starboard the deck was most often at a rather steep angle. A coffee cup might slide. We both were holding on to the safety rail welded to the bulkhead. It showed signs of often being used.

Chief Petty Officer Cutter came stomping along the port catwalk and into the tub. He loudly bawled, "I want Scott!"

"I'm here." I stuck my hand up. I had an instant feeling of dread. *Surely, I was in trouble for going up on that ladder!*

"I'm Chief Cutter from X Division." In a rather loud clear voice, "Scott, I have you down as a volunteer for the paint party. Right?"

"No sir! I did not sign that chit! I just wanted to know what type of painting it was."

"Don't sir me!" He snapped.

"I did not sign that chit!" I had been ridiculed by some of the gas crew for volunteering for the Landing Party, now this! I had recently learned that usually the painting party was over-the-side painting the ship while others were on shore leave. Now they were cheerfully chuckling about what I was now getting into.

Chief Cutter spoke slowly, clearly and loudly, "Oh - yes - you - did!" He had a piece of paper he held up and waved.

"Hey Chief, I'm a new guy here! Give me a break! I'm just out of Boot Camp! Without the benefit of a Chief Petty Officer to tell us about things like working parties and such, I thought they would be events like football or baseball ashore when the ship was in port. I know about those."

A lot of the gas crew had heard the loud voices and were now rushing out of the cabin into the gun tub. They wanted to hear this and many were giggling.

Cutter was pointing, "Can you see our flag?"

"Sure."

That flag pole sticking out to port needs painting. Can you do that?
"Yeah!"

My crewmates made a variety of sounds of surprise. With a little indignation, "I can do that! I'm not going to Hell for lying."

Turning back to Cutter with certainty, "Hey, I have done steeplejack work! I don't fall apart if I'm out on a limb! You must have missed my wing tank exercise just a few minutes ago. It was a bit worrisome but I handled it."

"It sure was!"

Chief Cutter was talking louder saying, "If you do this task I will see that you are off this and some of the other work parties you signed up for."

"But I didn't sign up for anything except the Landing Party and I'm doing that!"

Then Cutter pressed on my back and motioned for me to go up to the flight deck he wanted to cross. We hurried across the flight deck as a disabled aircraft was starting its turn onto final approach. The returning Corsair was smoking as it approached. He had dropped most of his munitions. There was a bomb dangling from its mount.

Everyone watched the landing. The bomb swung well forward on the landing, but stayed attached and did not explode. That was what we were looking for. There was a need to be alert for any loose objects skittering down the flight deck. They could easily explode, cut a leg off or worse.

Cutter pointed out the flag stanchion. I also pointed at the flag while I made a few waves and wags with my hands.

"We really should be off this deck. We may be in trouble. I have no idea what they can do to us, but it won't be much fun."

I led him to a tower door. As soon as we were a few decks below he asked quietly, "What the Hell was going on out there?' Why were you up on that Panther's wing tank?"

"The guy in the yellow cap is my boss. He ordered me up there."

"Is there something wrong going on in V-7"

"Yeah."

"What might that be?"

"Yesterday I had my first check out in the pump room where he and two others wanted me for sex. I did not appreciate that one God damned little bit! I gave them a definite, no thanks and got out of there!"

"I have heard a rumor about something going on in the pump rooms. You know that the Navy has a zero tolerance for any homosexual activity?"

"Sure I do! It is also immoral and not Christian. We were clearly told that in Boot Camp first thing on day one and we got that message several times."

"Good to hear that! The Navy finds that homosexuals are very disruptive. They use devious and deadly tactics. So, now tell me. What in Hell is a steeple jack?"

"At home I sometimes worked high places to repair and paint things like crosses on the top of churches. That is where the name comes from. I also climb up radio towers and such for whatever."

"I'll be damned!" He had a hand on the middle of my back firmly pressing me along. We were coming up to the Executive Department Offices. "Now, if you will tell Lieutenant Mason more about what we were just talking about I'm sure he will be very interested in your comments! He is a Navy attorney and insists on substantial facts."

I nodded my understanding, "Okay."

Lieutenant Mason was waiting for us. There were introductions and comments as to why I was there. Cutter excused himself saying. "I need to talk to someone for a moment."

Lieutenant Mason said, "You are excused Chief Cutter." He moved to a recorder. "Scott, let's get straight to the point. This is a recording device." He moved and turned a switch up so I could see.

He spoke into the mike, "Airman Zakary Scott, do you give me permission to a record your comments?"

"Yes sir, you have my permission."

"Airman Scott, do you object to this recording being used as evidence in a court of law, military or otherwise?"

"Sir, I have no objection."

"Do you Airman Scott, swear that you will tell the truth and nothing but the truth so help you God?"

"Yes."

"Scott, are you aware of what the Uniform Code of Military Justice says about sexual activity?"

"Yes sir, generally, but not precisely."

"The Uniform Code of Military Justice, Section 925, Article 125 is the sodomy section that mandates a court martial and current case law says to be invited to participate in sex is a felony."

"Yes sir. That is my understanding." I answered all his questions fully and accurately.

After his questions Mason said, "There was no question that those men wanted to have sex with you. Is that true?"

"Yes sir! Doing fore and aft was made very clear to me from their comments and actions."

"That is the substance I need! To date we have only heard about suspicions, with no authentic information. Just the way they were acting is not substantial evidence. Now with a clear offer of homosexual activity I can go forward and get more usable evidence and get rid of them."

"You are welcome, sir as that is exactly the way it was with no embellishments. Just facts."

Lieutenant Mason said, "Thank you Scott." He turned the recorder off. "Starting now you will have our protection. We will get you off the ship very soon while we investigate further."

Chief Cutter had returned and had been standing outside of the door momentarily. He now stepped inside. "It is our general consensus that you could be in a hazardous situation. Those queers would consider you to be a snitch and will want to get even. That could be deadly. That is why these pretend to be meek freaks are so God damn dangerous here and everywhere."

"Lieutenant Mason you may not know that last hour I was commanded to fuel the starboard wing tank which was well out over water of a Panther as we were starting to turn to port into the wind.

"I heard about that. That is intentional endangerment and I will be able to do something about that! We have several photos."

A very large muscular Marine with a square jaw was standing by the door. His white wide web belt held a holster with a pistol. It was very outstanding against his green uniform. He would accompany us.

Chief Cutter introduced us, "Scott, this is Sergeant Olofsdotter. Olofsdotter this is Seaman Scott." We shook hands and both said, "Hello."

"Olofsdotter will be your guardian and as such he is in charge of your safety. He or someone he assigns will accompany you everywhere."

Sergeant Olofsdotter leaned towards me and quietly said, "Everyone calls me Sergeant O."

Chief Cutter said to me, "I can point out where to find school postings. There are several recently posted on the bulletin board below deck. Are you aware of them?"

"No, I have not seen the bulletin board since I first came aboard, but I intend to find it today."

"Get familiar with it right now! I will walk you down to show you, but you have to read it and you have to file the chit if any announcement looks good to you. If nothing is attractive to you we will do something else."

We went below decks to the bulletin board where the announcements were posted, just outside the Personnel Office. Sergeant 'O' followed just one close step behind.

Chief Cutter mentioned that he had seen my file including the interest form and work history that I had filled out in Boot Camp and aboard ship. If I had a hard time making a decision, they would have a suggestion. Gently he said, "I will twist your arm! You are not safe where you are!" He paused then he announced, "I have one more person to talk to. I will be back in five minutes. Wait here for me."

Sergeant 'O' stood at parade rest a few feet from me.

There was a table and a few chairs in that open room space. I sat down to review the announcements in a ring binder. My mind had gone back and forth several times between applying for Aviation Mechanic or Hospital Corpsman.

Sergeant 'O' leaned over and asked, "Are you okay?"

"Yeah, thanks! I'm okay, I was just wondering what the folks at home might think of my choice." He nodded that he understood. A second marine also with a sidearm came into the room. He took up a position on the other side of the room.

I took a big breath and I prayed, *Lord help me do the thing that will please you most.* Finally, I decided it was medical! *I'm halfway there being checked out with the Marines and I was accepted as one.* With some purpose, I picked up the chit, Transfer of Divisions, and filled it out for the Hospital, 'H' Division. I also filled out a chit to go to school. I gave them to Chief Cutter when he returned.

Chief Cutter took my application saying, "Very well, this squares very well with the information you have provided the Navy about your interests and training. This form looks very good, but you did not get all the questions answered correctly." While pointing to the form, he asked, "Now do you really want to put a mark of acceptance by this one?" The question was to agree to extend if I was not able to get into a class early enough. I had put a check mark in that space and signed my form. He had a bit of a smug look about him as he pulled a form from a folder he had in hand. He presented a typed chit. With a little flair he pointed to where I should sign. It did not have a mark in the extend time square. I signed that one. Chief kept the one I had made out, just so he could show my choice in my handwriting if he needed to do that. He could be asked to show someone up line who may ask if he had to twist my arm.

Commander Baker, Executive Officer of the ship was standing by the counter in personnel.

"Hello Scott, we appreciated your work ashore with the landing party." He quickly signed the request of transfer and my chit to attend school. "As of now you are transferred to our Medical Department and you will continue as the Medic for our Marine Detachment while you are aboard ship. You are in protective custody until further notice. Thank you all. Good day gentlemen." We all stepped aside as he departed.

Without delay we were striding our way to my berthing compartment where I stuffed my belongings into my sea bag. There was an orderly way to stow our belongings so a quick move could be made. While I was doing that both Marines were standing close by. In two minutes we were on our way to the medical department with my sea bag on my shoulder.

At the Medical Department I was introduced and interviewed by Dr. Redman. "Tell me about your experience with the Red Cross." Then he asked several questions to test my knowledge. He was hoping to get eight in the announced apprentice 'strikers' class, which was scheduled to start in six or eight weeks. "I will add your name to that list."

Hospital Corpsman First Class Petty Officer Trainer, "Swede," assigned me a bunk and a locker. Then he took me on a tour around the Medical Department. He introduced me to all the corpsmen, and all the men in the dental department for a total of twenty introductions. We were standing around the reception counter and had started some talk about the college basketball finals.

The telephone rang and Swede answered. There was an emergency in the forward pump room. He said, "They needed a Medical team on the double!" Swede asked, "Where is the forward pump room?"

I said, "I know exactly where it is! I was down there yesterday."

Two Corpsmen with med bags instantly appeared.

I said, "Follow me." My two Marine guards, and three medics double-timed it to the pump room. I was loudly calling out to men in the passageway, "Emergency make way," as we ran to the forward pump room.

The Chief Master-of-Arms and a fire team were there when we arrived. A fireman was down in the pump room. The gas division was excited because the fuel was still on which was pressured and could create an emergency.

The firemen called up loudly, "They're both nude and look dead."

Chief Master-of-Arms recognized me and asked, "Can you turn the gas off?"

"Sure. I was taught that yesterday."

He presented a camera and asked, "Can you use one of these?"

"Sure can!" I have one just like this."

"Here's a roll of thirty-six. Shoot the whole room and get shots from every direction."

"Let me put a new roll in before I go down there. It may create static electricity and a spark if I were to change film down there. Let's be safe!"

"I will do that. Take your shoes off." I removed my shoes and socks.

Swede also removed his shoes and socks. We descended into the pump room. Swede took their vital signs. "I can't find a pulse. Can you?"

I got none. He was surprised that I knew how to do that correctly by using my middle and third fingers.

He asked, "Where did you learn how to do that?"

"I had a close friend who was a registered nurse through the last years of high school. She taught me lots of things." He raised his eyebrows in surprise and he nodded his head in understanding.

Then I took photos of the two victims' bluish lips and fingers, the table and magazines. Photos were taken of the entire pump room, including the pin-ups. It was there I discovered a shutter release cord and a camera that was taped to a bulkhead and well concealed with tape. I removed both and put them in the med bag. Then I put tape where it had been and drew a ring to resemble the lens with a soft lead marking pencil from the med kit.

A gruff call on the closed circuit intercom blared, "We are done, cut the fuel pump off! We don't want to bust a line." All the stations were closed and ready to be drained, purged and stowed.

I answered, "Aye," then went to work turning the gas off and the drains on. I used the pump room intercom to inform the gas crew as I worked the lines by their numbers alternating port to starboard, fore to aft. The open nozzles would drain back into the main aero fuel tanks, just like I had done yesterday. I finished about half of the draining process of the forward lines when an experienced gas crewman came down and finished the job. His comment about the dead guys was, "They finally overdid it." I think he did look over to where the camera had been but he didn't notice its absence. While he was securing the pump room, Swede and I strapped a body onto a wooden rack. I shouldered the med bag and went up with the first body to keep it from hanging on the many places that it could have gotten entangled on. Swede would follow with the second body.

I gave the Chief Master-at-Arms the camera, "This should be very revealing. I found it concealed by tape next to a purge valve. There is likely to be another in the aft room."

"I'll bet you ten to one this film is used for black mail."

That seems odd. Here is another thing I may not fully understand, better ask. "Isn't that the collection of money for protection or extortion like the gangs do?"

"It started out that way hundreds of years ago, but in modern times it is used to gain involuntary servitude. The way I see it this crap amounts to sex slavery and may be unconstitutional, but I'm not an attorney."

"I think that's the sixteenth amendment."

"It is!"

We hastened to the aft pump room and found another concealed camera.

I spent the night in the brig with an armed Marine guard standing watch.

Chapter Twelve

FROGMEN

Early the next morning I worked out with the Marines doing calisthenics and jogging on the flight deck and then went to chow with them. Later we went to the Medical Department where I watched the proceedings and did some filing of patients' records. I had two Marines at my side at all times. They watched everyone closely.

During that time a small boat from an Underwater Demolition Team carried Lieutenant Courier the Commanding Officer and Navy Diver, Chief petty Officer Carpenter. Both boarded our ship.

High Command ordered them to seek two replacement medics because five teammates had been injured in two different Jeep accidents and three were Corpsmen. All were hospitalized with injuries that would have them laid up for several weeks or longer. Command felt that because what they did was hazardous duty a search for medical assistance should be made. However, the team felt they could manage very well without replacements because they all knew first aid and untrained personnel could be a hazard.

When the morning Sick Call line was finished several of us took a short break while the blood tests and such were being processed. We went up to the flight deck for some air. While wandering along I exchanged a wave and a nod to Commander Baker who was on the bridge. Soon after that we were called to the Personnel Office for an interview. My Marine escorts went along too.

Swede was called to the interview because of his independent duty training. He could hold sick call at the base. I had the words swimmer and diver prominently displayed in my records due to that incident in Hawaii. *Perhaps they picked up on the words 'first aid' or did Commander Baker remember our interview?*

The two Marines who were my escort went with me into the interview room. Lt. Courier and Chief Carpenter had just finished interviewing Swede. They told him that he was preselected because of his training and experience and he had volunteered to go ashore on independent duty. Before my entrance Swede told the panel, "Scott is a volunteer swimmer who has recently passed a field orientation with the Marines and he has my recommendation."

When I entered the room I was introduced to the panel and I nodded my recognition of Swede.

Lieutenant Courier said, "Scott have a seat, we have a few questions of you. We don't need to get unqualified personnel who will become an endangerment to all of us during a mission. Do you know anything about Frogmen?"

"About as much as I know about submarines."

Navy Diver, Chief Carpenter said, "Frogmen use SCUBA. Do you know what that is?"

"Yes, SCUBA is an acronym for Self Contained Underwater Breathing Apparatus."

"Have you ever used SCUBA?"

"I did a little recreation diving using SCUBA tanks and I dove for abalone a few times close to home."

They asked more questions about first aid and my swimming.

Lieutenant Courier said, "First Class Hospital Corpsman Anderson has told us that you had just qualified as a Medic for the ship's Marine Landing Party and had satisfied their requirements. We have a similar mission. We would like to have a medic in the water on watch while we free up some fishing nets offshore that the Commies put up to interfere with the South Koreans' eating habits. You seem to have some of the attributes we need. Would you be willing to give it a try?"

I never thought of this! "Yes! I just love being underwater." *I think I'm capable of this task.*

Swede was happy because he was able to hold sick call on his own and he wanted to see some action. The Marines and several others were happy too as I was going off ship. We all went below while we picked up a few personal items and I was soon requesting permission to leave the ship on a temporary assignment. The Marines stopped at the head of our gangway and bid, "Good luck!"

"Thanks!"

As usual, we requested leave, saluted the Officer of the Deck, turned and saluted our ensign flying from the stern's main deck, then descended the ladder let down on the side of our ship to the waiting boat.

We were on our way to a shore base several miles south of the 38th parallel. It took us a full hour running at a high speed. We docked at a landing in a cove. We were assigned berths and met the team members. Right away we started with stretches and exercises, a practice swim and free style diving. Later we would use tanks filled with air. Initial testing and training was to last for two days. During that time I would clearly demonstrate my abilities or lack of them.

One exercise was to free dive, pick up a tank, open the air, clear the mask and put it on. Another was doing a free dive to twenty feet and pick up a weight, then surface. I then went down deeper to pick up an object, put the several parts together, and surface at a certain point. There were a series of dives to various depths, surfacing each time. Each dive was deeper by a fathom. Twelve fathoms, or seventy-two feet, was the maximum depth needed for these next few missions. I took to the tasks and water decently.

After the water exercises Chief Carpenter took me into a med exam room where he talked to me like a Dutch uncle. He discussed in detail the medical aspects of diving. He was very intense.

"Despite what the anti-war protesters and the politicians are saying, **this is a God Damned war!** They may say and think we are standing around merely on a watch with no involvement or enemy contact or that this unit is just doing recreational diving!" He emphatically pounded the examination table with his fist bellowing, "**We are not**! We often have to move out of a danger zone. We often have to manhandle the enemy." He would later teach me how they did that. "We may not have the luxury of time to decompress after a dive. We have to do that very soon in quieter water away from the underwater explosives. Time is always of the essence!"

"These men are a proud lot and are unlikely to complain. You have to be very observant. You will have to take charge to insure the divers were properly decompressed. Most of the time you will be keeping them company underwater because physical changes can occur quickly."

We discussed all the diving issues of decompression illness. There were neurological, psychological, and cardio issues all intermixed. We discussed in great detail all of the special issues connected with combat anxiety, trauma and panic. Those last three are referred to as the usual unseen combat illness. I listened intently as all our lives were at risk. I felt so honored that he thought enough of me that he could dump all the information and I would remember what he had said. A few hours after each session he had me recite and demonstrate the lessons. We would go over what I had missed or left out until I could recite every detail without hesitation.

In the water a new maneuver for me was rolling off a moving boat into the water and from the water back onto the moving pickup boat. Getting back on was the hard part for me. I got a fair idea of how to grab hold of the pickup ring, but the swing up into a fast moving boat was hard for me to do. I would only get part way up. That needed practice. I did learn how I had to swim with one hand out to change depth and use it as a bumper. That was for night diving, which was also new to me. I felt so privileged to know that I had been temporarily accepted as one of this elite group. They gave me a little friendly dunking. I was having fun and perhaps fitting in, but I felt like I was falling short.

On the third morning, while we were waiting to be briefed on our mission, Chief Carpenter asked me, "Scott, what is your first name?"

"Zakary, but only mum calls me that. I answer to Zak."

Chief explained that one reason for needing a short name in this kind of a unit was if one of our men had to call to you the sound should be short and harder to pinpoint by anyone listening, such as the enemy.

I was very pleased that I was now thought of as a man, not a kid. "We will call you Zak, Okay?"

I cheerfully answered, "Okay!"

Lieutenant Mann briefed us on the mission. Local fishermen reported that nets were set in a bay between two points they estimated to be about half a mile off shore and the same in length. The nets greatly interfered with their fishing and the locals were highly dependent on fish for food. It was a huge area to search. There was a muddy stream flowing into the bay. That lowered visibility and it spread far out into the bay.

We were a team of fifteen led by our Lieutenant Courier and Chief Carpenter. We were taken out to the bay in a high-speed low profile and low wake boat. This was not a bay it was a cove. It sure was not any half a mile. An enemy patrol of eight was spotted on the encircling cliff.

Off the inlet we got into rubber boats with a hard deck and dull black round rubber sides. We were to be in the water during a slack tide. Our dive window was ten minutes. The swim depth was at twenty feet so the air bubbles would not be easily seen on the surface. All divers were dropped inside the fog bank off a moving boat in pairs, a buddy system, and were to swim toward shore with flippers on. I was dropped early to listen for a tank tapping, a signal of a stress situation. I was to patrol the line and stand by after the call to surface was made.

The nets were located in less than ten minutes. They were about fifty yards off shore and perhaps fifty yards long. The top line was about ten feet deep right off the stream in murky water. Large cement blocks were on the bottom and several underwater buoys held the trap net in place.

Chief struck an iron pipe placed in the water to signal it was pickup time. We counted heads right after the pickup to make sure no one was left behind. It would be easy to become disoriented in the murky water. We all had watches and compasses on our wrists.

The next day a team of eight went out to set demolition charges under the large cement cubes holding the net in place. I would swim back and forth along their line to see if all was well. Lt. Courier wanted me to surface and signal with one flash of light when all was well and three if not. I thought it would be very easy for the gooks to see us as we were moving in and I would be coming up about the same place along a line and very close to the cliff. From where we were it looked like low double-digit yards. There was a high thin scattered overcast so the gooks could easily see us in the water.

I suggested, "I can bark like a seal and not disclose my position as much and you would get the message. A bark would have a short exposure for me. Then I can slip under water quickly like a seal. Also our black wet suits would look a little seal like." I provided a bark as an example.

"Okay, that sounds reasonable. Let's try it."

I surfaced and barked once like a seal when all was well, three barks or more if it was not and then slide back underwater. We dropped off inside the edge of a fog bank and our crew carrier boat disappeared deeper into the fog bank.

This time our slack water would last fifteen minutes. We were dropped off a minute out and it would take a minute or two for us to swim back after planting munitions. When twelve minutes had passed chief struck a pipe. I swam the line a final time. I was swimming in a crab, as the current had started flowing out to sea at our depth. Two men at the end of the line were being pressed against the base of a planted concrete cube. They soon could be pressed enough to severely interfere with their breathing. *This is not going to improve!* I tapped my tank to signal for help as I rose to the surface and barked three times, and then slid underwater. Two divers were en-route to assist as they returned a tank tap signal after answering my distress call.

I increased my crab swim around until my feet became pressed against the side of the cube. The current was strong enough so I could stand straight out from the side of that cement cube wall parallel to the bottom with my feet about a foot below its edge.

The team was trying to back off that block into free water, but they were now lying almost flat against the cube. Their air bubbles looked to be larger and irregular. *They are being pressed and the tide is increasing in strength.*

It's an insipid thing. It's much like a horse pressing you up against a rail. Soon you become aware of the pressure and poke the horse. A horse will move. Not the current, it just keeps on pressing.

Their movement off looked to be slow and unsteady and they seemed to be working hard at it. The current was now holding me firmly onto the block. *Should I do something rather than just watch?* I remembered a Marine sergeant in Boot Camp bellowing, **"See it - do it!"** I sidestepped over the first guy, bent my knees, grabbed hold of his tank, and straightened out my legs and crab walked towards the edge. I shoved him and he swam around the net's end and into the free current flow. The other guy was a step or two further back. I picked him up the same way and carried him along toward the cube's end. That was a little harder to do and took a little longer. One of the rescue divers was on the cube's end and pulled us around. We were all off the concrete cube and moving toward our boat.

The last team had not been happy with the placement of the last charge. It had moved off so they returned to replace it. That took longer than expected. One of the guys said, "The current did come up quite fast and it pressed on us so we did move a little slower, but I didn't think there was a real problem."

Chief looked around to see if we were all aboard, then blew the charges. We had drifted out to sea by then and were well into the fog. The end result was it worked and a lot of fish were saved.

Chief asked, "Zak, how in Hell did you know what to do?"

"Well, while in high school I worked on a turkey farm during the holidays. Sometimes the birds would crowd up to a fence. The ones in close to the fence could be suffocated, so, we pulled all those turkeys out of the crowd. This looked a lot the same, so, I pulled them off the wall, but they are not turkeys, they were much heavier and the out-flowing tide didn't help at all. They were not all that pressed but could soon be in trouble. I just helped to hurry them along a little. The current increased a lot and the rescue diver did help."

Chief nodded his head. He gave my shoulder a little chuck and said, "Good observation Zak. That is what I want of you, and by the way you make a good seal."

The following day we went out with four divers to check our work. Those charges did the job. Three days after our fish net destruction exercise we went out on another net removal job. It was much like the first one. Everything went smoothly as it should. All I did was swim from team to team and bark once. The Chief easily heard the seal bark. He signaled back with a short light tap on a smaller pipe, a higher note. We would have several more of these missions down the coast. Soon the seal bark was dropped in favor of something else.

A few weeks later just before reveille we got a call to, "Saddle Up! We have a pick up." We were briefed about a plane that had just crashed. The pilot did not eject and it created a brush fire.

Three teams of two guys in each were ready for each chopper as soon as they arrived. There were two bubble nosed Sikorsky S-52 Choppers that could carry two of us. They were to drop us off and one would come back for the last two men. The first team out was a fire crew with hand tools and a few fire extinguishers to put out the fire. The second team would help the first and then secure the pickup site. They had a radio. My buddy, Mike was ordered to remove the secret device and my job was to extract the pilot. We were on the third trip.

It was a given that Commies would see the fire and could arrive on scene before us. More of our team members would be moving in behind us in case we needed backup. The gooks wanted to get at our secret bombing device as badly as we did. The report said that there were no Commies in the area, yet.

When our chopper arrived at the crash site the first team had the fires out with the second team's help. Now they were looking through binoculars at Commies who were looking through their binoculars at us. The crash area was in a pile of very large rocks close together among large bushes. The breeze was from us to them

Mike and I went over to the plane and pilot and saw that both were burned to a crisp. The smell was indescribably horrible! It made Mike vomit on his first whiff. I got some of his splatter. Then I could not resist his guidance and puked too. Mike stepped off the plane as soon as he could and joined the team who was watching a patrol of gooks about a mile away downwind.

I took a few steps away and took a few deep breaths. After a few minutes I pulled myself together and took a closer look. Extracting the pilot was my job and I couldn't just turn away because we never leave anyone behind and nothing would improve with more time.

The pilot filled the cockpit. He was huge. His left side was burned to a crisp. His helmet was partly melted. His mouth was open and his face was very badly burned. The left eyeball was burned and swinging out of its socket. Blood had poured all over his flight suit. His left leg was badly burnt and his left foot was stuck under a rudder pedal that was twisted and firmly held that foot. I tugged and wiggled it a few times, but it would not move.

My kit had some Vicks, which I put in my nose. That cockpit was horribly stinky and was a very tight place to work. It was starting to get hot. The port side was caved in. There were a few burned chunks of body tissue attached to protruding pieces of metal. With my bare hand, I picked them off and put them in a body bag. Next I took a good size rock and hammered some of the protruding metal down flat.

I held my breath and dove to the foot. I pulled and wiggled the pedal and foot but neither would budge. The place was very close. I felt like it was closing in to suffocate me. I got dizzy and came up for a breath. It took several breaths of air to clear my head. I enlarged a break in the plane's side by bashing it with a rock. That allowed air to get in. It seemed to push the stink up and out of the cockpit, but just a little.

I held my breath then dove back down. I cut his bootlaces and down to the sole of the boot. No amount of wiggling of that foot made it come out of the boot or away from the bent pedal. I surfaced for air, and again dove back down with a knife. I did some aggressive boot cutting up the boot's heel and along the sole of the boot. Then I wiggled and pushed the boot to an angle, the foot finally came out.

Another one of my teammates came to see how I was doing. He too immediately turned and vomited. Before he departed he did say, "The gooks are still out-of-range of our rifles, but they are moving closer. You need to get this done."

I called and went over to Mike and the others to ask for help moving this guy. I was refused by their use of many vile negative words. It was clear that they would have nothing to do with my task.

I went back and cut his harness away. The canopy had more protruding pieces to be bashed down to keep from cutting me to ribbons and hanging him up. I climbed into the cockpit to try to pull the pilot up to the top and over the side. It took several attempts to get him to where I could grab his belt and work his huge body around. I was able to start putting the corpse trunk in a body bag. I put the bag on from top to bottom so as not to disturb the severe burned tissue any more than I had to. It was difficult as he filled the seat area up and it was a tight place to work in. There were more pieces of metal and of burnt flesh sticking onto the cockpit where he was rubbing as I moved him. The pilot slid back to his seat several times. I bellowed for help. The answer I got was "Fuck you!"

It was a huge struggle to get him up and half way over the cockpit's side. I climbed out on the wing where I could get a foothold and tugged on his belt. His body finally slithered over the edge. His weight pushed us off the wing, which was bent sharply down onto the ground. His body had me pinned down between two large boulders. I got snagged and so did the bag on the wing's torn tin. Using my best voice projection I bellowed again for help. I'm sure the Commies could hear me. I heard, "Fuck you!" from our guys and I'm sure the gooks echoed the same back. The breeze had increased. I struggled for a long time in close quarters, but finally inched out from under.

I went over to the guys and pleaded for help. I was again rudely refused. They did see that I had made some progress. They said that they had called for a chopper pick up. I went back to the body. The wing's edge had peeled some more flesh off and that went in the body bag, and then I was able to finish pulling the bag over him and secured it. I had to pause for a few breaths.

Just then a chopper landed and shut down in a depression well out of the way and out of sight. I saw the chopper blades waving in the stiffening breeze as it shut down. Bushes that were depressed by the blades during landing raised up a foot or so to further obscure the chopper. There was some water collected in the depression. Many bugs were flying around and lots of mosquitoes.

This was a Dragonfly. It could hold one litter, or two passengers. I pushed through the thicket to the chopper. I told the chopper pilot, "My patient has expired. He is a very big guy. I have him bagged and ready to be placed on a stretcher. We still have to remove the bomb device."

He exploded in rage, "I was told that you were ready to go! I don't have time to sit here all fucking day! Get your damn fucking ass in gear! I have to get out of here!" He jabbed his fingers in the direction of the gooks coming this way. "Why in Hell do you think I put down here in this fucking stinking hole?"

I looked him right straight in the eye and spoke evenly and firmly, "I am not all alone! There are five others sitting behind those rocks. I need help and I can't get those fucking bastards to help me! He is very badly burnt."

"Dead?"

"Yeah! He is big and stinks!" I yanked the stretcher out of the chopper.

He bellowed, and pounded his thighs, "They said you were ready and waiting! Move your fucking ass out of here!"

"They sure didn't ask me if I was ready. They didn't even come close enough to see me."

I went directly over to my team buddy Mike. "I need your fucking help moving this giant. I was pinned under him for over five minutes! I hollered for help. I got none! There is no way on earth I can do this myself!"

"Fuck you! I'm not touching any fucking dead body! You got him that far you do the rest!"

"Go to Hell! You are a gutless pussy, a spineless asshole and you are no fucking good!"

I hunkered over a little to keep low trying to keep a little out of the sight of the gooks as I hustled back to the crashed plane with stretcher in hand. I would remove the bomb device myself. The cockpit had an extra amount of acridness stink in the increasing heat. Again I struggled a few minutes to regain self-control. Once again, I got smeared by some of the body fluid on the bulkhead and seat. It made me gag. I put some dirt on it.

Our chopper pilot was stomping his way over boulders and through the heavy brush. I was sure he saw and heard the exchange between Mike and me. He was in a rage. He grabbed Mike by the collar and stood him up, glared in his face and loudly commanded him to get over and lend me a hand or he would see to it that he would face a court martial for disobeying an order under fire from a United States Marine Corps Lieutenant. Then he shoved him backwards. Mike fell over a rock in a twisting motion and landed with his face down and ass up. The pilot sent a kick towards Mike's protruding ass, missing it by a very small margin. In the process he fell backwards and onto a rock. He cursed much more. Neither was badly injured, they had nothing more than a bruise or two. Perhaps their largest injury was a bent ego.

The pilot roared, "All you fucking bastards! Move your fucking asses to that fucking crash and lend a fucking hand! Do it NOW!"

I had started working with a metal cutting blade that Mike had handed me. After much frantic sawing I cut the black box out and put it in the wire basket at the foot of the body.

They just stood there as I drug and rolled the body in its zipped up bag onto the stretcher. I tied it on with the baskets straps. Finally, we gathered together including the choppers crewman. Six of us lifted the wire basket. We struggled and strained towards the chopper stumbling over rocks and the rough terrain. Our feet were on a mucky bottom. We had to wrestle to get the basket into the chopper.

The pilot provided a rather loud harshly pronounced long and understandable discourse. Translated, he thought we should have been able to do everything much faster and that they all should have pitched in to help early on. As he spoke his face was red and his veins were standing out on his neck. He made several well put gestures to each of us. He then started the engine and engaged the rotors. A breeze had come up more which made the blades move up and down somewhat as they started up. We stood close to the chopper as they picked up speed, slowly waving up and down at first, and then stretching out more evenly as speed picked up. Everyone looked exhausted. The air was filled with cursing of all sorts. I added a few comments of my own during this fruitless exchange of cursing, waving and finger pointing. *Personally I call this kind of activity, 'Doing a Donald Duck.'*

Nodding towards the body the pilot asked me, "What's your guess of his weight?"

"I think he is close to 250 pounds."

"Yeah, that was my guess too and you go about two hundred?

"Yeah, close."

He said, "I can only take you and him to a morgue." He ordered his crewman to stay here by saying; "I'm too close to gross weight in this heat, with the body and doc to take you too." He told the team in more understandable language that he did not want to see lead coming his way on his return. If so he would fly away and leave them. We were up and away in an instant.

Our flight must have taken ten or more minutes. There was a fog bank moving inland over the entire costal area. The chopper pilot was cursing as he flew close to the fog bank's edge and top and landed in the middle of a dirt road. I was ordered out and told to take the body with me. I was to replace the basket in its bracket. I pulled the basket to the roadside where I rolled the body bag onto the road and quickly climbed back aboard to replace and lash the basket in place. Then I tied the bomb device to the wire basket. "Your basket is strapped in its rack and the device is tied to it!"

He shouted, "The morgue is in a Quonset hut about a half of a mile in that direction. Half is new and the other end is old. You can't miss it." He was pointing the direction I should take to find the morgue "I can't return to pick you because the fucking fog is coming in." He nodded and gave me a thumb up. I stepped back away from the rotor blades arc and gave him a thumb up.

Rotating blades seemed to be pulling fog towards us. He promptly departed straight up to retrieve the other team members. Fog had quickly rolled into the hole the chopper had made.

The down flow from the helicopters rotor blades on takeoff churned up a lot of dirt and dust. The dry dust whipped and stung my skin. Dirt had swirled inside my clothing and all over me, even in my boots. I sat down, took off my boots and removed a few chunks of gravel.

I looked at the body bag. I was alone with this big heavy body. It was too far out in the middle of the road. Some odor was coming out of the torn bag and I didn't have another bag.

I looked around for something I could use for leverage. Seeing nothing, I sat on the ground and pushed the body with my feet using my legs. I held my arms behind me for a brace and some more traction. It took many small movements. *He is one heavy sucker!* I felt like I was pushing a piano. I pushed with my feet until the body was at the side of this dirt road. That worked well. I pulled torn bag places together and secured them with a few rocks to hold the tears together and plug up a few holes.

I don't think it is even nine in the morning and I'm already pooped! I stretched out away from the body and lay there for few minutes, then rolled over a few times for more space. I found some clean dirt and laid my scratched upper back on it to stop the bleeding. Then I took some slow breaths and took several drags from my canteen. I could not shake the feeling of inadequacy. I prayed for strength.

In a while I started slogging along the dirt road in the direction pointed out by the chopper pilot. I sat down several times for a few minutes and finished the water in my canteen, as now there was no urgency. It seemed to have been much more than any half a mile! Here and there I saw where artillery fire or bombs had hit making holes of various sizes including the road.

Chapter Thirteen

THE MORGUE

A Quonset hut came into view. Part of it was old and weathered; the other end was new construction. *This must be the place.* A small amount of smoke seemed barely able to move out of its chimney. A heavy musky odor hung in the warm humid air. It was a dreary atmosphere and matched how I felt. On the older closer end of the building there was a larger than normal wooden door. I leaned against it. *I'm not going to make a very good first impression. I'm filthy and physically drained. I'm not enjoying this, but I have to do it.* I took a few deep breaths, and then I firmly knocked on the hinged side of the wooden doorframe.

I heard shuffling of feet approaching at a steady pace. The door hinges creaked as the door was opening rather slowly. A tall thin woman about thirty years of age with blue eyes and light auburn hair opened the door. Behind her was a blue-eyed blond. Both wore lab coats, and were thin. They did look haggard, drawn and pale. Their eyes were dull and had circles under them. Their posture was slumped, their hair a bit scraggly. They were lacking energy and really did look like morticians.

The first one said, "Hello, is there something I can do for you?"

"Is this the morgue?"

"'Tis."

"I was dropped off by a chopper with a badly burned body about half an hour ago. It was too foggy for the chopper to fly us here. I left the body bag by the side of the road. It has a couple of tears."

The first woman spoke in a soft smooth voice, "I'm Jane Boston, a Medical Doctor with the British Army Medical Corps." The second woman stepped forward beside the first, "I'm Ingrid Florence, a Nurse in the British Army Medical Corps. We heard the chopper come and go."

"I'm Zakary Scott temporarily stationed at a navy base west of here, I think; but I may have lost my bearings. It's so foggy everywhere."

Ingrid slowly said, "You are filthy and you smell! - - Do you need a drink?"

"Yeah, I do need something, anything will do!"

Ingrid stepped away momentarily then presented a half can of beer. "This is all we have. Want it? I have taken a few swigs."

"You don't look like poison." I took it and gulped it down. "Thanks a lot."

Jane said, "There is a community cart right over there." She held her hand up part way to point to a shed behind some shrubs some fifteen yards away. Whisks of thick fog swirled around the shed. "You can haul the body on it." Her hand returned limply to her side with a small lifeless bouncing motion.

Without energy Jane said, "Follow me Zakary." She had an hourglass figure. Her hipbones were pronounced. She walked listlessly towards an open-ended shack that was partly covered with thick bushes. "You really stink!"

"I rubbed against the pilot's burnt body several times trying to remove him from a smashed up cockpit and his body fell on top of me while I was getting him off the plane. That is where I got my shirt ripped up and back scratched."

She stopped, "Turn around and let me see. Good Lord! You should have said something."

The cart shed was empty. Weakly she mumbled, "Oh! I forgot. Tis Tuesday our trash collection day. A villager uses the cart to pick up community trash every week."

Jane drew a long breath and said, "Our community cart will be back some time after lunch. You will just have to wait." We started a slow walk back toward the morgue.

"What about the torn body bag? Will it be a problem with animals?"

"Not much we can do about that now, is there?"

"I put some rocks on the tears."

"That should help." Jane took a deep breath and straightened up then continued, "Thanks to the war there are very few animals around. Most have been killed or driven off. If it is bagged they are likely to take some time to find it. For that matter, there are few vehicles along this road or in this area. Then there is another little tidbit, few people would be attracted to a very burnt up corpse. This fog is cool and will keep him cool so he will keep for awhile." She paused and seemed to be gaining some energy. "So, when are they going to pick you up and take you back Zakary?"

"I have no idea. This morning right after liftoff we were flying over a fog bank. The base I'm temporarily stationed at is on a small bay. My guess is they are fogged in by this time. I would expect the chopper pilot to do for our team as he did for me, which is to drop them off at the fogbank's edge and point which direction to walk."

"Do they know which morgue you are at?"

"The pilot knows. He told me, "It's half a mile that way and described the building.'"

She mused, "Hmm, so you have been thrown to the wolves."

Jane stood back and looked me over and had me turn around. She had several negative comments about my general appearance.

"You desperately need to be tided up. You need to get your wounds bandaged and a good scrub. Here, let me look at your back." She ripped the back of my torn shirt open. "That one will need a couple of stitches. When was the last time you shaved? You need a haircut!"

"I won't pass any inspection Ma'am?"

"I will give you a medical examination after you get cleaned up!" Her voice didn't sound like she was all that happy with me.

"I shaved yesterday morning and my hair was cut a few weeks ago. I didn't have time this morning to do anything because we were called out very early."

"Zakary, stay out here." She went into the hut for a clipboard, paper and pen. She asked the usual questions: name, rank, serial number, unit, and specialty. I answered those and added, "I am a new medical trainee on a temporary assignment from a ship at sea. I should call the team."

"We do not have a telephone but I will send a memo by messenger after I get enough information. There is a Navy base right over the hill. Some of them come here to patronize the girls. That building over there is a whorehouse, the village bar and café." She was pointing to a building.

"Ingrid would you bring along shampoo, towels a blanket and med kit? We are going to fix Zakary up. Oh, how would you like us to address you?"

"Zak will be just fine."

I asked Ingrid, "Do you have something I can use as a mouth wash? I puked while handling the body and I can still taste that."

"We have brandy. We can all take a swig to deaden our noses and do we ever need to do that!" She bent forward staggering from side to side holding her nose and waving her arm limply as she started to go inside.

A minute later she came out with a basket full of things and a large half full bottle of brandy.

Umm. She is very efficient and thoughtful, quite cute and she will be fun to be around.

Jane told me, "Strip to your shorts and throw those dirty torn rags in here," pointing to a trashcan. "Put this on." She held out a lab coat. "Follow me." Her walk had picked up considerably. She had a swing that was easy to follow. Her hands were swinging and her head had risen.

There were two hot pools about a hundred yards away down in a hollow, which were secluded by tall brush. The pools emitted a light sulfur rotten egg smell. The warmer air dissipated the fog around the pools. The two pools were linked together. The upstream one was the largest being about five yards wide and maybe ten long. It was the hottest one and was usually used for soaking. The second pool was for bathing about the size of a dozen bathtubs. Both emptied into the river a short distance away.

"Is it time for the mouthwash?"

Ingrid held up a bottle of brandy and quickly took a big swig. "Here," as she handed it to Jane who took a short swig and she passed it on to me. I gargled with it and swallowed and then took another longer swig.

"Do I smell sulfur?"

Jane said, "This water has medicinal properties. I think it has some sulfur, iron and magnesium. People come miles to take this water home when someone is ill. Sometimes it is rather strong."

I asked, "Won't a little more brandy be a help to numb the pain?"

"Why, yes it would for all of us." Jane got up and retrieved the brandy. She stood in front of me, legs slightly spread, and her coat opened a bit as she leaned back while she took a long slug. She moved back a little to see if I was looking at her. Her coat opened a little further with that movement. I saw a nice pair of legs. My interest indicator made a movement. Jane then handed the bottle to Ingrid who did the same thing, but she opened her coat further and sooner, and then placed the bottle out of my reach in shallower water. My interest indicator moved up more.

"Don't I get some more brandy?"

Teasingly Ingrid said, "In a few moments it will be warmer and do you more good. Besides I want to see how well you take a little needle prick without very much of it." She spread a blanket out, "This is usually a nude beach, but now it is past our usual time of day and the locals like to use it starting midday. They may be using it soon. We should keep our underwear on." We removed our lab coats. *Wow, they looked so much better in their underwear!*

Ingrid beckoned for me to come to her. We entered the wash side and took a few steps where the water was close to calf deep. I sat down as Ingrid washed my hair and shaved me while Jane poured warm water over my scratches and washed them out. Jane gave me a short explanation of the stuff she was going to use called Yunnan and the fact that she was going to suture one cut up.

Jane cautioned. "Here we only deal with bodies that feel no pain. So, we have nothing here to use to deaden the pain that suturing will cause. Also, there is no penicillin here either."

I put my hands on my knees as I knelt in the pool and lowered my head. Jane gave my skin a little wiggle and a pinch, and then quickly inserted the needle. Both looked to see my face. I kept it straight. My arms continued to press on my knees. Jane did the same to the other side. They bent over again for the next half suture. They both looked at me with each needle prick. They were both cute doing that. My interest indication had waned.

Jane got serious and said, "With these cuts you will be here for a few days. So now we will give you a physical exam! You need to be fit as this is hard work and there are heavy bodies to be moved around. We are going to work you hard."

"I'm a hard worker."

"I hope so!"

They started at the top. One was on each side, ears, eyes, mouth, teeth, chest and abdomen percussion, reflex response, and then a short arm inspection. They both checked for a hernia. They tarried there momentarily. My natural interest indicator had increased to full up with their attentions. Both gals were smiling broadly.

"Jane brightly said, "You pass!"

Ingrid's comment was, "He will do just fine."

At this moment, several Korean kids let out some howls and shrieks as they bounded, jumped and ran down the path towards the pools. Their parents watching their step started to tromp down the dusty path towards the warm pools.

Jane was pointing to the visitors. We turned our backs and put on lab coats as we each muttered something negative about the interruption. Jane said, "We'll continue later!" We hastened towards the Quonset hut on a different trail. In a few steps we were concealed by tall and heavy brush. This path went a little further around and away from the heavily trodden path the family was using.

Jane was now very determined to send messages out promptly. In earnest she said, "Sit down and let's get this done before they take you away from us!" We all sat down and continued right where she had left off. "Your Navy base is right behind us over this mountain a few miles. I have had conversations with some of the men when they visited next door. They say it is a few miles south of the river's mouth. On the road it is about a dozen miles more or less. Your doing a recovery job on your own seems to be rather odd for a trainee. Fully trained specialists do that."

"They are short of help."

Jane went on, "Now, about our accommodations, they are rustic and meager. We have no vehicles in the village. There is only one bicycle and that belongs to a local boy, Jay. We use him as our messenger. We are not set up for guests, don't you know. We could put you up in the supply tent."

We went over to it. It was close by and about eight feet square, a single ridgepole tent with a canvas door and a dirt floor. Jane pointed to a thin shoddy mattress, which had water stains on it and several shabby blankets.

"There is no heat in here and it does get quite cool with all the evening fog and dampness that blows up this valley. When it rains a bit of water might get under the door."

"Hopefully I can get a cot soon."

"I will ask for a cot for you from the Navy. All our food and drinks are over at the local bistro. It is actually a house of ill repute. Right after payday, they have two or three working girls. You could stay there, but if you got caught inside you would be arrested on the spot, hauled off and sentenced for a jolly good term." Jane nodded her head in emphasis. "They do have decent food, however lately all allowances have been cut down to the bare bone. Thanks to the war the water is contaminated and the only drinkable beverage in this village is beer."

"Such a pity we have only beer to drink."

"Getting it is the problem because alcoholic beverage is strictly regulated at United Nation facilities, which this morgue is. By the way, our bistro owner will charge you for your food and drink and may ask for some personal service of you."

"I wonder what will be asked of me?"

"Definitely your money and perhaps some chores like getting wood and maybe supplies."

"Oh my God! My pants!" *My wallet is in my pants.* "My money and identification!" I rushed out to the trashcan.

Jane followed gushing, "The trash must have been picked up while we were at the pool. The wagon goes down this road," pointing to the back of the hut. "He has several stops to make after ours, so he is down the road some distance by now. The dump is someplace on the other side of that hill."

The trash wagon came in sight moving out of the village and had crossed over a small wooden bridge. It was a cart pulled by a donkey attended to by an elder. I ran after the trash cart up on my toes in a sprint. That felt good! *I haven't done this in awhile.* My lab coat burst open flying behind. I was able to stop him, then dug through the damp stinky trash and retrieved my wallet and my identification. I had quite a bit of money in it, a full half a month's pay; one twenty dollar bill, one ten, two fives and three ones. My identification was most important.

I put both hands together bowed, and said, "Thank you Sir." I presented a dollar.

He smiled, nodded his approval and wiggled the reins for the donkey to move.

I jogged back. Ingrid said. "You are a fast runner!"

"Yeah, when I have to. I really need my identification and I have some money, which I need to pay for essentials while here."

We went over to their supply tent where they had a good supply of uniforms for internment. Jane gave me a uniform and scrubs. I put on the scrubs. Then we went to the local bistro, as they preferred to call it. We sat around a wooden table on benches.

A young attractive Korean girl, Ae Cha, brought us tea. Ingrid said, "She is the local cook and speaks English. She will talk your arm off just to use her English. They have so little we take what is offered. The tea is drinkable as they always boil the water before pouring it over the tea."

"That is the way my Mum always made it."

We were early for lunch at the bistro so it would be a while before the sandwiches and tea were served. Some cool tea was available. We each had a cup of that. I wandered around looking the place over. There was a round potbelly wood stove. Several feet away there was a place where wood had been piled on a reed mat. There was no wood inside and the area was picked up. I looked outside and saw that the woodpile was depleted. "I'm not seeing any fire wood."

Jane said, "Getting anything from the Supply Depot lately has been a huge problem. The bistro is able to get supplies because it is on a list of war torn villages that receive aid and the bistro is the town center. They can get beer since it is not a United Nations facility. Last week on a visit there Ingrid and I were turned away. We were not on some kind of a list. They became a bit huffy so we left. Could you give it a try?"

"Sure. Hey, who wants to starve or be without anything to drink, especially beer?"

Ae Cha brought each of us half a baloney like sandwich.

After the first bite I lowered the sandwich, "This baloney has a rather strong and odd taste."

After a long pause Ingrid looked at me and said, "It is not baloney as you know it in America."

I had taken a smaller but good size second bite. "This is pretty strong stuff!" It nearly didn't go down. It seemed to swirl in my mouth, liver like, which I hate with a passion.

After a second rather long pause she continued, "They add their special spicy stuff." She paused again then carefully said, "I think it is more like blood liverwurst."

With that statement my eyes widened with disbelief. I had actually swallowed it! Not just one, but several bites, although each was smaller than the one before. I did not like anything with blood or liver, or any internal organs!

I started to gag. My posture stiffened, then came a wretch! Vomit came up my throat. I swallowed hard and took a sip of tea. Then I took a larger gulp of tea and was able to hold it down. Slowly, I put the remaining sandwich back on my plate.

My hands were flat on the table, eyes very wide. Jane was bursting and shaking trying not to laugh out loud.

I shuddered, then quietly asked, "Doesn't the Bible prohibit our consuming any blood?"

Jane was now grinning from ear to ear, "Yes it does but, here we are not at home don't you know. We have so little to eat we take what is given. I don't really like it either."

Ingrid leaned over extending a hand and softly said, "We do have a few "C" rations in our tent."

I vigorously nodded my affirmation. The canned, "C" ration was cold beef stew left over from World War Two. The "C" rations tasted much better than those sandwiches! Like lead, it went down and stayed there.

After lunch I went to look for the wagon. I saw the same elder walking his donkey back to its barn. I ran after him to see if he could help me pick up the body. I spoke to him in English. He had a rather blank look as though he didn't understand. I used my hands and managed to communicate that way. I hoped that I could get him and the donkey to help me pick up that body about a mile back up the dirt road.

Softly he said, "Elder."

I nodded my understanding but didn't understand its full meaning.

We walked to a storage shack where the two-wheeled cart was. He had a puzzled look. He placed one hand on his forehead and made a face like he had forgotten something. Using his hands he asked me how big was this load? I tried to tell him much bigger than I am. He waved his hands down shaking his head. He then stood up straight, and then he motioned with his hand for me to follow. He led the donkey and me to another shack several yards away also obscured by large bushy shrubs. They looked thorny like blackberry bushes. In this shack there was a four-wheeled cart with wooden spokes and larger wheels than the first cart. Its bed was several inches higher and longer.

I thought the wagon's bed was a bit too high for me to lift that big body up onto the cart all by myself. I would need leverage, a hoist or a crane. A slide would be good.

I looked around. Along the side of the shack there was a headboard and two sideboards. I secured them to the wagon. I found two more boards about eight feet long and a strand of wire and I tossed them on board. There was an old block and tackle hanging in the back of this shack, so I removed the cobwebs and shook off the dust, then loaded them onto wagon.

Elder was hitching the donkey up. First I used English again. He didn't seem to understand. I gestured can we use these? He nodded vigorously. Soon we were on our way. I pointed the direction. Now he had a self-satisfied look on his face.

When we got there, I put rocks behind and in front of a wheel as a brake. I placed the block and tackle in the center at the top of the headboard of the wagon, removed the sideboards and wrapped both together with the wire to make the incline less. I wrapped a line around the body with several hitches. Then I pulled on the block and tackle line. Elder was up on the wagon pulling on the line also. The pulleys were free running. They did not have a stop. I picked up a rock so he could put it between the line and a pulley to press on the line and act as a brake that was needed for the next pull on the line up the incline. It took many tugs and stops but we did it. We pulled the body into the wagon up close to the front with the block and tackle. I replaced the sideboards, and then secured the body bag with pulley line just to be sure that it would stay in place as the roadbed was quite uneven. The elder nodded his approval. We were both exhausted.

I said, "I would sure like to have a beer."

Elder was nodding and smiled as he pointed down the road. *How did he understand that?*

Donkey was looking back at us nodding his head. We sat on the front of the wagon and the donkey started walking. I did not see any command from the Elder for donkey to go. In fact Elder did not have the reins. They were dragging in the dirt. *Donkey could step on one and get hurt.* I hopped off the wagon. The donkey stopped as soon as I was off the wagon. I picked up the reins and gave them to the Elder. I then went up to give the donkey a little pat and climbed back on the wagon. We rode back in silence. On the way back the, donkey seemed to be going faster. Occasionally the body did strain against the tie down lines. Elder pulled our wagon alongside of the morgue tent. The wagon would remain where parked. Then he unhitched the donkey. I gave him a five-dollar bill. It was too much, but two dollars was too little. This was extra work for an elder and he had worked hard and greatly helped.

He said in English, "Thank you. You managed to communicate very well with your hands." He put a hand beside his mouth and spoke behind it; "The women here have been without a man for a long time. They are crazy in the head. They make everyone crazy too. Perhaps you can be of service to them." He winked and left. He was very pleased with himself.

I called after him, "Thank you for your help and advice." He turned smiling and raised a hand in acknowledgment.

Inside the morgue hut there was a heavy and distinct smell of formaldehyde. Jane had typed a requisition form for a cot, and a second memo to the Navy team about my staying here for a few days while my wounds were healing. My wound had been contaminated and should be observed by a competent physician, such as herself. She would send me to their base for a penicillin shot tomorrow and a second in three more days.

Jane wanted to type another form. As she was typing I picked up a bottle of formaldehyde and was reading its label. There was a warning on it that mentioned that it could be an aphrodisiac to female users.

"What does aphrodisiac mean?"

"She said, "In a moment let me finish this. I'm not used to all these interruptions. Our clients are dead quiet." She rolled her eyes.

Ingrid had arrived and sat down. "So!" she asked, "What do we do with our guest?"

I answered making a face and going, "Shh! She wants to finish typing first. I have interrupted her several times."

Ingrid said, "Oh," as she sat down close beside me. We clasped our hands and looked like elementary school kids who had been naughty and were waiting for the schoolmaster's lecture.

In a few minutes Jane was finished with the typing. Then she turned to us and picked up a note pad.

"Zak now I want to question you about your medical training and what brought you here." Jane urged me along by asking lots of probing questions. She wanted to know about everything and was given all the details.

"We can teach you a thing or two that will be of value on the line." She discussed several useful field procedures such as body handling, venal punctures, and lots of cutting and suturing. We will evaluate what was done in the field and what might have been done to keep those bodies out of here. You can learn a lot about fieldwork here. Some of the bodies come in bits and pieces. Your background sounds very useful, but these are humans and that is very different. Can you handle that kind of carnage in humans?"

"Don't I have to develop a stomach for all of it sooner or later? I'm willing to give it a try."

With assurance, "So are we." She paused. "We are scheduled to be relieved in ten days, so we can give you a start towards field applications, that is if you decide to stay with us that long." She said in a lower voice sounding rather disappointed, "The Frogmen will probably come and take you back as soon as you heal in a few days and possibly before."

"Well if they do come, maybe I could lie on a gurney under a cover and they could be told that I was off somewhere getting wood, supplies or something. They aren't likely to be turning the covers back in here."

"I love that!" Jane exclaimed.

"Good thinking!" was Ingrid's comment.

There was a quiet pause while Jane finished typing another form, then she asked, "Ingrid, would you go find Jay and see if he can deliver these messages this afternoon?" Ingrid assented and departed taking the messages with her.

Jane said, "Zak there will be a small fee, but he is dependable and they will get there this afternoon. You may be able work the fee off by doing some chores for the bistro. Jay is closely related to them. Would you be willing to do that?"

"Sure, I'm handy. I will do anything asked of me."

Jane smiled and looked amused and softly said; "I will hold you to that." Jane and I went to their tent, which was across a hill and upwind from the morgue. On the way she pointed out the latrine, which was an open ditch surrounded and covered by old canvas draped over a wooden frame. Their tent was partly concealed by heavy brush. It seemed to be quite a bit larger than the supply tent and it had raised wood flooring and two hospital beds, a potbelly stove, a kerosene lantern on a small table and an open wood frame for clothes. The hospital beds were sturdily built higher than a normal bed and wider. Jane sat on her bed and she patted it for me to come over and sit on it. It had a nice soft mattress. She leaned back and gave her hair a swing backwards. At that moment Ingrid entered the tent.

Jane then said, "Zak now is a good time to answer your question about the term on the formaldehyde label. Aphrodisiac means it is a sexual stimulus. While working around formaldehyde women often become quite sexually stimulated. It doesn't seem to affect men that way at all. I know for sure that is true!"

"Ingrid, do you think that label is correct?"

"Definitely! It winds me up so much I could just bust! Combine that with all the shelling it drives me half crazy. When they fire those damn cannons we are not able to sleep at night. It stirs our innards. Both sides fire lots of shells. That makes me extremely in need." She slowly moved up to the bed and stood between my open knees and was looking me right straight in the eye.

I looked straight back saying, "That sounds terrible. If there's anything at all I can do, I will certainly do it. Just let me know."

Ingrid gave me a hip nudge and said, "I hear someone outside!" She then darted out the door.

Smiling Jane mentioned, "She has the eyes and ears of a wolf."

Then she said, "Oh! I have an Oriental Robe that you could use. I got it for seductive purposes, but that guy turned out to be a total dud. It has never been used. Would you like to see it?"

"Sure! Bring it out!" I removed my lab coat and stepped out of my pants just to see how it would actually look on me. She had it on a hanger made of reeds in the open clothes rack. It was red with embossed golden dragons front and back. I put it on with a little flair, "Very nice. I like it." I turned around giving it a swirl.

She said, "It's perfect!" Then she jokingly added, "I charge!"

I cheerfully answered. "I pay!" Then I quickly added, "Ah, - can we barter?"

"We should be able to work something out."

Just then Ingrid stuck her head in again and urgently announced, "Jane, there are two families of customers waiting at the morgue. They are the ones who were at the pool. The both want their kin folks' bodies so they can bury them properly in their family cemeteries."

Jane uttered, "Damn! - Are there two families and two bodies?"

"No. There are three bodies."

"Then, I will need your help Ingrid. Zak this will take half of forever."

They quickly departed. Jane was in charge of internment. The families found their kin on the plot map. Ingrid went to get a few local laborers. Jane took the parents to the temporary graves, where the laborers would exhume the coffins. They had new South Korean flags. This was part of the service to causalities and was the purpose of the temporary cemeteries in Korea. It would take all afternoon for them to complete this task.

As they departed the tent I removed my robe and got back into work clothes.

Chapter Fourteen

CHORES

Ae Cha was coming my way as I stepped out of the gal's tent. She said, "Mama San said you can do at the supply depot what they could not do as she waved at the gal's tent. I must give you free fuckey fuckey. She wants you volunteering very good. I pay before you go, yes? We do fuckey fuckey here now! We use this." She held a condom in her hand.

"Not just now. I want to get wood for tonight's dinner fire. I want some hot tea and some rice tonight. Can you show me where there is some dry loose wood?"

Ae Cha pointed, "I will take you there. We can do fucky fucky there."

There was a trail that led to a gravel beach at river's edge. "So, just what might I do at the supply depot that they did not?"

"You crazy guy." She gave me a little nudge. Women run the supply depot. They are crazy wanting to do fuckey fuckey. I know that for fuckey fuckey they will give you many more things. We need so many things. Mama-San has very long list. You will see. You do fuckey fuckey to them they give you much more than an old haggard begging woman. At that place one is very fat and ugly. The other is very skinny and ugly. Her face looks very sad, like an old dog with many wrinkles. You close your eyes and do fuckey fuckey to them. Yes?"

"Yeah, - - If I have too."

The beach was littered with a lot of wood washed up during high water in the stream. We both gathered up an armload of stove size loose wood and trudged up the hill back to the bistro. Some of it had some rot and would burn fairly fast. After our second trip with arms full of wood Mama-San was very happy. She asked Ae Cha, in Korean, "Did you do fuckey fuckey with him?"

"No he wants to do that when he returns tomorrow with much stuff."

Mama-San pointed to the wood. "Did you ask him to do this?"

"No Mama-San! He asked me to show him where some wood was. As soon as we were on the bank he just started picking up wood. He gave me some to carry. We have gathered enough wood for the evening meal, yes?"

Mama-San looked at me with narrow eyes. She moved up close, her long fingernail was poking my chest.

"We need you to do a very great performance tomorrow! You need to act like those women are beautiful and the best in the world! You must pretend you feel much more than you do! I coach you now. Every woman I mentor needs coaching. This is something everyone thinks they do so well when they are only so so. Must please customer very much, yes! That very good business, yes! First, I will tell how to make much good noise. You will please every woman much better by making much good noise, yes!" She provided examples. She had me copy what she did. We worked on making noises and heavy breathing for nearly an hour.

Ae Cha said that Mama-San was psychic and is able to know what men could do. She said, "You are successful tomorrow! You on right track - almost."

The sun was lowering before the gals returned from the exhumation chore. Jane would be free in a little while, after some paperwork.

Ingrid said, "Okay! So, now let's get started on your pilot while there is still light. We will work on him outside as the ventilation is poor inside and the burn cases are smelly." She presented a jar of Vick's Vapor Rub. "Put a little of this up your nose. It helps reduce the stink and we do get quite a few bodies. We will use these heavy rubber gloves to keep the yucky and stinky stuff off of us."

We measured him. He was six feet one, and then she estimated his weight at two hundred and ten pounds. He was not quite as big as he had seemed. His flesh was too burned to make a normal venal puncture. It is much harder to insert a needle in a corpse, as the veins do not have the heart pumping pressure through the system.

"Now we insert the needle like this." Then she put a small square of gauze under the needle, and then wrapped it with a roll of gauze. "Tape won't do well on this charred skin. I will wrap gauze under and over to hold the needle in place. Now you can roll a few wraps of gauze around his arm, and then secure it by placing tape on top of the gauze. Also you can pull gauze apart and tie a knot when there is no tape. It's just as good. Sometimes it is faster, especially in the dark. On the line you will be working in the dark and low light. We will be training you in both." She started the bottle of formaldehyde with a few other chemicals. "The differences in formulas are complex. You can learn about that later but there may not be enough time. We will drain his blood into this container. The locals can use it." She cut down as that leg was very badly charred and put the needle in on the exit flow. "This is the best place to learn as they do not complain and we can always repair the damage. This guy will have a closed casket."

The corpse had an abdominal wound that had some fat showing.

"Zak let me show you something." She took the scalpel handle and ran its flat side over a roll of belly fat tissue with a little pressure. Dark yellowish fluid oozed from the fat. She held the handle for me to see the fluid. "He was a heavy smoker. This is what smoking creates in most tissues throughout the entire body. In the thick fat places it can form pools of this stuff." It looked bad and smelled worse. I was quite surprised. She pointed out cigarette stains on his fingers and that his mouth was tainted and slightly dried. "It would get worse if he were to live to an old age. That is all for now." She stepped close and smelled my breath. She was close enough to kiss. I resisted my mounting urge. She stepped back, "I do not smell smoke on your breath. You don't smoke?"

"Only when I need to get a break. Usually they only allow 'smoke breaks.' Then I let it burn. No inhaling, just some puffing to keep it lit."

"Even that is addictive, it just takes longer."

"Zak you should take a nap as the cannon firing should begin again tonight and that means no one gets any sleep. We play cards. We are not likely to be receiving bodies today due to this morning's fog and now it looks like it will rain. Koreans do not drive in fog or on wet roads. They make ruts and get stuck and it makes big messes for them and for others to deal with."

The fog had cleared hours ago. Now there were heavy clouds gathering. The wind had picked up and was blowing up this valley from the coast.

We washed our hands, and then went to our respective tents. I did not sleep. After an hour of tossing about on that thin pad I went over to their tent. It was dusk and Ingrid was awake, sitting on the bedside swinging her feet. She smiled brightly when I peeked in. She motioned me in.

We carried flashlights with a sheath to check on the pilot's body. She made a few adjustments telling me what and why. He would be fine here in the cool air for the time it takes to finish this job. We carefully put a waterproof cover over the body.

Then we went to the bistro and each ordered a beer. Hers went on my tab.

Ae Cha said, "We are very low on beer. This is the last case."

"Did we get enough wood Ae Cha?"

"Almost. Mama-San said it would burn fast as most of it is small and old. There is enough wood for some hot food this evening and a small fire all night. I have more sausage. You likee sausage?"

"Not all that well. It has a strong taste!" *This is no stateside café!* I paused, held my head down, then pulled it up and firmly said, "No! I don't like it! I will have rice and hot tea if that is possible."

"Maybe yes, but tonight is a cold rainy night. Perhaps we go to bed early to keep warm. Maybe do much fuckey fuckey?"

"Thank you for the offer, but no thanks. If I get rice tonight, I will bring many supplies back from the depot tomorrow, maybe then?"

Ingrid said in a surprised voice, "You didn't take her up on her offer!"

I leaned towards her and quietly said, "I don't have quite enough energy."

"Aha, I think you are telling me a big fat lie."

Jane came in and sat on the bench beside me. *She feels so good.* Our knees lightly touched.

Ingrid said, "Zack just told Ae Cha that he didn't have enough energy to have sex with her. I think he is lying!"

Jane answered Ingrid, "I sure hope so." Then she turned to me, "I asked for wood, but was told there would be no more deliveries until October."

"I can walk to the supply headquarters tomorrow. It's just three or four miles and it won't hurt to explain our needs." Then I asked, "Was the clerk female?"

"Yes. She is big, fat, and ugly."

I made a horrid face then, "Maybe she really needs a smile and a little attention from a guy as an incentive. Tomorrow I will try to be persuasive! I will close my eyes and think of you, love."

Ingrid rolled her eyes saying, "Sure you will."

"Hey, I have a good imagination and will have to do my duty as I see it. Tomorrow I will have to do everything I can to get us enough supplies. Correct?"

"Well, a guy might possibly do a bit better with a female clerk. I might be able to get Jay's bicycle for you, for a price of course."

Dinner was meager with a small bowl of rice and tea. A few slivers of that sausage were passed around. I handed that along taking none. *No wonder they are so thin.*

The shelling started, as did the rain. The shelling sound seemed to be much too close for comfort. It seemed to be very close, within striking distance. I was told that there was a South Korean unit stationed a few miles away. Most of the bistro customers came from there. We ordered more drinks. These were from the last case of beer in the house.

I listened intently as both women talked about close shelling creating extreme anxiety and how it created unusually high desires of procreation. They were not able to shake it. In this state they would become very demanding and they would be inclined to do unusual things.

Jane said, "I think what we have is a form of shell shock. In men the reaction was all too often the opposite. Most became dysfunctional. Some others will become boastful but still unable to perform."

My being new to the shelling this close, young and interested in women and their problems was worth a little something, but alas, of no material help at the moment. Listening was only one small part, but it was a start of a bridge to the basic problem.

I was not hearing any suggestions, not even words that could be twisted, bent or stretched. They were officers and I enlisted. I understood that I had to be asked, better to be ordered, before I made any move that could be remotely construed as having any sexual implications. They were in the driver's seat and firmly held the steering wheel. Their talk was all so very clinical. They were just talking shop.

We were on the last of the beer and soon would be getting ready to retire to our respective tents. The gals had half a mug of beer or more. I had drained my glass and was fiddling with it on the table. There I sat. *I would not be getting an invitation tonight or any time soon.* I gazed into my empty glass and said, "It's time for me to retire. - Good night." They echoed my comment.

I opened the door. It was pouring down rain. I picked up an umbrella at the door and walked to my tent. There was a huge puddle in front of my tent. When I opened the door it was flooded in there also. I returned to the bistro. *I will just have to stay here. The military police are not likely to raid this place tonight.*

As I stepped up on the wooden porch in front of the bistro, Jane was coming out the door with umbrella in her hand.

"I'm flooded out. I will stay in here tonight."

Jane had her hand on my chest and was pushing me back. "Such a pity. If you stay in here they will arrest you. They will take you away, toss you in the brig and throw the key away. You don't want that now do you?"

"That would be a huge waste of time." We embraced and moved towards their tent.

"I am so full of lust."

"Me too!"

Our pace quickened. As soon as we went through the door the open umbrellas fell to the floor causing streams of water to run down to the floor.

Chapter Fifteen

❖

SUPPLY DEPOT

In the morning Ingrid and I went to the pool, "I don't want you to have cuts and missed spots when you approach them for rations. You need to look good. It is a first impression." She used a straight razor.

As I departed there were some puddles and a ground fog from last night's rain. It took about an hour to get to and locate the supply depot. The entrance was partly concealed by shrubs.

I introduced myself to Darren, a male Transportation Clerk, and presented our wish list. His first question was, "This is only a grocery list. This isn't the correct form and it doesn't have a name or number on it. Where are you from?"

"Presently a morgue a few miles up this valley by a sharp bend in the river."

"I don't have a morgue on my list." He called the Captain Steward to whom I repeated the directions. "I sent supplies for its reconstruction after a shell had hit it. The restored unit was to be managed by a foreign command and they had not yet provided forms for supply service." He got out a chart and I was able to point out the location because the river made a sharp turn there. It did have a number and that was where he thought it was. "Is it open now?"

"Yes, it has been for a time. I don't have any idea how long. I just arrived yesterday."

A tall busty blond, Sara attached to the Swedish unit joined our chat group and said, "Last week two emaciated snippy British women had made demands without a unit number, a name or a requisition. They quickly got upset and left in a huff."

Meekly I asked, "Is there any possible way it can be registered for supplies?"

"Sure. All you have to do is ask. You just did!" Darren promptly presented a form and we filled it out right there at the counter. "Sign right here on all five copies."

"But it says the commanding officer and I'm not an officer and not in command."

Captain Steward stepped up to the counter. "Zak, one of the duties of a field commander is to care for his charges by asking for adequate rations and to stand up for his and their rights. That is what you are doing. Sign the form."

"Yes sir!"

"Have you ever driven a ton and a half Chevy truck?"

"Yes sir! Before I joined the Navy I often used them for hauling hay.

"Good, I have a proposal for you. If you will take those dead bodies to the morgue I will process this form and fill this list and send you a full load of wood."

"I can do that."

What is your full name?"

"Zakary Scott."

"Watch how I do this." He took a pen and scribbled a big Z and a few wiggles then a large S and some unintelligible wiggles. "Observe", he wrote MD more legibly. "We all understand that means Medical Department. Believe me it will never be questioned and I do want to be rid of those bodies as soon as possible! The locals are not willing to handle our dead bodies in any way. They just won't do the job! Around here dead bodies give everyone the willies. I must discharge my duty concerning the deceased."

Since loading the truck would take a few minutes Captain Steward thought this was a good time for me to hear about the duties and responsibilities of the Quartermasters' Corps. We went into his office where I got a good lecture from him. It went something like this.

"The Quartermaster Corps is in charge of all processes of those who had lost their lives in and around combat areas. In every battle around the world we require that all bodies be treated with respect throughout the process and with the highest possible dignity. The morgues are to restore the deceased to as lifelike and natural as possible. There are no short cuts or mutilations allowed. It is mandatory that all bodies be removed from the field regardless of the circumstances. No differential treatment is made because of race, rank or religion. Special advances and attacks are routinely made to recover a single body. Very rarely do we ever demolish a body by friendly fire, if so, then by disintegration. There are an unbelievable number of territorial, political, religious and moral issues in these policies."

He went on, "As a medic you will be in places where you can be of great help to the troops. Chaplains are very scarce on the line. Grieving and honors for the deceased are very important. These men are closer and more dependent on each other under fire than can be imagined by the average person. As a medic you can do a great deal for the troops by reading a passage and showing empathy."

"Sir, I have no problem doing that."

"There is a real need for those bodies not showing a definite cause of death to be held in a warm area for a minimum of twenty four hours. They are called sleepers. Sometimes they wake up! That justifies a whole lot of extra care and expense. We value life! The enemy does not!"

"I understand! Thank you sir."

The Korean laborers had piled three rows of wood rail high against the cab and hitched up a large trailer full of supplies. The Captain was happy to present the keys to the truck. I thanked him for the use of the truck. I parked it alongside the loading platform, carefully pulled the bodies onto the back half of the truck and promptly departed for the morgue. This truck was nearly new with less than five thousand miles on it.

At the morgue there were several papas-sans who helped unload the wood. I carried the bodies inside the morgue and laid them on tables. Jane and Ingrid started working on the bodies as some were in need of their immediate attention.

I was able to be back at the supply depot in time for noon chow. There I was able to talk to several of the guys I had seen earlier. They wanted to know how I got into a morgue. I told them a short version. The guys that I was talking to were very much in agreement with the Captain's policies and happy to help us out. They understood that without a requisition and a number why wood and supplies were not sent to the morgue. None of them wanted to be a "sleeper" either and buried alive. That thought was horrifying!

"None will be sleepers while I am there! Each body will be definitely one that has perished."

I mentioned how pathetic the town's people were. They too needed a requisition form. I filled out and signed a form for emergency assistance for the village.

I politely asked for the use of a jeep so I could get my penicillin shot from the Navy base. They could do that. Again I had some more paperwork to fill out. I was on my way in a few minutes with a map in hand. I thanked them for the use of the Jeep. As I was driving to the Navy base I wondered, just how far I had stuck my neck out. *I guess I will find out sooner or later.*

At the Navy base I asked, "By any chance did you received a memo from Jane?" They had it. Since I was going there for supplies they gave me the clothing chit that Jane had typed up for me. Maybe I would be able to get into a proper uniform much sooner. The cot request was under review. It would have to go up line. A medic looked at my wounds and gave me a penicillin shot, "Come back in three days. It is red and swollen so don't over exert yourself."

Chief Carpenter said, "All the injured men have been returned to base and all are on light duty. Swede has gone out on a scouting patrol this morning. Where did you get the jeep?"

"From the Quartermasters."

"Aha, the Quartermasters. They are good at keeping track of things."

"I am doing some light duty around a morgue. Today I'm getting supplies and taking bodies back. The morgue staff is willing to give me some field medical training while I'm healing. What do you think?"

"Get all the training you can. I am very sure you will be using it. How long will it take?"

"They did mention a few weeks."

"That is good. I will send your ship a message. Incidentally those cameras you found are being effectively used."

How did he know about that?

I did run into Sara when I returned to the supply depot. She was a big boned girl, not fat, and not at all ugly! She had classic features, nice eyes and her breasts were nicely shaped and larger than normal. She asked me, "Did you handle those dead bodies?"

"Yes, I did."

She shivered and shook all over, "How could you do that?"

"Well I will pick you up and show you how."

"Don't touch me!" She quivered again.

"They can't hurt anyone and I won't hurt you." I stepped back with my hands up. "Okay."

We exchanged a raised eyebrow look. My gaze did drift down to her beauties. I said, "Nice!" On my way out I took several steps before I looked back. She was looking to see if I would turn around. We both smiled when I did.

I got substantially more food for the village than I had asked for. Also there was a trailer attached with several hundred gallons of water. Sara was not present when I returned the truck.

They told me I had the jeep for as long as I was in the area so I put Jay's bike in the back. It had a trailer loaded with barrels of beer. I thanked them earnestly.

I arrived late for dinner. Ae Cha warmed some up for me. The trailer was very quickly unloaded. Many villagers remained to make a toast to my success. It seemed like everyone crowded around to find out how I was able to get everything asked for and more.

"I simply filed some forms and said, thank you."

Chapter Sixteen

TRAINING

Jane, Ingrid and I had a lengthy discussion on hysteria and about a treatment regime. Jane had several special massage techniques she wanted to test. Both had their special needs and requests. They described in detail what they wanted, and then we practiced until the art was mastered.

They had me take care of every corpse as if I was in the field and they were alive. We discussed what was done and any change that could have been done. I did some cosmetics and nearly all of the cutting and suturing. I became very quick and good.

Jane's medical degree was in Holistic Medicine and her experience was extremely valuable as was Ingrid's nursing. I listened intensely and paid strict attention. The activity was high and I vigorously pumped information from them and they generously gave of it. My mind opened and absorbed nearly every word they said. All this was so much more than what I had ever imagined or had hoped for.

Toward the end of the first week a body of a young Korean female arrived from a village some distance to the west. We guessed she was about eighteen to twenty years of age and had received huge pelvic damage. Apparently she had stepped on a mine and been cut with large sharp pieces that were blown straight up between her legs and sliced up her middle. One chopped up to just below her naval. She had drained very quickly. In the vulva area there were three major cuts revealing an incredible number of nerves exposed.

Jane said, "The text books used in medical schools were amazingly short of information on this part of human anatomy. Most of the cadavers used in medical schools were older women who had been embalmed for quite some time, both of which skewed the measurements and observations because of the shrinking and drying effects on body tissues. This fresh normal young woman has much more fullness of tissue." Jane wanted to get details of this young woman before embalming and closure were started. I held the tissue apart while she took photos and Ingrid wrote notes.

Jane strongly advocated using Yunnan, a Chinese powder that was their great contribution to medicine. It stopped bleeding promptly and promoted healing of wounds and was used to treat a host of other ailments. They taught about holistic and oriental procedures, wounds and trauma, as I would not be treating ailments in the field.

By the end of their first term the gals were asked to stay a few more weeks before they were sent home because there was such a shortage of qualified personnel. They got an extension for me too. That was a good thing as I had so much more to learn. We got along exceptionally well.

My learning curve would never be this high again. I would never again be so mentally sharp or zealous.

In the last hour of the last day there remained one last body that was on line receiving fluids. It needed to be moved so we could clean up that part of the building. I tugged on the gurney. It wouldn't move. I knelt down to see what the problem was and saw that a wheel was stuck in a knothole. Ingrid came over to help. As I pulled up she gave the gurney a tug back. The stuck wheel jumped out of the hole. The bottle of formaldehyde banged against its holding stand, broke and poured down all over my neck and back and down my left leg and into my boot.

Jane said a few words that I didn't hear due to my muttering. I was doing a Donald Duck. She then came over with a new bottle of fluids. I picked up the broken glass. Ingrid sopped up the formaldehyde and threw the rags out. Jane said, "We will just have to wait. He is running very well."

Ingrid told me, "Go to the pool and wash off with shampoo." She presented a bottle of it.

Jane said, "Just jump in the river. The cold water will be good for that."

It was still quite cool outside and the river was running cold. I went to the warm pool with shampoo in hand and jumped in. There seemed to be a reaction of some kind. My back and left side felt a little bit warmer. This was such a lovely combination, formaldehyde mixing with the smell of the pool water! The odor was overwhelming. Jane looked at my back seeing that I had a few small blisters and told me, "Now, you just take a good dip in the sea when you get there. Several minutes in cool salt water should do it up quite correctly."

While I was changing clothes their relief arrived in a helicopter. They promptly climbed aboard and were flown east.

The new guy quickly opened all the windows and doors further. "Never mind the body, I will care for it. Get off to wherever you are going. Trot right along now."

I drove the jeep to the supply depot. They said, "You can take it to the Navy base. We will be along in a few days to pick it up. Be sure to leave it outside."

I arrived at the Navy base in time for noon chow. I was sent outside and downwind from everyone. My services were no longer needed, as everyone was fit and back to full duty status. Also, my time had expired. Very soon I was transported at the far end of their speedboat to a supply ship off the coast ten miles or so. That ship refused to take me aboard, so I was taken much further out to sea to my ship at a very high speed. As soon as I arrived in the Medical Department they sent me directly to the shower to scrub up. The pharmacy made up a concoction, but it did little good. Very few of my shipmates enjoyed the slightly changed smell of whatever it was. At the evening chow I was ushered to the fantail. I felt like Le Pew, the Disney cartoon's Stinky the skunk.

I tried several soaps and shampoos. Nothing worked. I skipped rope to work up a sweat and then showered for a third time. One of the guys, a former well digger, had worked with stinky water and made a solution of bleach and water for me. I rinsed all over with that. It seemed to work right away. Now I smelled like bleach and something else that was indescribable. My dog tags were discolored and I had to have new ones made. I went to the metal shop for that. Their service was quite quick. "They will be ready in the morning."

I put fresh green scrubs on and socks as one of my boots smelled of formaldehyde. I had to buy new ones. I was not very welcome at ship's store either as my new smell was a bit strong. I put the new boots on and went up to the flight deck to air out my new offensive odor. On the way up to the flight deck my stinky old boots went over the side. A few shipmates thought that my new smell would evaporate quickly in a stiff breeze.

While wandering around the flight deck I ran into a few of the guys I had come aboard ship with and exchanged a few "How ya doing?" comments. I stood downwind while speaking to the guys. One told me that after my departure he had heard that some guys were quickly transferred off ship and that most admitted to and were convicted of homosexuality and were discharged.

We watched as our helicopter landed on the ship's port side aircraft elevator with a sick or injured sailor from one of the smaller ships. It shut down and was lowered to the main deck, and then soon it was lifted back up to the flight deck minus the sick sailor. We watched as our helicopter was refueled and was starting up. I loved to watch helicopters start up, as it was now, their blades waving in a breeze, and then standing out as they gained speed.

While we were standing there chatting I caught the eye of Commander Baker. We exchanged a friendly recognition nod and waved. He turned and quickly disappeared. Just as fast he reappeared. He had a bullhorn in hand and called, "Scott! Get in the chopper! NOW! GO! GO!!" He was thrusting his arm portside and pointing at our chopper. Again he commanded, "GO!"

I ran over to our ship's copter, which was now turning up very fast on the port aircraft elevator. I jumped in. We were airborne instantly. Its nose turned sharply down and its speed went up and turned towards land at full speed. I had to hang on with both hands. They had just heard a radio call from an injured pilot in a damaged plane preparing to ditch.

As I was strapping in the crewman told me that the duty swimmer was not readily available for this mission. He had been dropped off while they flew to the other ship for the sick guy and he was not in the ready station. The crewman said, "Lieutenant Gardner and I recognized you and Baker did too. Welcome back!"

"Thanks!" *Wow! I really felt honored!*

"A pilot is heading for the water as we are speaking. He will bail out in a few minutes. His target is to land beyond the breakers." I nodded my understanding.

A person could remain conscious five minutes in this cold water dressed as I was. It was likely that the pilot would require my help getting in the harness and perhaps some first aid.

Lieutenant Gardner asked, "Are you able to do all that?"

"Yeah, sure! I've done that before."

"Great." He stuck his hand back with his thumb up. The plan was that I ride the harness down to the pilot and secure him in it and fix his wound. When he was secure I would wave. Then they would start hoisting the pilot up and toss the life raft down to me. I was to get in it and paddle a few miles down around a point of land that marked the demilitarized line. I was told to stay well off that point as it had lots of sharp rocks. We could faintly see it through the haze two points off our port side about four miles away. "We will pick you up on the far side of it. It will take us about half an hour to get back. We have to refuel. You should be there by then. We will look for you on the beach."

The crewman said, "At last look the raft had a reflecting mirror and flares you can use when you hear the chopper." As he was talking, I unconsciously put the med bag over my shoulder, much like an infantryman would take hold of his rifle.

"Okay, I understand. - By the way, why is there a strip of fog under us?"

"There is a stream of warmer water and the air above is colder."

The pilot of the damaged plane was trying to get close to that point marking the division line. He had turned his plane towards that point. His cockpit was filled with smoke. His plane had a fire in the instruments. He used the fire extinguisher to put that out. It was still smoldering a lot. His left leg was burned and it was very painful. He was choking and gasping for air. He had radioed his intentions. There was too much smoke to go any further or make a water landing. His goggles were speckled with dark oil, which streamed onto his face in the strong wind from his open cockpit. He would bail out soon after as the nose of his plane crossed the water line. He wanted to be a little further out due to the possibility of his being shot at from the ground. In order to get a little more time he raised the port wing up a little and had trimmed the plane so it would fly ahead about a minute and slowly start a turn, which would turn into an increasing bank and a spiral dive. He climbed partly out straddling the cockpit edge. When he was sure that he could land in water beyond breaker's edge he bailed out. As he descended he was able to see his plane in a spiral dive a mile or so further out to sea. The gooks had taken a few shots at him as he descended. He let air out from his parachute on one side, which made him swing from side to side. That way he was harder to hit with rifle fire. Losing air made him drop faster. He hit the water in a side swing well beyond the breakers. He was able to get a breath of air as the edge of his parachute fell over him. He removed his harness and swam underwater out from under the big white parachute canopy. He removed his shiny gold helmet, put a little water in it to keep the top down and tossed it in from the parachute's outer edge. He then inflated his life vest. The current would pull him out to sea faster than the parachute and helmet resting on the surface. They would be good targets for the squad of gooks he saw on the cliff. They had fired at his plane when it went overhead. They were running towards the cliff dodging some large brush as they went. They fired at what they thought was him after he had hit the water. They saw the shiny golden helmet and were shooting at it. The pilot had taken several underwater swimming strokes out to sea so his orange vest was visible to sea. He was moving away from the gooks. Water made his dark green flight suit harder for the gooks to see, so was his wet dark hair. Their shots did not hit him.

I was hanging onto a line with my feet on a harness swinging from an arm sticking out from the chopper and was lowered down to just above the water. I dropped into the water just a few yards from him, put the harness around him then pulled the cinch up. I slipped underwater to look at his wounds. The burn looked bad. I pulled some gauze pads out of my kit and sunk underwater again. It was so very cold under water! I tied a protective bandage around his leg, then came up and waved to the crewman.

While the pilot was being lifted he was swung out from the chopper as it moved sharply to starboard. As soon as he was clear the crewman pushed a life raft out the door inflating it as he pushed it out. The raft quickly blew open, then came floating down. It flipped around and landed upside down its yellow belly up.

The gooks on the cliff were firing at the pilot being pulled up. Our chopper was hit on the windshield in front of Lt. Gardner who turned towards the fog bank at full speed. The dangling pilot was swung violently from side to side as Lt. Gardner flew a hard to hit staggered up and down pattern. They were soon out of range of the gook rifles.

The raft hit the water upside down and I took a few underwater breaststrokes towards it. As the chopper moved out of range the gooks directed their firing to the yellow life raft. It attracted enough lead to tear it to smithereens and it sunk in a minute after it hit the water. Bullets slow very fast after entering water. They zigzag and leave many small air bubbles trailing after them. I swam sidestroke at an angle to the shore so I could see the gooks on the cliff and I was a smaller target. It took several very long minutes for the gooks to leave.

Chapter Seventeen

OUT-OF-BODY

I was making progress to shore using the sidestroke. I could keep my arms underwater, not splash, and swim pretty fast. When the gooks were out of sight I started using the Australian crawl, a racing stroke, face down for two strokes and up for air on the third. My boots helped keep my feet underwater and the surface splashing down. I was getting cold. I increased my swimming as fast as possible. *I've got to get out of this cold water!*

Finally, I was in a wave. The outflowing tide shortened its break. I tried to stand up but there was such a strong undertow it pulled my feet out from under. I staggered to get up. I had lost ground and had been swept further out. I was floundering and in a mild panic. I started to see red. I took a slower stroke to take a longer breath. I saw two children playing on the beach. They saw my efforts and they urged me to go faster but I had slowed. The girl let out a shrill scream. They were running at the water's edge. My vision went from red to black. I was rising up looking down at my body, which was face down drifting out to sea. I saw the two children splashing as they ran toward me into the shallow water.

I looked up and saw a tunnel of white light. I was heading into it at a terrific speed. A figure in white suddenly appeared saying, "Not yet! Help is coming." A long finger was pointing as I was being turned back towards the cold water from where I came. The largest voice in the universe deeply thundered, **"Your work is not finished!"**

WAR WOUNDS

I was receding back at a tremendous speed. What was pointed out came clearly into view. I saw two dolphins racing towards my body. The first dolphin hit my left rib cage. Instantly I zapped back inside my extremely cold body. The second dolphin thrust me into a wave. That wave deposited me partly on the shore. Its turbulence swirled gravel and sand around me. I was conscious.

I had dug my hand into the course sand and pulled. I raised my head and saw the two children very close. I held an arm up. "Help me!" They took my arm and pulled me a little further up onto the course sand. Water from the wave was tugging at me. I was slowly slipping back out to sea. That felt dreadful! The girl screamed again in a high-pitched shrill. Their father came running at full speed. He plowed into the wave, grabbed my arm and pulled hard. Everything went black again.

An elder was sitting out of doors enjoying a pipe. Directly overhead he saw a pilot bail out of a smoking plane. He had watched all the events including my being pulled out of the water. He asked a man who was near by to get a donkey and take that wet man to a certain feeding trough at the other end of the village. They did that and put a feedbag over my head to hide my face, and then covered me with hay. I remained passed out for sometime. When someone shook the trough, I awoke. I could not see because of the feedbag they had put over my head. I heard harsh voices asking questions. They were probably North Korean troops who had come to search the place. They poked bayonets through the hay. I could feel the pressure of hay moving as they bayoneted hay just above me. That woke me up! They finished poking the hay and were looking around. The troops finally departed. Their voices had been very stern and had a warning sound.

After the troops departed and were out of hearing and down the dirt path some distance the North Korean farmer tipped me out of the trough. That really made my side hurt. He excitedly said something to me in Korean. His voice was stern. I was still wet and so cold I could barely move. He pressed me along and waved good-bye. I took a few steps, turned and bowed with my hands together. He did the same thing. He repeatedly and rapidly pointed to the road. He was very anxious for me to leave. It was some distance to the road. I was

149

shuffling down the path to the road when a small child toddled up to me. He wore a heavy coat that touched the ground. A commanding voice came from a shanty house several yards uphill. A canister slipped out from his coat. He just stood there looking up at me. I took a quick step closer and gave the canister a quick kick with the side of my boot back towards the house. It was a poorly directed kick as it went towards a small shack and rolled out of sight into a depression. The farmer who had been urging me to move along now fell flat on the ground. I did too only much slower. I reached for the child and pulled him down where I could shield him from flying particles. In a second there was a blast. No particles reached us. I pulled the child up as I rose. He was crying. I gave him a few gentle pats and hurried along. The farmer directed his screaming at someone in the shack.

It hurt to breathe. I was breathing through my mouth. That didn't work very well. My ribs were moving too much. I switched to breathing through my nose and that helped some.

I staggered up the road several hundred yards or more. I heard chatter and stopped to listen. It was getting closer from ahead. I saw some blackberry like bushes nearby. I crawled under them using my right arm and my legs to move inward as far in as possible. As they came closer I lay quiet. Tears from pain were running down my cheek.

Three gook soldiers stopped to pee in the bushes, one only a few feet from me. Some of his piss spray came very close to me. A drop of his pee landed on leaf just inches short of my boot. I shivered as he was looking over his shoulder talking to the others. I forced off a second shiver as he turned back towards me.

I heard the sound of a large aircraft engine flying slow and low. The gooks hurried under some trees just down the road to take cover from the plane. The sound faded. The gooks continued down the hill and around the bend I had just come up. I waited a few minutes. I listened. Hearing nothing, I slowly slithered from under the bush and continued over the hill. In awhile the sound of low and slow aircraft was clearly heard again coming from another direction. Those sounds made me feel like I was being looked for.

I tried to divert my attention from my side by thinking about my new boots. I tried to walk on soft dirt so they would make less noise. One way to break boots in is to get them wet, then walk in them. Yeah. That's what I'm doing. I did not expect to break them in this soon or this way. *Yeah, I got that saltwater dunk Jane wanted me to do. I'm not stinky anymore!* I said my thanks to God for his help. I also asked for the sun to shine and its warmth.

I staggered along for a while and paused at the hilltop. I desperately looked around. The road turned to the right up into a broad canyon with an open field with oat like green grass more than knee high to offer some protection. I took a few more steps and could see the ocean to my left. I saw a path going left. That was where the Navy wanted me, but there was no place to hide on a beach. I could be easily seen and shot. The cliff lowered as it turned towards a flat portion further ahead and then it rose again as it turned seaward towards the point. I saw some very jagged rocks well out and many more in close. *I should be on the other side of that point right about now.* I was so anxious I peed.

I turned right and was on a narrow road inland where the sun shone lighter and brighter. I had prayed for this sun and warmth. I better not walk away from my prayer.

I spied a straw hat just inside the field I was passing, picked it up, dusted it off and put it on. I saw a Corsair fly by about half a mile off shore, but I was not able to see the pilot. I waved at it with the hat in my right hand. Not seeing me, the plane flew on.

The path curved around a hill to the right. It became warmer as I got further inland. In what seemed to be a mile there was a fork in the trail. I was not sure which direction to take. My head was very foggy. I was weaving quite a bit. I took the road to the right as it was most traveled. I took a few steps then stopped to listen. I stood there until I steadied myself. I heard the drone of several high-powered aircraft far away. I strained to see them, but I could not. I continued struggling along.

In a few minutes I heard a vehicle coming. I walked wide-legged so not to leave an easily to be seen trail into the field some ten yards or more where I slowly knelt down and laid flat to hide. In a long minute the vehicle passed. I stayed put until its dust settled and I could not hear it, and then moved back on a different track, still with feet wide apart making another path.

I saw a village some distance away. The sun went behind a cloud. A man dressed in black and white was slowly walking towards me. As we approached I saw that he had a stovepipe hat with a brim straight out. It looked to be too small for him. He wore a robe with very large cuffs. His hands looked to be held together inside them. The sun started to reappear behind me as we drew closer. It shone on me and it felt warm. We stopped some three or four feet apart when he put his hand up. He waved his finger back and forth, and then pointed in front of me at my shadow. His hand motioned for me to turn around. I got it! My shadow was pointing northward and I was heading in the wrong direction!

The Elder looked me over closely and then at my scrub tunic. It had a caduceus symbol imprinted on my left side. On each side of the staff there was a letter, M to the left and D on its other side. Those letters meant Medical Department and there was small print below saying that, but that would not mean a thing to him. USN was also embossed on it in large letters. He said, "Ah so." He smiled gently and then noted the dampness of my clothing. He made circles over his head and then made a swimming motion. I nodded, pointed to myself, "That was me." I nodded my head in affirmation.

He placed a finger alongside his head and bent it to one side. He was puzzled. I tried to tell him that I was not a doctor, by pointing at my tunic and making a cross. *Well, that didn't work!*

I placed my hands together, bowed and said, "Thank you." He acknowledged and pointed south again. He waved his hand to the south to show good-bye and that way.

We both turned around, I was now heading in the right direction. I walked some ten yards and turned around. He was standing in the road further along towards his village. He was looking at me. We waved then continued on our separate ways.

When I got to the fork I continued south. I had looked ahead and picked out a mountain as a guide. The sun was warm and I felt a bit better. I walked slowly and quietly, as I wanted to hear everything.

I heard the drone of huge engines, closer this time, coming from the coast. I caught a glimpse of two Corsairs fairly low and slow. *Perhaps they were looking for me along the shore.*

I waved my right arm and hat, but soon stopped. They were a mile or so away. I could not see the pilots so they could not see me. It made me feel better that they were looking. *I should be on the shore but I am shivering cold. On the beach I could get shot by one of the many gook patrols. I need to warm up. It has not been all that long. It is not noon as the sun is not yet overhead. I sure could use a jacket!*

The road had turned towards the ocean, almost parallel to a distant row of shrubbery. In about half of a mile I saw a stream. I was quite thirsty. The stream had a narrow bridge. Along side was a railway bridge. Its rails were shining as the sun had reappeared. It seemed like an eternity but I got there. There was some water in the stream and it was flowing. I carefully walked upstream using a wide stance to prevent trampling the grass and making a clear visible path. In about ten yards there was a deeper puddle where I washed my hands. Then I walked a little further upstream and used my right hand to scoop water up to drink. This river would be a good place to hide, warm and rest. I found a dry place where the sun was shining between some tall brushes. I sat down and gave thanks for being alive.

Chapter Eighteen

AH LEE'S VILLAGE

It was some time before I heard a faint sound like wood rattling. I thought it was likely coming from a wagon going at a slow pace. I would wait for the wagon to pass. I found a rock that was warmer, so I moved over and sat on it behind some high brush.

The sound grew clearer and louder. After a few long minutes the wagon came into sight and stopped at the bridge. I was looking through some reeds. That wagon was off the road for some reason. The small load of reeds had shifted as it moved off the road. A man wearing light clothing made quite a show about getting water, drinking it and giving some to his donkey. I was wondering about all his antics. He was looking my way. His hands went up as he said, "Oh! There you are!" He waved, and then started to come my way. *Rats! I have been discovered!*

I could see that he had no gun. He had nothing in his hands but a cup. He stopped after he had walked half way and called, "Hello!" I was surprised that he spoke English!

This is dreadful! I had been seen and discovered. How? I thought I was fairly well out of sight and concealed.

"Are you a doctor?"

"No."

I rose and walked a few steps towards him. Now we were only a few yards apart. "I'm not a doctor or a nurse. I'm just a trainee, and very new to the Medical Department at that."

"Ah so, I am called, "Ah Lee," he bowed his head.

"I am called, "Zak Scott," nodding my head.

"The Elder told me about you. He pointed at my tunic. You have M D on your shirt right there."

"It means Medical Department, not medical doctor.

"You are not a doctor!" His voice lowered, he was visibly disappointed. "My village needs a doctor." He turned and pointed north. "The Elder at that village told me that the Communist Army has taken all doctors, nurses and staff away by force. We have none in this area." He waved all about showing exasperation. "There is a woman in my village that will give birth very soon, maybe today. My daughter has a very large sore that looks bad and it is painful! She needs attention very soon. I don't want to lose her." His voice trailed off, "I love my daughter!"

"I understand very well. Is there no one who can assist with the childbirth?"

"Yes there are, perhaps too many. She has lost two at birth. She thinks too many have done wrong things and her babies end up dying. She has no trust in them."

"That is very sad indeed."

"Elder says you are a doctor, a man of God as the sun light shines only around you. We trust you. An American will do the right thing." He brightened with hopefulness; his head was nodding with assurance. Then came the word, "Eventually."

Wow! That pushes the do it pressure up!

"I do trust in God, yes! Me, I know so little of these things, especially birthing. I was trained in a morgue."

The Ah Lee looked very sad. We were walking slowly towards the wagon. The donkey had moved the wagon back onto the road and was standing patiently looking at us.

We pushed on the small load of reeds. I just used my right arm, and I held the load while Ah Lee went to the other side and cinched it down. I went and gave donkey a pat. Slowly, I climbed up into the seat.

"I see your side hurts."

"I was drowning and a dolphin saved me by hitting my ribs and a second one pushed me to shore. I think that one or two ribs may be broken. - What do you call your donkey?"

"Ah, donkeys are jackasses, so I call him Jack." Jack started walking without any words being said or any rein movements that I saw.

"How did you know where I was?"

"The High Elder told me where to find you. He said that you have had a hard day. You have big pain in your side and are tired and thirsty. Your mouth looks dry. Did you quench your thirst?"

"Some."

"From up here on this seat I can see very far. I saw a reflection from a big puddle in the river. One spot moved."

The first part was true, but the second was simply that I was not concealed very well and he did not want me to know that or make me feel bad. I did move!

"Aha so! You have a very good eye! Very good observation!" I nodded several times to add emphasis.

"You have nothing. How do you expect to survive? You are in your enemy territory."

"I was supposed to have a life raft and paddle towards the beach and around that point." I was pointing to it. "They were to pick me up on the beach on the other side, but that yellow raft was a target for the Commies. They blew it to bits and it sunk, so I swam toward shore."

"The Elder told me that a helicopter came back but was shot at and left. He said I should tell you."

"Thank you. It is nice to know that they tried. Listen!" I heard the drone of aircraft engines again.

"Aha, I hear them. They are looking for you on the beach now. Many Commies are patrolling it. Everyone wants you. Since you have no identification you will need help getting across the line and back to your ship."

I replied with confidence, "My dog tags will be my pass."

"I didn't notice them."

"Oh my God! Where are they? I had them on when I left!" I was exasperated! "I will not be able to get into any base!" A feeling of dread flowed through me.

We rode in silence for sometime. Ah Lee broke the silence.

"We both need help! I will help you get into South Korea somehow if you try to help my people. Neither of us can guarantee anything. We can just do our best."

I don't like doing a birth by myself. Not at all! Even though Nancy did take me to several classes given for emergency staff on that subject, but it was just until medical help arrived. Here, I'm the medical help! On the other hand women have been giving birth without medical help for eons. God, help me!" I raised my right hand and said, "I will do my best."

"So shall I."

We were climbing up a shallow grade on the side of a hill and had just turned a corner on top. We went on that stretch a way when Jack stopped and turned a few steps to the right, his head tossing to the right. Jack took a few short steps into a turn then brayed, pawed his hoof, tossed his head a few times then lowered and raised it a few more times.

"What's Jack doing?"

"I do not know. I have never seen him do this."

I had an urge to look around and slid off the wagon. Slowly I went up to try to calm Jack. He gave me a push with his head. I took a few steps backward off the road. Jack bared his teeth and tossed his head. Animals know things we don't. I saw an outcropping of rocks. I would go that far and return. When I got quite close there were skeletal remains of three Chinese soldiers lying fairly close together. They were sprawled out and mostly turned up.

I remember the gals in the morgue had told me that the Chinese soldiers all carry a packet of Yunnan in their left breast pocket. I looked in their pockets and found that was true. I rescued their packets from any further deterioration. While I was kneeling down plucking their pockets, a small truck passed going north. It was going fast and raised a huge cloud of dust.

I slowly returned. Jack had moved to his down-the-road stance and was looking straight ahead. When I got close Jack turned his head towards me. I held up the three packets. Jack tossed his head. I went over to give him a big hug and a pet. He liked that.

I looked north. I could see where I had been earlier, the small village of eight or ten shacks where I had washed up. It wasn't all that far. It just seemed like many miles. Standing in the sun was good. It was warming me.

To Ah Lee I said, "This is Yunnan. It is a healing powder that the Chinese think highly of. Can you hold these for me? I don't have pockets."

"Oh yes, it is the best medicine in the whole world! We have Yunnan you have Penicillin."

"Tell me, how did Jack know all about this?"

"A truck hit him and he was hurt so bad he could not walk. They wanted to shoot him. I used Yunnan and he was better very soon. They are not dumb. I think they can smell better than we can."

Ah Lee pointed to his village and said its name. It ended with a dong, song or something, as many do. For me, those names go in one ear and right out the other. Much like Korean people, they look to me to be so uniform, and so much alike with the same basic body frame, height, haircut, and clothing.

His village was less than a half-mile away and Jack was moving faster down a slight grade.

Several people were working in rice paddies close to the village. We could see two women leaving and walking down the road ahead. One woman stopped us. She and Ah Lee talked a moment in Korean.

Ah Lee had Jack start by wiggling the reins and saying something, Jack started trotting.

Ah Lee told me, "The woman with child had broken her water and has started to have contractions. A friend took her home a little while ago."

"Should we be in a hurry? It is likely to take some time for her to deliver. Jack can walk. It's not very far." He thought a moment and pulled Jack to a walk. Jack walked a few steps, and then started to trot again with his ears back. Ah Lee tried to hold Jack back, but he continued to trot. He moved his head up and then down, wagged it and then held it down while he continued his trot. Ah Lee shrugged and let him go. We arrived at the shack of the pregnant woman.

The mother to be was standing in a doorway leaning back against the doorjamb. She was taking deep breaths, held them for a moment then let them out. She looked tired and her face was drawn.

Ah Lee talked to the woman and introduced me all in Korean. She looked apprehensive and was perspiring.

"Worried? I don't blame you! I'm not a doctor and I know so little."

A woman came with a reed mat. The pregnant woman lifted one leg then another. The mat was placed under her. She took a few more breaths, and then nodded. She pulled her dress way up and slid down the doorjamb onto her knees with her legs apart.

I prayed, *"God help me! I don't know what I am doing!"* I knelt down in front of her.

She had a pelvic bulge with some bloody water that dribbled onto the mat. The woman made a great grunt and she was pushing hard. The protrusion became larger. More moisture and bloody matter dribbled on the mat. The woman grunted again. She let out a painful cry and pushed long and hard. The protrusion was a head. My fingers seized the small wet head and pulled gently. She again grunted longer, louder and pushed. The baby smoothly slid into my waiting hands. It was a boy. I pulled back a bit further and the umbilical cord was pulsating. The baby was rather bluish. I held his head in my right hand and his trunk along my right forearm and then wiped his face with my left hand. Then I rolled him over to remove some mucus from his mouth with a finger. "Come on Mack, take a breath!"

Two women came up one on each side of me. One had a cloth and she wiped baby's back. He was now facing down. From the other side a woman appeared with a knife. "No, not yet!" I held her away with my out stretched arm. The baby cried a little. I turned him over so his front could be wiped. I raised him up a little, then down again. He let out a small cry. A moment passed. I was feeling quite apprehensive. "Come on Mack, take a breath! This is the first thing you have to learn." I gave his chest a small squeeze with my thumb and forefinger, and then tapped his foot. He contracted and cried louder. He took a few more breaths, with those his color quickly improved. I held the woman with the knife off again. In a long moment I gave him to his mother, he was still attached to the cord.

After a few minutes the mother handed the baby to one of the women beside her. Another woman placed a pan between the mother's legs. Mother grunted several times and a large glob slid into the pan. I noticed that the cord was dangling. *How did that happen? I didn't see any clamps or it being cut.* The pan was quickly removed. Mother returned to a sitting position. A blanket was placed around her. Her hands reached out. The baby was returned to her. The mother held him smiling.

Many women crowded around the new mother. There was much chattering. I stepped back and was given a rag to wipe my hands. I nodded and said, "Thank you."

Thank you Lord for making it easy!

I slowly went over to Ah Lee. Jack was standing nearby. Both were watching. Several women were excitedly talking to Ah Lee. He was making large positive hand movements as he spoke. He was enjoying the attention.

Donkey was looking my way with his ears forward. I gave him a few pats with my right hand. I had a huge urge to pee. I walked to the other side of the wagon out of sight of the women and watered the wagon wheel's rim.

Ah Lee and I slowly walked to my next patient who was a middle-aged woman. She had had severe diarrhea for several days. I looked around her place. There was a huge pile of dirty glasses and dishes. I asked Ah Lee if I could get some water that had been boiled for a few minutes or longer. He returned to the new mother's house. In a few minutes Ah Lee appeared with the mother's younger sister who held a teakettle. Ah Lee introduced us. She was Yea Woo, a very lovely young woman indeed. In English, she said, "Thank you for all that you have done for my sister."

I said, "God was in control, I was just there." She smiled and nodded her understanding.

I asked, "How's the mother and baby?" *Hello self! Just what would I be able to do if they weren't doing well?*

"They are both doing just fine. Thank you." I was very relieved to hear that!

"Yea Woo, would you watch as I examine this patient?" I felt her forehead for a fever. She felt a little warm. I checked her mouth. It was normal. I pressed the woman's abdomen. It was tight, and sore in some places. When I pressed firmly and held it, something seemed to soften and move. *Gas? I don't like this! It could be dozens of things.*

Yea Woo translated and said, "She has problems."

My nose verified that right away. I gave her the skin pinch test for dehydration. She was quite dry, as her skin did not recede very fast. "How much sake or wine does she drink?"

"All she can get."

I cleaned a glass using the boiled water with a clean looking rag and poured it full of hot water, swirled it to cool, then heat tested it on the underside of my wrist. I told Yea Woo, "Please tell her to drink the water while it is quite warm." *That should start her intestines moving and the gas.*

I thought of my half brother. He drank quite a bit and had lots of gas. When he drank the hard stuff he would get gas and gout. He used a half of a teaspoon of baking soda, in a glass of water, which worked very well for both.

I took the glass back and asked Ah Lee for a box of baking soda. I was surprised they had some. I tapped some in a glass and filled it again with water, stirred it well, and then gave the glass to her motioning for her to drink. I got a blank look. I told Yea Woo, "Get her to drink to the bottom as that is where the best medicine is."

A neighbor lady came in and asked how she was doing. I asked Ah Lee, "Can she be asked to help this lady in the morning?"

"Yes she can."

Then speaking through Yea Woo, "She needs a lot of water and cleaner utensils. All of these need to be washed." I wagged my finger at this patient while I said, "You must not drink any sake or wine for a week! Only boiled water." It was translated. She had a horrified look on her face. *Just as I feared, that was a total waste of breath.*

There was quite a clamor outside. Ah Lee told me I was needed outside. A young man was rushed into the village. He had gotten a severe head cut while working in the fields. Yea Woo's questioning revealed that he was working to move a crashed Navy Panther jet off a field. He had slipped and fell against one of its sharp metal protrusions. His friends had tied their shirts on his wound to slow up the bleeding. He was sitting on a wood bench.

It was a long and deep gash. This wound would take several sutures. I would have liked to tie off a small bleeder with suture, but none was around. I applied pressure. I needed some clean water and asked Yea Woo to get the kettle we used for the woman. There was some dirt down deep inside this wound. Yea Woo was happy to do that. I picked some dirt out of the wound by using my fingers and blood to clean it. I asked Ah Lee for some Yunnan and then I washed it out with some water that had boiled and was now warm. After the wound was cleansed I sprinkled a package of Yunnan in it. That stopped the bleeding on contact. Yea Woo produced some tape and some scissors. I cut enough hair so tape would hold the wound closed. Then I put clean rags on top and many wraps around his head. He was a classical wounded man. *Shucks, no camera!*

My next patient was Ah Lee's elder daughter, Ca Lee. Yea Woo wanted to come along too. Ca Lee had taught Yea Woo and several others English.

"Welcome! You are a great help."

Ca Lee had a large boil on her behind. I asked Ah Lee for some sake. He had a partly used bottle. I dribbled some all over the head and around her boil as a septic. *That should shrink the tissue and sanitize it a little.*

Ba Lee, Ah Lee's wife provided a sharp knife. I used Sake on it also. In a few minutes I incised the boil's head and the contents started to rise out. Ah Lee saw an opportunity for a toast. He had a toast for everyone! I took one small baby sip. It was awful!

It took about an hour for the boil core to move out. I asked Ba Lee for narrow chopsticks.

She was puzzled, "Why did I want them?

"I want to pull out some stringy trash from the bottom of this boil." I dribbled Sake over them and then started to use them.

Yea Woo stopped me. "You are not holding them correctly."

"I'm trying to get that stringy stuff out of this hole."

"I can do that."

"Very good." She carefully removed the trash.

"Very well done! Thank you."

Now for some Yunnan and I had one bag and a half left. I applied the half bag into the hole. "Yea Woo, can I get you to spread some Yunnan along the inside wall?" Again she did a good job. "Perfect."

Afterwards, I got Yea Woo to tape up my left side. I asked her to put strips along and beyond each end of my rib, and then put alternate the strips up making a step with each strip. That was continued along my left rib cage. It strapped the thing down and helped a whole lot.

"Yea Woo you do very good work!" I took some cool water and rags and then wound them around my feet, as they were sore from my new boots. Ba Lee got a pair of sandals for me.

I stood up and looked around. Surprisingly, I was seeing great differences between the individuals. They were not all exactly alike and Yea Woo was beautiful!

Ca Lee was drinking some sake too. She was up walking, even acting silly. She also wanted to attend the celebration of the new birth. They would eat some of the placenta, which was now being prepared in a special way. A High Elder would be there. I tried to opt out as eating placenta was against my religion. *That didn't work*. I was told that the Senior Elder wanted to toast me. I felt humbled but honored.

Ba Lee prepared dinner. I had much rice. Ah Lee was feeling much better with his people taken care of. He invited neighbors over to celebrate and of course to keep the sake from turning into vinegar. Much more sake was poured. More townspeople arrived. More toasts. The Lees were the center of attention and were delighted. The oriental face really lights up when they are so very happy!

Someone provided me a nice warm dark red robe. It was made of a heavy towel like material. They all thought I should wear it tonight. It was warm and I was still cool, but well above the shivering level. Warm sake was provided. It did seem to help with both the cold and the pain. I too was feeling better. My side hurt when I laughed. They liked my laugh. *O, Lord help me!* With the setting sun the party got bigger and louder.

By the time the bell tolled for the ceremony we were all quite high. Yea Woo held my right arm, "You need to be held up. You walk wiggly."

"I would be just fine if you would stop pushing into me every step or two." So in retaliation I was forced to press her right back, but not very hard. We weaved and pressed our way to the meeting place. We laughed quite a bit.

The High Elder was the man who had given me directions to go south. He was the master of ceremonies. Mother was there with her baby boy. She looked tired and drawn. She would name him Mack, as that is what I had said to get him to breathe. I was touched. I had no intention of naming the baby.

The woman with the intestinal problem was there. She toasted me. Yea Woo translated her comments; "I am disobeying doctors' orders by drinking toasts."

I drew a long breath and shook my head. I tried to explain, "You are not disobeying any doctor's orders. "I'm not a doctor! I just made a friendly suggestion. You are just naughty!" After the translation by Ah Lee there was much laughter.

Yea Woo was close at my side when it came to the toast to baby Mack. This was something like a combination of a christening; a communion ceremony and a baptism sprinkling led by the Chief Elder. Another toast was being made. There was a woman with a tray passing out what looked like deep fried pieces. There was another toast with the partaking of that placenta. I was able to palm it and pass it to Yea Woo, to her great delight.

A person who had rooms to rent received a toast for letting me use his number one room. Sake was flowing like water and it creeps up on you. I was very drunk! Yea Woo led me to the provided room where I fell on the bed. She piled several blankets on top of me just as I passed out.

I had a day to rest as the best tide and weather was tomorrow. Today was quite windy.

Yea Woo took me to see the crashed jet. I opened the gas and other fluid caps so they could evaporate. The villagers needed the field to be in production.

"I would suggest that you get a big tractor or a crane to drag it off the field because it probably weighs about fifteen thousand pounds and there are several bent up parts driven into the ground. It was difficult to move using hand tools and leverage like you are doing."

I still felt a little cool. We walked inland some and looked at the options to cross the border. It warmed up several degrees as we moved away from the coast. We saw no useful trails. The foliage to the west was low or burnt brush providing little or no place to hide. All along the line I would have to crawl over or under high fencing with lots of barbed wire and sharp flat curly metal stuff piled up high. The railway was heavily guarded, as was the local road. A second road was two mountain ranges over and several days walk from here. Also if I were to get across the line there would be a huge language problem with the South Koreans who were quick to shoot. I could see no effective or half safe way for a land passage. I decided on swimming as the best solution and then I could walk the shoreline south and have more brush cover.

Ah Lee encouraged many villagers to take advantage of the minus tide at sunrise the following morning, where they could pick up several edible items and provide a distraction for patrols. *Wow. All these people were doing this for my cover!* I was amazed by the friendly and helpful attitude of the people in this village had toward me. Okay, so I did try to 'treat' a few skin rashes that looked like poison ivy with cool mud and some acne with aspirin paste. I did not know if it would do anything or not. It worked. I guess a lot was due to my trying to do something for them. Over a dozen eagerly came with buckets in the early morning mist. I was loaned a robe and a straw hat like theirs to wear. Low light and mist would help me blend in.

There were three armed North Korean soldiers on the cliff above the point. They watched us for a while. They mostly had their field glasses trained on the young girls who were running, dancing, splashing and having a good time. In a little while the North Korean troops departed inland.

Ah Lee and a few others went out to the point with me where I returned the hat and robe to them. I bowed and said, "Thank you. You have been wonderful." They bowed back.

I did not have an easy time going from one rock to another due to the slippery growth on the rocks. The point had ridges of rock that looked like a bunch of knives with sharp edges up, and close together. There was a very narrow passage. I carefully passed through it and noticed that the swells were making the underwater growth move from side to side, more in than out, a sign that the tide was moving up again.

I climbed up several feet higher to see if there were any places where the water was swirling to indicate a rock below. There were a few near by but I would be able to avoid them. I didn't see any further out in my swim area. There were some rocks protruding out of the water some twenty or thirty yards further out to the south and some ten to fifteen yards to my right. I would have to swim around all that and more. My swimming track would have to veer left some to avoid possible shallow rocks. I would have to keep away from what is visible now for some thirty yards to keep the inflowing tide from carrying me into the outcroppings and any unseen shallow rocks. I should start to get a small push from inflowing tide to help with a final sprint.

Here, the water was cold. I would have about five minutes survival time. With my injured rib I would use the sidestroke with my right arm pulling down, left arm for the short strokes. *This should take about three or four minutes.*

Should I strip and move faster or wear my scrubs and boots? Some attire would be better than none after getting out of the water. There is no telling whom I would meet or how far I would have to walk after getting out of the water. *Having boots and scrubs was best.*

I was standing on a two-foot ledge. I did a few calf raises, stretches and knee bends to warm up a little before my dive. My competition would be the cold. Just before I dove off the ledge I said a prayer for His help in this effort. I made a very shallow dive into a swell crest and went into a strong right hand down sidestroke. I counted my right arm extensions, as I needed to do about thirty-five sidestrokes to be clear of those visible rocks. It was not a comfortable feeling having my back to them. I saw something dark under the water so I made a few more strokes before I made the turn. By now I was quite a bit colder. I put more power into my right arm, and widened my kick. I headed straight to shore and with the swell. *I must just keep swimming, no slowing down.* Swells and the inflow were increasing and they provided some forward movement. I caught a wave at sixteen strokes. It pushed me onto the course sand beach. I was able to crawl out of the water. I was severely cold and shivering. While I staggered out of the water, I gave thanks to God for seeing me through these past several days and this swim.

Chapter Nineteen

A TURKISH UNIT

I staggered out of the water and cried out in a shivering quivering voice, "Help!"

There were a few men on the beach kicking a ball back and forth. One came over to me with a blanket that had been thrown out on the beach and wrapped it around me. Another guy came up. I was fading. It took both of them to hold me up.

"Vou er ya?" One asked.

"American Navy." Shivered out between chattering teeth.

"Vee er ze Turkish. Vee take vo to ze Fraunch Narse."

They drug me up a short cliff and let go of me at a tent entrance. I stumbled into it. They hurried away while holding their noses. There was a strong odor of sweet perfume drifting from inside.

Just inside the tent I saw a pair of beautifully sculptured legs with a lovely face looking at me upside down between them. Her dark red hair was brushing the floor. I tried to talk but only a single sound was uttered. My head was swirling and then everything went black.

Monique was about thirty, a French nurse now serving with the Turks. She had been on the front lines serving with several different units for a long time. She was often transferred, as her knowledge of many languages was highly valued. She was a very charming and beautiful woman. To keep her figure she worked out for over an hour three times a day. She loved the smell of sweet perfume. Vainly she used more, convinced that it would help attract men, but here it failed and she could not understand why. She saw herself as a natural person. She did not shave off any hair or use makeup on her eyes or eyebrows. She didn't have to.

Monique had been under heavy shelling and had all the yearnings of other women who served on the line. She craved attention and had a deep-seated need to propagate. She was suffering greatly from ostracism, depression and hysteria.

The Turks thought Monique stunk worse than any living creature. They stayed as far away from her as they could. Her tent had been moved twice. Each time it was always set up several yards further out of the main camp and further downwind. She was not allowed at their tables or around their tents and they spoke to her only at a distance while they stood up wind. They brought her meals to her tent, then hastily retreated backwards bowing and saying, "Shalom."

I was her man captive. She was absolutely determined to be successful with me. I was an answer to her hopes and prayers, brought to her door and tossed at her like a bone to a dog.

She shook me awake. I was shivering very hard. Monique touched my quivering body, took my temperature rectally as my teeth were chattering too hard. It read ninety-two degrees. My pulse was weak and my fingers had a blue tint. She promptly removed my scrubs and boots. Later she would take them out and drape them on the tent's mooring lines to dry. She took a towel and dried me off and rolled me up in a blanket. She got several more blankets, spread them out on the tent floor and wrapped me up in them. Monique placed me where the early morning sun shone fully on my front side. She put more wood in the small potbelly heater and set a metal teapot on it. She said a few amorous things in French, some I understood, but I was not responsive to anything. I tried to say something but only slurred and then fell back to sleep.

In a few minutes, Monique unrolled me on my other side and lay beside me and flipped a blanket over us, so my left side was getting the sun. She held me gently, blew on my face, and then blew her breath down under the blankets. That was not very effective. We stayed there about two minutes. When I drifted off to sleep she shook me awake and unrolled us. She stood up, took her shorts off and her outer blouse, then lay next to my skin and rolled us up. She tried to move around but the blankets were too tight. She lay still about a minute, no more than three. I dozed. She stood up and removed her panties and bra, got next to my skin, held an arm next to me and we rolled up again. She blew her breath between us. She was not able to move enough. She wiggled this way and that. Again she unrolled us, placed both of my arms on my chest and got next to me with both of her arms next to mine. Not quite right. She moved her legs above my groin, stuck her butt out, crossed my arms, held her arms out, and we rolled up again. Now she could move and wiggle. She blew her breath under the blankets. Her wiggly activity and her warm breath began to transmit life. In about an hour my heavy shivering had subsided considerably.

The tea would be warm by now. She rolled me over and propped me up facing the direct sun under the blankets. I faded off. She shook me awake. She sat on my hips and wiggled back and forth. She wrapped her legs around my back and squeezed repeatedly. She made me take a few sips of quite warm tea. Speaking in French she urged me to drink more and more, "*de plus en plus.*" Down it trickled until it was all gone.

Monique got up, dressed and put a lab coat on and then took the teapot to the mess hall where she put more tea in it. She picked up a few scraps of wood to put in the firebox, then stopped at the supply tent and got a cold weather cap. She placed the cap on my head and tied the earflaps under my chin, and then she moved me to where the sun would continue to shine on the full length of my body for a while.

Monique sat in the warm sun for several minutes. She realized how cool she was, so started to exercise to warm herself up. She put on warmer clothing and went to the beach to gather wood. Fog was laying offshore less than a mile so it could drift ashore soon. Fog would make everything cooler. It was not predictable in the spring.

Monique stretched my arms to stir blood flow and worked my legs, then moved me from side to side. Her hands were all over me. Those movements woke me up! I was able to stand and stagger about. We marched in place to stir the blood and warm up. My ribs were hurting from the many movements. I asked for an aspirin. I was given two.

Monique wrapped blankets around us, and then we staggered down to the beach. The morning sun had burned the fog further out to sea. The warm sand felt good. We lay on it. When it cooled beneath us we rolled over to a warmer place. We were well down the beach after several sunbaths and warm sand soaks.

I think she has nasal congestion as she has redness around the nose and some drainage that she swipes unconsciously. In an hour we wandered back to the tent and put a pot of water with some Vicks in a bent spoon to make a small tray that went over the spout. I put it on the stove. I didn't think direct inhalation was required as the tent was not all that big and was fairly well closed up.

It had warmed up quite a bit. We wandered down the beach some distance to a protected cove. There was a stream with warm water flowing into the cove. It took a little encouragement to get her to take a nude dip in the ocean but she finally dove in and caught a wave to body surf on. As the wave broke she got a mouth and a nose full of surf, which caused her to expel great amounts of mucous. With that Monique regained her ability to smell. When we got back to the tent she opened the vents to let air flow through to help remove some of the perfume odors and then we sat outside the tent in the sun and talked.

Our noon meal was brought over to the tent. The delivery party had their faces mostly covered. They backed away. Monique said, "That is what they usually do." We ate what was brought. After eating we went further down the beach and started up where we left off. I provided lymphatic and foot massages to help lower her stress level. I was able to provide some French techniques and some of Jane's. She responded very well. Monique would demand a lot of my attention during my short stay.

Two Turk troops had a knife fight early the following morning. They were brought over to the tent but refused to go in. They each required several sutures. Monique had some Yunnan. She absolutely refused to suture. I shrugged and wasted no time sewing them up. We did it outside several yards up wind from the med tent. Captain Waters came over to review our work. Monique translated. She said that he had said, "Well done!" He then went back to his tent with his swagger stick held behind him tapping his hand with his stick.

A little later Turkish Captain Waters interviewed me and again Monique was our interpreter. He did not believe what I told him, especially that I was a trainee. Soon I was fitted head to foot with army field clothing and briefed on their secret way to kill gooks quickly and silently. "Very often we can't give our position to the enemy or put ourselves or fellow troops in jeopardy by firing weapons at the enemy." I received a pistol and was briefed in its use, just in case.

I was soon on patrol with them as their medic. This mission was a repetition for the Turks as they were watching an enemy encampment every day. The gook troops were gathering in a valley about four or five miles north. On this trip they said that this encampment had added a lot more troops and artillery pieces. That news was whispered over a hand held radio in Arabic to their base camp.

The following day we made a similar patrol on the same trail. The time was later and the day was quite hot. I wanted to carry a second canteen on my right side so I put the pistol on my left, its handle was pointing forward. This day we saw many more new enemy troops busy setting up tents. On returning from this patrol we stopped to radio back our findings to base. Thorny brush had scratched up a few men so I was busy patching small wounds during this stop. It was soon over and they quietly continued down the ridge.

My left boot had untied, so I paused to use a rock as a prop to tie it. Just as I finished I stood up and stepped back when a bayonet was thrust into my belt buckle on my left. The pressure twisted and pushed me to the right. I was suddenly looking at a crazed ugly face nose to nose. The pistol was in my right hand and went up under the toothy grinning face just inches from mine. I gagged on his foul garlic breath. His gun went off firing over the bayonet stuck in my belt buckle. An instant later my gun went off under his chin. I was losing my balance. A second gook was just a few feet behind the first. My gun went off a second time. He was hit center chest. His backward motion caused his rifle to fire straight into the first gook's back. That momentum pushed both of us close to a steep hillside. A third gook was several feet further behind the second gook. My pistol fired a third time. He was hit in his left shoulder. My bullet's hard impact caused his right hand to extend. He held a grenade in it. The grenade came out of his right hand flying in my direction. I saw it strike the ground and tumble towards me. I was starting to twist and slide but was able to give it a little tap of a kick back in his direction. It would explode in about two seconds, close enough so it would cut him up. With that extra movement both of my feet completely slipped out from under me. I was sliding headlong down the steep gravel slope. The first gook's dead weight was also pulling us down. We slid down several yards. The grenade exploded as I was sliding. I was shielded by my footstool rock on the hill and by the first assailant.

I was terrified! I had an involuntary discharge of body fluids.

My left side was killing me and I had a powder burn on my lower right side. I slowly started to claw my way back up to the trail grabbing at bushes along the way.

The second gook got a heart hit. The third gook got a good blast as his lower groin was split open with a dead center blast. He had drained a lot and his upper left arm and shoulder were mangled.

I listened and looked for other gooks. Hearing none I started running down the ridge. The jarring sent a clear message from my left side that this was not what I wanted to be doing. I settled down to a striding walk. There was less dust walking, far less jarring and it was much quieter.

Three Turks were running up the hill. They had to verify the shots, any kill and then look around for more gooks. They waved me aside and pressed on uphill.

The other Turks were scanning the hills with field glasses. They saw many gooks coming over the back ridge. About a mile away they looked like ants. The Turk patrol leader called their base camp on a walkie-talkie about my ambush, kills and the swarming gooks. Our unit hustled down towards base camp at double time about a mile or so away. I followed at a brisk walk.

During this day the Captain invited Monique over to his tent for lunch and a glass of wine. Today she did not smell of strong perfume. Her swim had cleansed the perfume.

The Captain said, "I notice that you have improved greatly since the American arrived. Why are you airing out your tent?"

"The American put some Vicks over the tea pot spout and my nasal passages reacted and much mucous came out. Now, I can smell."

"I am puzzled. Why does he say he is a trainee? It is obvious to me that he has had a lot of experience. You just don't suture that fast and do that well without much experience."

"He asked me to suture and I refused so he just picked up the tools and went right to work. He knew just what to do and asked no questions. A trainee would be scared stiff asking all sorts of questions and begging me to do it for him. Also he knew about my congestion without my complaining or an examination. That too is peculiar."

"He lies"

"He does!" After that they agreed on many other things. They would talk a very long time. He got up to go into his tent for more wine. She followed. They didn't come back out anytime soon.

When I came down the hill into the Turks' encampment Captain Waters had a jeep and driver waiting for me. Monique translated and said he commanded, "You must go to the next camp. They have several officers from headquarters that are very sick and need a doctor."

"I'm not a doctor! I'm a very new medical trainee."

With obvious agitation Waters said, "So you say. You go there now! You will do what is necessary for them! I told them you could do it!"

"Aye, sir!" I got in the Jeep and we were off with my dirty pants and all. On the way I saw that most Turkish tents were down and had been put on trucks. All camp followers had departed south. The med tent lay flattened and was set ablaze as I was driven off. The main body of Turkish troops did not look like they were going south. They were standing by in full battle dress. My driver said the US Army was moving up and there would be a huge confrontation here very soon.

Chapter Twenty

GOUT

The next encampment was a mile or two away on an unimproved trail. It was Dutch and their medical staff and other support units had been ordered off the front lines and had departed south.

I said, "Hey, take a look at that sunset!" It is beautiful!

The driver turned to take a look, "Wow!" Just then a tank popped out in front of our Jeep. My driver was going rather fast. He jammed on the brakes and turned hard to the left. I was flung out of the open jeep. I landed right in front of that tank, which had come to a sudden stop, its dust rolling out in front. Now, all that dirt was on a partly damp me. I had a fresh coat of mud. My left side gave me a message that took my breath away. As I picked myself up a chubby blond nurse hustled up.

"Doctor, are vu Okay?"

"I am not a doctor! I hurt in a few places, otherwise I'm okay."

"Come." I followed. My leg got twisted from the jeep dump, so that had me hobbling.

"Vo er ze mass! Vo can't see ze stoff vooking like zes!"

"I have not been standing at parade rest all day, I've just returned from a patrol."

She led me to a tent and gave me a wet towel, and green surgical scrubs, which she tossed onto a cot. I could not get the bent buckle unfastened or pull my crappy pants down.

"Vow vid zees hoppen?"

"I was ambushed by three gooks. One stuck his bayonet in my belt. He managed to bend it up quite well."

She tried to unbuckle the belt but she could not. Then she picked up a knife and cut the web belt, pulled my pants down and tossed them in the trashcan. She took another wet towel and aggressively wiped drizzly shit off my stinking ass and down my legs. Another towel appeared and I gave it a quick look to see if it was dirty, then wiped my face and arms, then took a swipe over my crew cut head. The scrubs went on and a white lab coat was tossed at me. The coat had a medical staff with M and a D on each side of the staff as did the scrubs, and again it meant Medical Department.

"Vot tes zees? She was pointing at the tape.

"I have a cracked rib which is still bruised and I am in pain from that landing I just made. May I have an aspirin?" She provided two.

"Thank you."

As I was swallowing the pills a US Army Captain strode into the tent and asked, "Are you the Navy Doctor?"

The nurse answered quickly, "Ya he zis!" She then stuffed a stethoscope in my lab coat pocket. That is where we carried them in the 50's.

He demanded, "What is your name?"

"Scott, Zakary Scott."

He quickly ordered, "Follow me," as he strode back out the tent entry. He gained several steps ahead moving at a smart gate.

The Dutch Nurse pulled my head down and gruffly said, "Vo fust act!"

I picked up his proud swinging gate and moved my nose up some and from side to side to show that I was reacting to her request. She had a big smirk. We arrived at a tent that was a temporary command post. The officers were busy reading reports and sticking various shaped and colored pins in charts mounted on a stand.

The Captain loudly announced, "This is our Navy Doctor!" He emphasized Navy.

This place would not be a resting area for patients. There was too much activity and the sounds of intense bombing and shelling was constant. There was the noise of trucks arriving with men, artillery and noisy tanks.

Four Army Officers were sitting with elevated bare feet. They were talking on telephones and radios about units, tactics and supplies and such.

The one with gold oak leaves bellowed, "Our fucking feet are swollen and hurt like all fucking hell!"

I stepped over to look, "Nicely prepared." The feet were covered with a damp undershirt. "Does that help?"

Another said, "Yeah some. The fucking nurse did that."

Everyone had quite a bit of unrepeatable to say. I took a flashlight and looked intently at each foot, lightly touching them. Their feet were red, swollen and warm to the touch.

I made several," Hums and uh-huhs." *I had seen this many times before. My half brother drank a lot and had bouts of gout often.*

"Painful?" I asked one.

"No! It fucking throbs like all fucking hell!"

"How long has it been doing this?"

"About two hours."

"When and where have you eaten today?"

"About three or four hours ago at mess and lunch was at a local establishment."

I smelled their breath as I looked. It smelled foul. I asked, "What were you eating and drinking?"

The announcing Captain offered some details. "We all had a local delicacy and some local beer."

"What was in the delicacy?"

"They all had chicken liver and kidneys with mushrooms, beans and peas in gravy over rice and three beers each."

"All local ingredients?"

"I think so. The bottles were in Korean."

"Thank you, Sir. I stepped up to him. "So, what did you have to eat?"

"I don't like innards of any kind. It was something like a gravy over rice with peas." I got a whiff of his breath too. It was stale but normal.

"I pass on the innards too."

I turned to the nurse, "Can you put a little more water on each foot wrap? I will be back in a few minutes with a remedy."

I guided the Captain out of the tent and asked, "Where is the galley?"

"Where is the what?"

"The galley or mess hall. It's the same thing."

"Yeah! You are Navy." He pointed to a huge tent. "Why the mess hall?"

"They should have an ingredient that is needed to cure this ailment. This was caused mainly by foods and stress that can be cured with a special food ingredient. I shall soon return with a remedy in hand." Then I added, "Hopefully they will have that special ingredient." *I was wondering if my acting was convincing.* The nurse seemed pleased.

The mess hall would remain where it was with the change of units. I saw a black US Army Sergeant. "Hello Sergeant, I am Navy Medic Trainee Scott looking for some baking soda and four eight ounce glasses. I have some staff patients with gout. Do you have any?"

He presented his hand, "Bill Banker." We firmly shook hands. "Say, that is an old gout remedy. My grandfather used to take that all the time. He had it often. He drank 'White Lightning.'"

"It's a simple and a very effective treatment. My half brother had it rather often also for the same reason as your grandfather."

"Here, take the whole box, Doc."

"I also need four glasses and a tea spoon."

"Yep, here they are! Take that tray."

"Great! Maybe I should set up for the second dose now, as that will be in four hours. So, can I take four more glasses?"

"Sure! Sounds like yer thinking ahead, - - Hey Doc, you hungry?"

"Yeah! I'm starved! I haven't had a chance to stop today."

"How does steak and hash browns sound?"

"Perfect! Let me pour this down my patients' throats. That should only take a few minutes."

I returned to the command tent, stirred up the contents in the glasses and gave them to the patients while announcing; "You must expect a belch in a few minutes and to expel some gas in an hour or two. Keep the flaps open and the air flowing."

The nurse had dribbled more water on the wraps and was making notes in charts. I prepared the next dose, stirred them up and placed them on a table. "Here is a second dose to be taken in four hours, but no sooner than in four hours. Be sure to stir it up first."

I turned to the nurse who had charts for each patient and had made notes. "Good girl. Good work. Thank you!" Then I turned back to the officers, "I'm going to chow now as I have not stopped for anything today. I will look in on you after I eat." I heard considerable grumbling, none of it worth repeating.

To the nurse, "I'm going to chow. Would you like to join me?"

"Yah!" We started walking toward the mess hall. "Vee hasn't been introduced. I yam Dotty. I yam ze Dutch. Vou vould vin der acting prize!"

"Thank you. Hello, Dotty. I'm Scott, Zakary Scott, US Navy, a new medical trainee. We were rushed a bit. Sorry about the dirty behind. I had a good scare and let loose."

"Vat happens all ze time on ze line." she replied.

"Cleaning up is the dirty part of the job."

"How is vat vo know vat being part of der job?"

"As a trainee what I do most aboard ship is clean up messes." We had arrived at the mess hall.

Bill Baker had a huge steak and an enormous pile of hash browns, enough for three. He said he grilled it up to rare because he didn't know how to cook it.

"Please cut it in half and do mine well done." Dotty wanted it the same.

He asked, "Why do medics always like steak well-done?"

"Well, because we see a lot of rare all day."

"Another question. Why do medics always say that they are a trainee or practicing?"

"That's because I realize how little I know."

After dinner Dotty went with me to see the patients, and then took me to her tent. She pointed to a cot. I laid down on it and immediately fell fast asleep. She set an alarm clock to ring in four hours so she could see that the next dose of baking soda was timely. At that time she was up and giving the next dose of baking soda. She was a stern one, "Take zees or suffer!" They took their medication. She checked their feet and was happy to see the swelling of the patients was receding. She made notes of that and the fact that their pain level and the swelling had lowered considerably. She also wrote notes that indicated the patients took their medication but did not sleep much. At five o'clock in the morning, Dotty was woken and told to take a car to meet up with her unit at a rear area. She woke me up as she was leaving. "Wake, so vo can do der mornink rounds." Then she quickly departed.

A little later I arrived at the command tent. They had their boots on open and untied, and were hobbling about. They had not slept except for a short nap. They were still busy putting pins in charts and talking about units. They were delighted with my treatment. One final dose was passed around with some finger wagging instructions from a United Nations Medical Representative, "Do not eat any food with internal organs or drink any alcohol for the next two weeks. What you have is gout and it can and will reoccur. A recurrence is likely to be more painful, last longer and be harder to cure." They were reluctant and grumbling, but nodded agreement.

The introducing Captain wanted to know, "Just how did you do this without all the lab work and full physical examinations?"

"First all medical personnel were ordered to go south, so I have to make do with what I have. I do know what I'm looking at here, and smelled the breath of each patient. It was sour. Your breath smelled normal. Then for confirmation I asked what you had to eat. It was different."

The Captain asked for my identification.

"I have none."

"For Christ sake, how the fuck can I describe you without your numbers?"

"Just say you ran into a guy who answers to Zak Scott." I gave him my memorized ID number.

Later he said, "Hey Navy, I sent a note to Mom saying you are here playing with us. Here is a copy."

"Thank you!"

"Hey Doc, you are going to play hell without any identification. I'll message a rear hospital with that same information."

"Thanks, Colonel!"

"Colonel! I'm not a Colonel!"

"You call me doctor and I am not!"

"I've got my rank on my lapel and you have MD on your shirt." I had scrubs on. I told him what it meant. He shook his head in disbelief.

A few moments later he said, "Navy, get in this Jeep." He gave me a note that I held in my hand. My scrubs had no pockets. The Captain conversed in Korean to the driver and the driver nodded his understanding.

The road south was far better than those across the peninsula and the driver was in no hurry. I soon fell asleep.

Chapter Twenty-One

LOST IDENTIFICATION

A bugle playing mess call woke me. I was sitting in a Jeep in a parking area on a base in front of a huge hospital tent that had an ambulance with huge white squares maybe four or five feet square with red crosses in the middle. There were platoons of troops marching to various places. *"Where was my driver? Does it matter? Here I am."* I stood there looking for the mess hall.

Not for long. Marching briskly up to me were two military policemen. One called out in a commanding voice, "Sir, we need to talk to you! You were let through the gate by mistake. May I see your identification?" My scrubs did not have pockets and I had lost that slip of paper.

"I have none. It was lost at sea."

"Come with us." We went to the Military Police's tent. I was ordered to sit down at a card table. Soon I was surrounded by eight unhappy people, two sat behind me, two on each side and two in front. They all had armbands and side arms. There was a bright light shining on me. That felt good as it was warm and I still felt a little core cool.

This was an interrogation. It started with name, rank, serial number, unit and circumstances. They thought I was a Russian spy or infiltrator of some kind. I was given a number, photographed from all angles and finger printed. There was considerable talk about what to do with me. The quick simple solution was to kick me off base. This was a war zone and I had no one to vouch for me. They were not willing, as far as I knew, to contact my ship about me.

"I haven't eaten anything today or much yesterday for that matter. When and where is chow?"

One MP said, "Forget chow you won't be here that long!"

"An Army Captain said he sent a message here about me."

Another MP said, "We don't have anything about you,"

They took turns asking questions. Many questions were similar, only asked differently by different people. It lasted what seemed a long time, probably an hour. They were rather abrupt and impatient.

"How long will the chow hall be open?"

A third MP said, "Forget it! We are not feeding you!"

My answers did not please any of them. *Maybe I should have gotten that tattoo with my serial number on it.* I was marched between two armed men and two behind me out the gate. A short block away was the Red Cross office where I was deposited. They made a brief announcement to the gal behind the desk and they marched right back.

She had a trim athletic figure. She was a blue-eyed, light brown blond with her hair pulled back and tied. Her nametag said Audrey Austin. She said, "Take a seat. I'll be with you in an hour or so. I have an interview right now."

Her small office had two chairs and some magazines all in Korean. I could wait here or wander around awhile. I chose to wander around the town a bit. Having no money I couldn't buy anything. I had no watch but I had a good sense of time and I noticed that there was a clock in the middle of the street up another block. I had a personal need that was quickly mounting. I had passed by the public privy used by both sexes of all ages. It was a sand rock building with a high over-head and was open at both ends. Two troughs were used for both eliminations. You went by squatting down over a trough. Someone dumped water down the troughs every once in a while. It was one gigantic stink house! It didn't seem to bother the locals very much. I had passed on that as a place where I wanted to hang out.

When I returned she was still working with her appointment. Behind her desk and to one side there was a sign on a door in English that said 'Private.' Below there were oriental marks so it was probably written in Korean also. It looked like a bathroom to me. I decided to go and see. Just as I was opening the door, Audrey shouted in a very firm and warning voice, "Don't go in there!"

I had opened the door. Sure enough! It was a small bathroom, a tiny place. Its porcelain bowl was right in front of me. Its seat was down and my need was way up. I was just in time!

Audrey loudly ordered me to go down the street to the public outdoor facility. I ignored her command and inched up closer to the bowl that my water was now flowing into. She yanked the door open and pulled on my waistband. I jerked it close. It ripped apart as it was only made of paper glued to a thin wooden frame. The back and forth movements jarred a few dildos off the shelves, I caught a dildo as she pulled on my waistband. My water stream sprayed up onto fancy linen on the tank top cover. Audrey forced her way in.

"Which one do you want to hold?"

She stepped back and screamed, "NO! You bastard!" She was shaking, her fists pounding my back. That woke up my side! Her whole body was shaking and her face was very flushed.

The Korean couple were laughing and holding their hands over their mouths. That made her madder. They backed out of her office saying, "So sorry. We come back tomorrow morning, yes."

Audrey was furious! She stepped back in and started to pound on my back again. I was still peeing. I dropped the dildo on the floor, reached around and grasped her left hand, then held her right hand. That stopped her pounding but she was still wiggling hard. My rib was sore from her pounding.

When finished I asked, "Would you like to put it away? I have my hands full of a wiggling you."

"No you bastard!"

Then I gave her a good butt nudge that sent her back into the office. I picked up some of the fallen toys and put them back on a shelf, rinsed the cover cloth with water from a small corner hand washbasin and used paper to sop up the few stray puddles of pee, then washed my hands.

Embarrassed and fuming mad she was now sitting at her desk. I went behind the counter in front of the entrance door. I was holding a gnarly dildo, "Congratulations, you do something for yourself. Hey, you have nothing to be ashamed of. I will bet that you have what every woman in a combat zone has which is hysteria at a time when men, for the most part, have erectile dysfunction. So, you have the good sense to do something for yourself." Her head was turned away. "Hey, I have no identification on my person and no funds, at your service."

She answered in a slow, very cool, level voice, "I don't want your service!"

"A boy is better than a toy," waving a dildo.

"I told you where to go!"

"Have you been there?"

"No!"

"I have! I stopped by to watch and gather in some of the local ambience. Perhaps I should take you down there. You are missing a valuable local experience. It is quite different from anything like we have at home and you are recommending it. It's a very smelly stinky place!"

"I'm not interested!" There was a very long pause. I slowly moved to put the dildo back on its shelf.

We introduced ourselves to each other.

"I will look at the broken door and see if I can fix it." *It looked like fixing a broken kite.* "I can fix this with a few sticks of wood, some glue, a few small screws and a bit of paper."

Audrey had some typing to do. It was a very long time before she started asking questions as to my predicament. I answered her questions. She found my name in the file of those 'Missing in Action.' She consulted a binder of forms. She found samples. "I can type your forms from these samples. They require sworn statements and notarization and will have to pass through every level of command." Audrey was putting five pages and carbon pages between for each form in the typewriter. It had to be set just right so all the typing would be on the same line. Also the carbon between each page had to be lined up. The manual typewriter had roller releases so that could be done with a hand on each side of the paper. She typed and asked questions from time to time. In about an hour she put them in front of me.

"Sign these. There are five carbon copies. Here use this new ballpoint pen. It's a new product and works like nothing else ever has. It can make impressions on the last copy if you press hard enough."

"All at the same time?"

"Yep! No more doing each page one at a time."

She went over to the broken door and shook her head. She was calming down.

"I'm sure I can fix that. You can call my mother and a lady friend or several others at home and arrange for sworn affidavits."

"That is on the second set of those forms."

"Okay."

I finished signing the forms and filling in the blank spaces. She looked and asked, "Where in California is Grover City?"

"It is about twelve miles south of San Luis Obispo, or approximately halfway between San Francisco and Los Angeles on the coast.

She brightened up. "I know a Nancy Arden. She is in the San Luis Obispo Red Cross. We have been to many training events and conventions together."

I replied, "Small world. I also know her very well. She is the lady friend I mentioned. We put on First Aid classes together. Perhaps you would believe her. She looked at three clocks on the wall. One was local, a second for Pacific Time, and a third was for Eastern Time. "Right now, it is after 10 AM here and it is yesterday at 5 AM in California. Audrey was dialing the long distance telephone operator for an overseas call slot. Overseas calls had to be placed several hours ahead of time in order to be able to call, and then it was for a timed limit of three minutes. By then it would be midday on the east coast of the USA. The operators wanted to know your rank or position, as military operations were priority. This call would have no priority, so it could be terminated at any time. She got her asked for time slot so her call was in line to be placed in five hours and she might have three minutes to talk. The operator would call this number when a line and time was open.

"I know of some fix it up projects at the hotel where I am staying. Perhaps you could work for your housing by fixing some shot up walls and a wooden bathtub."

"That sounds like something I could do, fix the tub and take a bath! I should clean up some time."

"You can do that later."

Audrey's attitude had really changed. She was now business like and civil. She was willing to loan me some Korean won for the repair supplies. I could get the stuff I needed around the corner. She had some more typing to do.

I had gone into a hardware store in my wandering around town and had spent a good part of an hour looking around in there. I went there and got a cheery welcome, bought what I needed, then went back and started to work fixing the door. Its hinges just slipped in and out, a very simple system.

She continued to type. She said, "I am going out on a limb for you. You owe me for this."

"I pay."

"The interest is high."

"I pay and pay, or work it off somehow."

"I will think of something."

"Yeah, I bet that it will be a doozy!"

As her guest we went to the base Personnel Office with my 'Missing in Action' forms and she presented my recertification forms. They would not accept any of it! "This form is out dated." They did have new forms. The finger print card was absent. Only security could do that. They would have to do my fingerprints and photo again. Their forms, the fingerprint card and photos would be sent to Headquarters in Japan and on up from there. Every page had to be embossed with the stamp of each level of command in the Far East including the Pacific Fleet. Everything had to be done correctly and sent through proper channels. Otherwise it could have just been typed up. I could be a spy or an impostor and she could be a collaborator. They had all the forms and would ask the questions and make an investigation. First they wanted to know where and how I had lost my identification.

"I don't know when or where I lost them. If I did I would have them."

I was told that since I had no priority or status these forms would take at least six weeks and probably several months to process.

During their quizzing Audrey went to another office and got a temporary visitor's pass, which would get me into the mess hall and the Enlisted Men's Club for a few days. Then she went back to her office.

Later I returned to Audrey's office and I finished fixing the broken door. Her telephone call to the states came through quite a bit later than what she had asked for.

"Wait outside for a minute. I have some personal things to say to Nancy."

I went outside and wandered down the street. On the corner there was a small park. It had a statue of an elder with one of those small stovepipe hats and another fancy item that I started towards when two Korean girls dressed in rather revealing and suggestive attire approached me and we started to talk in English. They thought it would rain very soon. We talked about the weather and the possibility of it raining. I was invited to their place for some tea or something stronger if I wanted to keep dry this afternoon. My scrubs had no pockets. A hand was softly searching over my backside for a pocket and a wallet. She said something in Korean. "So sorry, but we must go now." They departed. *Nice girls, nice to talk to.* Audrey was walking towards me and saw the girls leave. She had a big smile, "You have a great smile!"

"Thank you! Were those girls trying to pick you up?"

"Of course. They made a ply for my trade. Well, don't you know, if there is no money, there is no honey."

Audrey took me over to her hotel and spoke to the manager in Korean. We looked at the damage I was to repair. There was a wooden tub where a bullet had gone through. It had a small hole on the outside and larger on the inside. Also they had a room that had been shot up. Two walls were badly damaged, but were repairable. They use reeds and paper for their interior walls in most places. It looked bad due to the mess that the bullets had made. My estimate was that it would take two or three days to get everything done.

Soon-bok, the manager asked, "I would like to have that room soundproofed if possible. It would be good to have a place for parties that could become rather loud and not become an annoyance."

"I think I can do that. It depends on the availability of materials. It will take another day or two, maybe three." So, maybe my housing was set up for a few days.

Audrey guided me towards the base and I was able to get on by using those passes she picked up. I was on time for the signing of those forms. I failed to understand all of what was going on. *If the ship acknowledged that I was listed as a member of that ship's company why did I have to go through all the reinstatement?* When they were explaining they seemed to talk in circles. I sure got the often-repeated part that my being a trainee put me at the bottom of priorities and status during this progress. I was told that neither my time in service nor pay would be in effect during this process. I would have to serve additional time. Someone would make a decision based on the forms. I think they call it red tape or was it a political explanation?

Chapter Twenty-Two

THE AUSSIES

Later I was to meet Audrey in front of the 'O' Club at a particular time. She pointed to a bench and commanded, "Sit - there." *I felt like barking.* Then she gave me a charge chit, "You can only buy beer at the 'E' Club and that will be charged to an account under your name and later taken out of your pay. A service charge will probably be assessed along with some interest and some other fees."

"How much will this cost me?" *I'm sure I will pay dearly later for all that.*

"I'm not sure. All that changes from time to time. Nancy will help by taking a notary to your parents so they can quickly get all the forms back to the Navy. That would save several days. I'm going to Seoul in the morning as my duty here expires tomorrow."

Glad to have that bar chit. After this day I need a drink! I returned to the hospital to clean up, go to chow, and then to the 'E' Club where it was crowded inside. There was outside seating between the 'O' Club and the 'E' Club. The two clubs were separated by a row of fair size plants in large pottery planters.

The 'E' club bartender had a problem with my chits. He did not have a tab for Audrey Austin at the Red Cross and that chit I had was only good for chow.

"Didn't they give you a second one for the bar?"

I was grumbling while looking in my fresh scrubs that had a hip pocket on the left side.

"You a medic?"

"Yeah."

"Thought so. Those rags give you away."

"Gee whiz! Look here! I do have a second one. It's stuck to the back of the first one."

"It happens all the time. Hey, this is the kind we like, unlimited!" His voice and manner rose to cheery. "Here, have the first one on me!"

I was pleasantly surprised, "Thank you so very much!"

"Hey Doc, there is one item. It's your dress. Those scrubs are not likely to pass as uniform in here. The military police just made a pass through but they will be back in an hour or two. Here take my jacket. That should help keep both of us out of trouble."

"Okay, thanks! Aha, but I don't have any cash for a tip."

"That is okay. Your being a ward of the Red Cross tells me that you don't have much of anything."

I took my can of state side beer outside and saw an empty table close to the end of those planters. I had to maneuver around a large crowd of men who were strutting around in front of a few civilian Korean females at the center tables. A big guy with a bushy mustache beat me to the empty table by a few quick steps.

"Well, I'm in second place!"

"It was close! Have a seat mate." He was an Australian. We introduced ourselves. He was Sergeant Major Adams and did he ever have a lot of questions and comments!

"What's up with the uniform Mate?"

"I'm a medic in training and I'm here as a Red Cross guest because I lost my identification"

"Well, we have a medic without any identification and no money?

"That is quite correct."

"Yur a stray and pretty well up a tree I'd say? We just lost two med's. They raised their heads. We surely miss 'em."

"I am working on getting the paperwork for reinstatement put in motion. It has to go in and back through all the proper channels."

"You are navy and they are army?"

"Yep."

"That could take half a lifetime. You might like to have chat with the brass? They are right around the corner over there." He pointed to the officer's area. "We take in strays from time to time."

"Why not?"

Captain Bass of the Third Royal Australian Regiment had just taken a seat a few tables over. Sergeant Adams saw him, got straight up and nonchalantly ambled over. *Hum, I'm getting the idea he has a few under the belt already. Hey, that's okay.* I followed Sergeant Adams as he weaved between the hedge pots towards his officer's table.

Adams said, "Captain Bass, I'd like you to meet a prospect medic, if you would like?

"A medic! Why certainly!" Sergeant Adams introduced us.

We all went back to the table on the 'E' side. We had left our full beers and his cap on our table. Captain Bass could come over to our table, but we could not go over to the other side of those bushes even if all of us spilled all the way out to the runway. We took seats at the suggestion of Captain Bass.

He said, "There is a great shortage of medical personnel all over this part of the world. Let me tell you about our contractual system for Australian Warrant Officers."

"I would like to hear about that."

"It is basically a separate slot for specialists and not directly attached to either the enlisted or command sections of our armed forces. However Warrant Officers do operate and cooperate between them. We do have replacements that are on the way, but it will take about a month to get them here and on the line. Even then not all can stand up to the job. Around here someone gets wounded every few minutes and we are very short of competent medical staff."

My background and circumstances were generally discussed. "I have had no formal medical schooling so I have no degree or diploma. I have had some First Aid training and recently I have done a bit of on-the-job type of training in a morgue."

"In a bloody morgue? Why there?"

"They were in need of help and I needed training."

"I say that is a rather odd way to train. I have never heard of such a thing. Well, here we are much more interested in what you can do than in diplomas and such as that." We all raised our glasses to that!

I noticed that they were drinking a large blue can labeled *Fosters*. "Is that an Australian beer you are drinking?"

Captain Bass replied, "Why certainly. Tis the best brew in a can and a mite larger one at that. Beyond that, the price is a tad lower. Here take a sip."

"Tis quite good!" A Korean waitress was passing by and I caught her attention, "May I have a Fosters when you are able."

She replied, "Certainly."

Captain Bass then continued. "For the Warrant Officer you need to be acknowledged and will be quizzed by an Australian doctor to determine if you are trained well enough to go any further. After that you'll go through an operational test to see if you can stand up to the job's demands. That same doctor or another will evaluate your abilities for two days. Then you will have to pass my inspection, part of which we were doing now. After the reviews you may get a recommendation for something between flunky and a specialist. In your case Scott, if all fails you can take a swing at me and I will have you arrested and sent to the brig. Either way you will have a place to stay while the paperwork finds its way through the system and eventually back."

These folks are quite genuine and practical. "Let's give it a go! I might pass your muster." I offered to buy the next round. They gladly accepted my offer. That improved my standing if it was ever in any jeopardy. It would go on my chit. We toasted our mutual success. *Maybe I just got to first base. Thanks to Nancy, Jane and Ingrid, I felt that I could do this!*

On Monday I was to meet a Doctor Green who retained a staff position as Professor of Surgery at Sydney University School of Medicine. He was returning Monday morning from a three day Rest and Recreation trip to Japan.

"That will be perfect. Audrey has arranged housing for me for two or three days." We agreed that if I was unable to get on base by Monday morning they would go to Audrey's office, gather me up and march me back. We chatted for quite a while.

Audrey came by the table with an unfinished drink in hand. "I have something I want to do before an early morning appointment. We ought to be going home. Is that okay?"

We said our, "Cheerios."

It was now pitch dark. I wanted to tell Audrey about what the Aussies had said but she had several other urgent concerns. On the way she said. "I was talking to Monique and she told me about how good you were to her. Are you going to treat me the same way?"

"Really! Do you have infected sinuses? I used steam inhalation for that."

"Not that." She gave me a little nudge. "You know what I mean."

"Aha, she liked the foot massages!"

She nudged me fairly hard and made me regain my balance. Our pace was quickened as a few drops of rain were falling.

"You are giving me a hard time Zak. She simply raved about what you two did together."

We were in a darkened place outside the main gate close to her office. She pulled me close in towards her and whispered in my ear.

"Oh!"

It had started to rain harder. We went from a normal quick walk to a trot crossing a street and ran into her hotel. She called to the desk clerk in Korean, "I told her that I am taking you to my room for a spanking."

Once inside we grabbed at each other's wet clothing and threw it over the metal railing at the foot of the bed. Rain was coming down in sheets and it was blowing through an open window. I quickly closed it.

In the morning Audrey said, "I should be back in two days. I have a ride to Seoul this afternoon. I will ask for an extension of six weeks. I'm sure I can get it. That way we can be together until the certified forms are returned and you are shipped out."

"Sounds like a plan." Then again I tried to tell Audrey about what the Aussies had said, but she was in a rush to get to an important appointment.

"How long can I stay here?"

Audrey quickly said something in Korean to Soon-bok. Her reply had terms that Audrey had not heard before. She started to ask what she meant. Soon-bok stopped her, saying; "You are running out of time."

Audrey gasped when she looked at her watch. It was nearly time for her appointment on the base. Audrey hurriedly told Soon-bok what I needed in Korean, and then bolted out the door.

Soon-bok looked me over closely. She looked puzzled and doubtful, but finally nodded assent. She had me go with her granddaughters while they gathered up the materials that I needed. Soon-bok wanted that damaged room to be soundproofed, if possible.

"This will take a lot of egg cartons."

After Audrey left, Soon-book's granddaughters watched me as I put a thin film of glue around the edge of the tub's hole and placed toothpicks as fill and as support for the cork. I made a brace to put pressure on the glue job.

That night I stayed in Audrey's room. The next day I worked on the shot up room. The girls helped me pick up the mess.

I glued the broken framework with support materials, put small screws in to assure they held, and then we papered the outside. I was still unable to raise my left arm above my head. The girls had a good time being my left arm by holding the egg cartons up to the asbestos ceiling so I could staple or glue them in place. The day following we worked very well together and finished the room, if late. I tested the job by turning up a radio quite loud. Sound was hard to hear in the hall except through the door. We glued more egg cartons to the inside of the door for more soundproofing. That helped.

Soon-bok was delighted. She wanted to have a party to celebrate. She had a special robe for me to wear. She would fix a special dinner and serve it in the refinished room. A woven pad was placed in the middle with a large pillow for me. The girls brought in a wind up Victrola, put some oriental music on, then lit a few candles and fragrance sticks and served me tea. A little later they would serve sake. They had light brightly colored robes that would fly open when they stepped high. They liked to do that as they danced all around me flashing some skin. They held long banners of silk like cloth attached to sticks that they waved around making swirls and curls of the streamers. It was quite an artistic show! They lit some other fragrances. Later they shed one of their robes and continued to dance in skimpy loose brightly colored attire. They looked so cute and were a delight to watch!

Soon-bok came in wearing a colorful robe. She carried dinner flavored with special and very hot spices. Those spices caused 'Dragon breath full of fire.' It was horrid! I was able to eat some rice.

Soon-bok lit another stick. It had a heavy scent and made smoke which clung low to the floor. The girls liked to kick it up and dance around with more dipping into the smoke with their streamers.

Soon-bok poured much more sake. We made a toast to something. I was getting lightheaded. They all danced around in the thick smoke. I was dizzy. The girls giggled. I passed out.

I slept well into the morning. I felt like a train had hit me. My head was splitting. My side stung like a wasp swarm had hit it and I was as hungry as a hog on a holiday morning.

I staggered out of the hotel and sat on a bench in a park across from the Red Cross office wondering what to do next. In a while I went to the culvert to see if I could crawl through, but a grate had just been welded to hinges. They were still slightly warm. A lock was in place. I tried my passes at the gate. My guest pass had expired and the others were not accepted as a gate pass. I went back to the park bench. There was a cool breeze.

I had a week of beard to shave and needed to clean up and get ready to meet Dr. Green tomorrow morning, so, just how do I get in the gate to do that? *A uniform would be nice for a first meeting. Well, the Aussies did say that they would go to the Red Cross office if I failed to get in.*

I sat in the sun for a few hours when a tall thin middle aged lady in a long gray dress with a gray cape topped by a short dark cap went up to the Red Cross door and fumbled with a large ring of keys while trying to open the Red Cross office. I went over to her and asked about accommodations. She sharply said, "I have just flown in and need to get oriented. It would be another day or so before she could sort things out."

In a day or two! Where do I stay tonight? I really didn't need another night like last night! It has taken the better part of today to sober up!

"Of course! It was just that I have some immediate needs." She made a huffing sound as she entered and sharply closed the door. I didn't wait around for an answer, just turned and started to leave.

She opened the door and called out, "Yes, we can! We can get you a loan at ten percent interest and you will have to stay at our approved hotels and eat in our recommended restaurants." She thrust a short list of places at me

"Thank you. I will see you in the morning?"

"No the next day!" She snapped.

Suddenly she seemed to become haunting. That hat now had a broad rim and went up to a point. Was that a wart on the end of her nose? Oh, her transportation; she flew in on a broom!

I returned to that same bench. It was now partly in the shade. I looked at the paper I held. These places were all in the high price part of town. I had heard about some of the places and fancy prices from the guys in the chow hall. They had said food and lodging was thirty to forty dollars a day and for me to do that for six weeks, or longer! I would be paying a full paycheck for well over two years! Better try something else. My face fell into my hands.

I prayed again, *"Lord, again I have needs and wants. When can I do something for you?"*

I stretched a bit, and then walked around the small park. *I could go back to that hotel and take Audrey's room or whatever was offered.* I pondered that. In a while I decided to walk around the block to see what I could see. There was nothing of interest for me. I came back to another bench that was now fully in the sun. I sat and just absorbed the sun's warmth.

Some time had passed when I heard the rhythm of marching boots. It was the Aussies coming back from a walkabout. Their slouch hats were pinned up on their left side and tilted a bit to the right. Their arms swung up and down a fair amount and very evenly. Smart looking!

I scurried and crossed the street ahead of the column. Medics march at the end on the right of marching units. I plucked a cloth cap from the end lad's pack, and put it on. I joined in the second platoon and picked up their step and arm swing straight away and marched right through the Main Gate with them. I remained in line until they were at their area and dismissed. I returned the cap. Then I approached Sergeant Major Adams. "Good afternoon Sergeant Major I need to tidy up a bit before tomorrow's meeting with Doctor Green. I have not been able to secure agreeable facilities. Can I bivouac here?"

"Glad to oblige you. We are a few lads short and have quarters to spare." We went into the tent and he pointed out a bunk. Your dress is quite right for Monday morning as you will be going to your test station and doctor Green will be wearing the same kind of surgical scrubs."

I went straight to the hospital and picked up a clean scrub set, then cleaned up in the hospital showers. So not to be a stranger, I decided to look over the receiving area. I watched the nurses assist, get supplies and made mental notes where things were. I was able to beg a couple of aspirins for my sore rib, and then I wandered back to the Australian camp. *I'm lucky to have been raised in many Canadian foster homes so some of the Aussie slang was a bit familiar, but still it was something of a foreign language.*

I saw Sergeant Major Adams. He waved me over to where he was talking to his troops. He introduced me as their new medic. I got several cheery comments like, "Good t'have ya mate!"

On the way into the tents Adams asked, "Did the Sally toss you out?"

"Aye, she did but not for the usual reason. She was called back to Seoul. It was her time to rotate. Her replacement was not all that helpful. She flew in on a broom, don't you know?"

You don't say." He chuckled his understanding. "We're going on a bit of a jog. Want to tag along?"

"Ordinarily I would love to, but my left side is a bit of a bother from a cracked rib or two and I've been reaching up quite a bit the past two days. So, I better decline the jog. I should ask about getting cleaned up with a proper uniform so I will fit in with you chaps."

"If you don't mind hand-me-downs we will get you into something when we get back. We have several lads about your size. We do allow beards in the warrant classification and yours seems to do you quite well. Don't bother with that."

"I was raised in foster homes and on hand-me-downs. It's nothing new for me."

Sergeant Major Adams led the group in some calisthenics. I did a few stretches with them. I had not been doing much in the way of keeping in shape lately. I would not do the jog. They went around the perimeter twice. One lap was over a couple of miles.

I chatted with Corporal Meyer after their workout. He had visited relatives in Little Rock, Arkansas. We were the same size. He loaned me a uniform so I could get into the mess hall with them tonight and Sunday. I was very happy to be with this group and I would have a day to rest.

Chapter Twenty-Three

PRACTICAL TESTING

Monday morning a little before eight o'clock I was standing at parade rest outside the receiving station waiting for Captain Bass. When they came around a corner I came to attention. He introduced me to Dr. Green.

Captain Bass told Dr. Green, "This is the lad I was telling you about. He is willing to be evaluated for a temporary warrant appointment under your command." He then introduced us. We shook hands. Dr. Green said, "I will be happy to do that. You will be working alongside me for a few days. Then we'll decide what we want to do with you, if anything." His voice lowered as he said, "If you fail you may be returned to your ship!" He made it sound as if that was the very last place on earth anyone would want to go.

"Heaven forbid! I would return to swabbing decks!" We smiled.

"Have you had any field medical training?" There were patients arriving by chopper.

"I got a bit of practice in a morgue."

"Hum, we shall see. We will take the worst patients as I have to evaluate you."

Two nurses were rolling a patient on a gurney over to us. This patient had a large chunk of shrapnel sticking out of his belly.

"Would you like a lap kit?"

"Definitely."

I went to the cabinet and got a general laparotomy kit, and a tin of gauze. On the way back I picked up a bottle of water. An IV kit went between my teeth, and I pushed a holding stand along using my foot.

"Should I start a water bottle?"

"Generally that's generally a good idea, but hold up on this one."

There was a nurse standing by at this patient's head. She told me who she was. I didn't catch her name, but I did notice that she had nice large brown eyes and was doing anesthesia. She announced to both of us, "I won't need much at my end as his vitals are rather weak."

I was concentrating on a quick set up. As I flipped opened the lap kit Dr. Green thumped the patient's belly. It looked like he was about to give birth. It had a very firm resonating sound.

I held out a scalpel and stood with gauze in hand to swipe the wound. Blood flowed out rapidly as he entered the abdominal cavity. It took a lot of gauze to sop it up. Doctor Green removed the long piece of shrapnel causing a huge gush of blood to flow from a large artery deep inside the belly. It took several handfuls of gauze to sop up the blood.

Doctor Green said, "Look at that, cut clean through." He applied a clamp to the spurting artery.

"What do we have here Zak?"

"That severed artery is the superior mesentery."

He nodded his head saying, "It's a real big gusher."

I sponged up the area. The clamp failed to hold. I offered him another hemostat. Doctor Green took it. I pulled the gut back further for a better view and wiped with gauze in the wound to sop up more blood. He applied a second hemostat and clamped, again I sponged. There was no leaking. The nurse had her hand on the carotid artery, the neck artery. "Nothing here," she said.

"I guess there is nothing more we can do. He has finished bleeding to death." He turned to me and said, "When you use three handfuls of gauze to sop up blood, the probability of survival is very low. A person one-pint low has a comeback chance. This guy had lost more than any pint before we opened him up. I knew that from the size and sound his belly made. He only would have lasted a moment or two one way or the other."

"I heard that percussion. It sounded quite tight. Was that from the pressure inside?"

"It was."

"Thank you. I couldn't get that in a morgue."

A nurse covered the body and moved the gurney. A second nurse joined her.

"Good thought about bringing the water bottle over."

We stood there a moment while the next patient was wheeled up. He examined this patient as I got an ortho kit, then pulled the stand and water closer. This was a badly burnt guy with a missing leg.

Another nurse was standing by the patient's head to administer an anesthetic to him. She looked up and said to me, "Hello over there, I'm Beth. I do this end."

"Hi, I'm Zak, a trainee."

Doctor Green corrected me, "No, he is possibly our next medical team member. We are doing the warrant testing."

"That is lovely!"

He asked for vital signs. Beth told him as Dr. Green examined the injury, and then told her, "Put him under."

A curtain on rollers appeared at the head end to block a light breeze. Without hesitation I started to do a venal puncture and then stopped, "Do you want to start a bottle of five percent?"

"Let me see you do it."

I moved a little to one side so he could see me work better. The venal puncture and tie down took only a minute. *That was by far easier than on a dead person.*

I picked up two hemostats in my left pinkie and a scalpel, its blade to my palm between thumb and forefinger. I had gauze pads in my right hand and three hemostats hanging on my right pinkie. There was an open tin of gauze pads on the tray table.

He looked about, "Good timing team. We are all ready at the same time. Now Zak since you are all ready to assist would you kindly pick up that empty tray over there and put it on his abdomen?" I laid the contents in my right hand on the instrument tray, reached over and seized the tray he was pointing to and placed it on the patient's abdomen and then scooped up my right hand tools.

Dr. Green promptly asked, "Scalpel." My left hand went forward and produced the scalpel without hesitation and pressed it in his hand.

"Sponge here, now over here. - Three gut, - snip." So it went. I passed the tools. I was able to anticipate most of his moves. *I thought of the gals and I was sure glad that we had roll played!*

"We will get rid of this burnt tissue." He excised that and put it on the metal tray on the patient's stomach. The stench was awful! Those fumes rose right in front of me and not very far from him. They were eye watering. It took several long minutes to cut and clean before Dr. Green made a second evaluation of the wound. He blinked and wiped his eyes with his sleeve.

I asked, "Would you like a little more air sir? I can kick the curtain back a little."

He looked at me through blurry eyes, "No, not quite yet."

There were a few more small bleeders to tie off and then he asked for a saw.

"There is no saw in this pack, sir. Should I get one?"

"Definitely."

I paused, "I can get some Vicks for your nose? It will help with the odor."

He answered, "No. That test is over! Now you can move the curtain and fetch a saw." We paused while we both wiped our hands on our butts.

"Say Zak, before you do that would you take this tissue tray over there and place it on their patient's belly?" He pointed to a team to the right and whispered, "Do it quietly and carefully and say nothing, be sly and just drift back away. I want to see the reaction of that big doctor and that blond nurse with the red headband."

The big doctor was slowly suturing a patient's thigh. The tray was quietly slipped in place with nothing being said. I was not noticed as they were facing the other way while both were looking at their patient's wound. I drifted away and then with haste went straight to the packing station only a few steps away and asked, "Do you have a saw? Our pack doesn't have one."

The gal said, "We don't have any sterilized saws."

Just then, the nurse with the red headband made a funny face and wrinkled her nose while the doctor was standing there. Just then that doctor got a whiff of the smelly tray. He moved back, made a horrid face and retched. His second retch brought fourth a projectile of puke. His regurgitation splattered under the gurney. He marched off saying something unintelligible, probably not repeatable. The nurse had departed in haste holding her hand over her mouth. That patient was abandoned.

A backward glance showed Dr. Green and Beth bent over trying not to burst out in laughter. Doctor Green called, "Can you finish that patient?"

"Aye. He just needs a few sutures."

"Can you do it?"

"Aye!"

I left the tray where it was and turned the gurney so he could see what I was doing, and then finished the sutures. It only took a minute and asked, "Can someone do the bandage? I still need a saw!"

Three Koreans rushed over with bucket and mop in hand. They removed the tray and the patient was moved away for bandaging. Several nurses near by made some disparaging comments and several others glared at me. I rushed over to ask a nurse who was putting packs on the shelves. She was giggling.

I asked, "Are there any saws available? We need one right now."

"They are all dirty."

"Are you sure there are no saws in those packs?"

She pointed to a dirty one. "That is the only one I know of."

"Thanks!" I picked it up, dipped it in a hand wash basin, took a hand towel and wiped it, then picked up a bottle of hydrogen peroxide and poured some over both sides of the saw and returned to our patient, "This is dirty. I wiped it off and rinsed it with hydrogen peroxide."

"We were watching you. Why a dirty one? Would she not open a kit pack?"

"She said that was the only one she knew of and obviously it was dirty. The patient will be getting Penicillin won't he?"

"He sure will, - especially now! Good try though, especially for telling us what you wound up with. It's better to get it done now than wait a week for a proper saw and make him go through a lot of agony twice. He is hanging in there. Here we make do with what we have or can get. Often we are not able to postpone much of our work, nor should we."

"The saw needs sharpening and will probably leave some rough edges. How do you smooth them out?"

"We cut or file them. Definitely the burrs have to go as they will tear up flesh and be painful forever." He paused, "Sharpen a saw! No one around knows how to do that."

"What's so special about a surgical bone saw?"

"Just that is gets sterilized. Ah, well, some of the time."

"If there is a file around I can sharpen the saws."

"Really!" Dr. Green stood back a half step. "Do you know how to sharpen a saw?"

"Sure."

"So do you know how to use one?"

"Sure on wood, not on a live person yet, but I did several in the morgue."

He pointed to the spot, "Saw right here. Let me see if you can do it."

I took the saw and promptly started sawing. Do you want a straight through cut or should I cut all around the outer side?"

"Why cut around the bone?"

"Well, with wood it would prevent most burring and splintering. That may apply here too, especially with a saw this dull."

"It is the same principal. Where did you learn about that?"

"At home while doing some finishing carpentry work. Lately, in a morgue where they had me finish some jobs and remove debris from several bone cuts. They didn't like burrs either."

Beth said, "Boys, we are starting to have a time factor here!"

I sawed faster, cut straight down for several strokes and then worked around on each side. I picked the leg up and continued to make a cut all around the bone. It was finished with a few more strokes. I removed a burr by dragging a scalpel.

Doctor Green ran his finger around to check. "That is good." He then started removing a large piece of skin from the lower leg to cover the stump. "His skin will heal fast and there will no rejection problems." The skin had a ghastly tattoo. We all wrinkled our noses at it and made disparaging commentary. I seized the end of his graft cut and pulled it close to the skin.

"Where did you pick up that technique?"

"While I worked in a slaughter-house skinning hogs and cows."

"Well, that just saved us a lot of time!" He arranged the skin so the tattoo was on the lower inside mostly out-of-sight.

Beth said, "Patient is waking up. Hurry along boys."

We both started suturing on opposite sides. Two nurses came to help. They cut the suture ends and passed us needles for the next suture.

"Should I remove some of the hair before taping the bandage?

"Why do that?"

"So the tape can be removed without hurting the patient."

"That is thoughtful. Do it."

Quickly I scraped off hair by using the scalpel like a straight razor. *The use of a straight razor was something that Ingrid had taught me.*

Beth said, "Good go gents! That was all done in a single dunking under the gas!"

After that it seemed as if we worked on less damaged patients. Dr. Green told me what he wanted me to do. Sometimes he asked what I would do. He asked what the various tissues we were working on, the muscles, bones and about other parts as we went along. I was grateful for the morgue training. It was sure important today. *I mentally said a prayer of thanks for the gals' help.*

We secured for the time being. We washed our hands in a bowl and wiped our hands on a clean cloth towel.

"Well that was a good morning's work! Was that your first passing?"

"Yes sir, of a human."

"Thought so. I thought you looked a bit anxious. It is a hard reality but all too often there is a limit to what we can do for them." He paused a moment and asked, "Where are your bags and such?"

"What you see is what I have. No identification, no dog tags, not even a tooth brush."

"Now pray tell, how did that happen?"

"Well, the short version is that I left the ship in scrubs on an emergency pick up and I had to swim ashore. I think my tags got lost in the waves."

"Oh I guess that is what Captain Bass was referring to when he said, 'You were plucked like a Jaybird!' Well, we will have to get you properly taken care of."

He hailed Beth who was walking by. "Beth, can you help Scott here find accommodations and something to wear? He is now a member of our Medical Staff and he needs everything. All he has is what you see. Can you get him fixed up properly?"

"My pleasure. Follow me Zak." Beth beckoned for me to follow as she strode off. Wow, did she have a stride! I had to stretch to keep up.

"Please slow down. My side is hurting."

We came to an abrupt stop. Beth asked, "What's wrong with it?"

"A few ribs were probably broken several days ago." I pulled up my jumper top up so she could see the tape.

"Did you get an X ray?

"No."

Why not?"

"I was in enemy territory."

"We are going to X ray!"

We went directly there. They removed the tape, took the pictures and then Beth taped up my rib cage. The X-rays fresh out of the development fluid showed a cracked rib. I was still bruised. A dry reading would be made in a few hours.

She then took me to a tent and pointed out a cot that I would be using. Beth gave me two aspirin and a small bottle saying, "You should take two of these every four hours for as long as it is painful. They reduce swelling and bruises."

"Thanks."

Captain Bass and Dr. Green were at lunch. As we approached we saw that their heads were gently nodding. When Beth and I arrived they had just sat down. Beth and I got our lunches and joined them. Dr. Green announced, "A reception unit on the line should be the next test."

Captain Bass answered, "Quite right." He then turned to me, "Zak, tell me if you will. What is your background? I am interested since you failed to faint or flounder with the first set of patients and that you were not fazed but moved along through all of that grizzly stuff. Many interns turn green don't you know?"

"Do you really want all that now while we are eating?"

He was insistent, "This is a part of the oral testing I mentioned."

I began with the requirements of the Scouting program and a neighbor nurse taking me under her wings, as she needed a 'dummy' for demonstrating artificial respiration and such. Then I mentioned that I worked part-time in an abattoir as a pucker.

Dr. Plum asked, "I'm not sure what that actually is, Zak?"

"An abattoir is the refined word. The common term is slaughterhouse. I was a pucker, the guy who cuts the guts out." Right then Dr. Plum eyes had bulged, his hand went over his mouth, and he quickly got up and hurried off leaving his tray. "Also I had to scoop all of them up and shovel guts out of the way usually onto a platform or into a rendering truck. Most of the time it was rather warm and there were swarms of flies all around that area. The guts developed a bit of a stink quickly. They were all supposed to have empty stomachs, but that was not always the case. They would split open a lot easier if they had food in them. The gastric fluids do have their own distinctive odor, don't you know." Here, Beth asked to be excused saying something about her lipstick. I was starting to say a bit more about that. Captain Bass had turned a tad pale. He raised his hand as a signal that I could stop at any time. He got up and mumbled that he had to attend to something not clearly specified and he would return in a little while. I skipped all the lovely details of my working in a slaughterhouse and went directly into what I had done in the mortuary and the wonderful training I had received there. My audience had expired. Only Dr. Green remained and he had stopped eating. I asked, "Should I change the topic to the weather?"

"No continue. I'm impressed. Now, I really want to know what you did in the morgue!"

"I will leave the morgue stuff out and concentrate on the field training." He was pleased at what was covered. He asked some questions.

"I know next to nothing about anesthetics. All the subjects were dead don't you know?"

We took a final sip of our tea. I noticed that Beth and Captain Bass were returning from the bar area and she was carrying a tray with four *Foster* beers.

When Captain Bass returned he asked Dr. Green, "Did I miss anything important?"

"Why yes, I would say so!"

"It got better in the morgue, eh?"

"Quite so! I have no doubt at all the lad is able to handle carnage and he has had some very useful training."

"That is very necessary around here."

After lunch Beth went about buying uniforms for me, which included a used pair of short pants, as was the custom of the Commonwealth countries in the summer. Beth had put my new clothing on my cot. I quickly got into them. They were a good fit. The bill would get to me later.

While she was buying clothing for me I had gathered up bone saws and was in the auto repair shop sharpening them. Beth spotted me as I was leaving the shop. We delivered the saws back to the cleaning and packing area.

Along the way I saw Dr. Plum and went over to him to apologize for describing the gruesome stuff and told him I had received a lot of useful training in a morgue.

"My Doctorate is in Microbiology."

"Oh!" *That is a good explanation for an aversion to this line of work.* I started to speak.

He held up his hand saying, "Thanks but I've had and seen quite enough! I am going to Japan early in the morning where I will be much more comfortable working in a biology laboratory."

"I wish you the best!"

"Same!"

When I returned to Beth she asked, "What was that all about?"

"I just apologized to Dr. Plum. He is going to work in a biology lab in Japan." She nodded her understanding. "Can I buy you a night cap?"

"It's time we should be sleeping. That would be cheery."

On the way we saw Dr. Green who said, "Captain Bass is making arrangements for us to go to the front line this evening where we can get some patients fresh off the line, hopefully without being totally swamped. We will probably go to a new Mobile Army Surgical Hospital, a MASH unit, or a similar Navy MED unit. Both had said we're welcome. The MASH and Med units have the best facilities of all! They are very well equipped with surgical lights, supplies and are very well staffed and can handle everything. They even have landing pads and a crew for choppers close by. You do know that both the copters and the mobile hospitals are experimental units and are rather rare, don't you?"

"Yes I do."

"Then you know that you certainly won't find either of those or that kind of equipment on every corner of this peninsula!"

After evening chow we were taken to the line in an empty ambulance. There were several items in them that I needed to be familiar with, so I snooped around as we went along. We were en route to a Navy MED unit that was fairly close by. En route I was silently praying for help, courage and guidance, as I felt inadequate.

We met Dr. Brown, a very renowned anesthetist who was on a research mission to evaluate the procedures being used in the field. He briefed us on nitrous oxide that he liked to use under these conditions. He said it is safer than ether and less invasive for the patient and has a much lower impact on the medical staff than our usual ether. Dr. Brown demonstrated and talked continuously as he was totally absorbed in his mission. I was amazed by the effectiveness of local injections. This was all new to me. The morgue had nothing like he was talking about, as it was not needed there. Jane did have me do subcutaneous injections using a substance to create a more natural look, often by filling up a depression caused by lost tissue.

Dr. Brown said local injections were less damaging to patients and they had a faster recovery. Most patients were taken to hospitals in ambulances as soon as they stabilized.

"I have never done this kind of an injection on a live person"

"You will, very soon."

Our tour was interrupted when a marine was brought in with both legs blown off by a mine explosion. His left leg was off close to the pelvis. On the right side the leg was severed in the middle of the femur. He had a lot of blood loss. We hooked up whole blood and a bottle of water. Dr. Green did debridement while Dr. Brown administered nitrous oxide. A nurse was assisting. I watched. In a while Dr. Brown announced that the patient had a collapse of his circulatory system. We quit working. We had worked on him for quite some time and then he was moved to an Intensive Care Unit.

Other patients seemed to be so much easier after all that heroic effort. Many patients came in with lacerations. Dr. Brown demonstrated subcutaneous injections. Then he had me do them. He followed me closely. We had a good number of patients that needed that type of anesthesia and I got to inject and suture many.

Dr. Green and I got back to the rear hospital in time for lunch. Beth met us and she stayed to chat for a while. Then I went to get some sleep.

Beth woke me up in time for an afternoon workout with my adopted unit.

Adams said, "This is much like yesterday."

My side hadn't been much of a bother today, so that was good. I did a light workout then stepped away as I didn't want to tempt the devil by running; however I did take a brisk walk around the premises.

The next day Dr. Green and I went to the front line again and looked at the amputee patient who was still critical but stable. I was happy to see him alive and on his way to a hospital in Japan.

Today Dr. Green had me remove debris from some wounds. We left bullets in place if they were not bleeding. The bullets were very hot and usually cauterized the wound, which stopped most of the bleeding. Dr. Green wanted X-Rays to see where all the bullets or trash was located before he went in hacking on human flesh like it was brush. We would not be chasing bloodless bullets. That would be done in Japan, then with the aid of X-rays. Banish all the thoughts and Hollywood scenes in the old western movies where they immediately extracted every bullet with ease and had it drop clunking into a tin container, after which the hero would soon gallop off.

We were back at the base hospital by mid morning. I felt a little stressed from being under the pressure of the inspection. Ah shucks we had missed breakfast, so we each picked up a beer and went out on a patio to meet with Captain Bass, Dr. Green, Master Sergeant Adam and a few others.

Captain Bass announced, "I am pleased to announce that Zakary has passed our Warrant testing." He had the paperwork in hand and I signed it. "You are now an Australian Medical Warrant Officer Second-Class." I was warmly congratulated. They also had an ID tag for me.

Chapter Twenty-Four

 ❖

SWEDISH HOSPITAL

I was napping when Beth came for me. She tapped my foot, "Zak, Dr. Green wants to talk to you very soon." I got up and went to him straightaway.

"Hello Zak. Since our attack procedure notice to the United Nations got hung up somewhere there is a pause in our deployment. I made arrangements for us to go to a Swedish Hospital where I can work with a renowned reconstruction surgeon and you can work with an orthopedic surgeon where you will be exposed to a great variety of procedures. Would you like to tag along?"

"Yes sir!"

"I thought so!" After a good lunch we departed by jeep.

On arrival two very beautiful Swedish Nurses met us.

I said, "Wow, this will be heaven!"

Dr. Green nodded his head and said, "This is the best hospital in Korea. That blond on the left was second runner up in the Miss Sweden contest"

She walked directly up to me, "I yam Gertrude! Are you der trainee?"

"Yes, ma'am."

"I yam der teaching for der scrubbin."

Her voice was loud, high pitched and staccato. She sounded like a machine gun. She ordered, "Vo follow me!" She marched me over to a table that had a pan on it and dunked my hands into it. It was bluing!

Gertrude jammed a brush into my hand and commanded, "Vu scrubbin der clean!" She took a few strides away, turned around, and folded her arms. In about two minutes she strode over and took my brush. She snarled, "Dummkopf! Vu know no thing about der scrubbin!"

"Hey, this is new to me," I pleaded. "They have only been wet a few times other than when I have been swimming."

"Ya volt! Vu never vash der hands!" Gertrude grabbed the brush from my hand, "Like thees!" She pressed the brush very firmly and scrubbed my hands frantically.

"Scrubbin!" She then stalked back to her former position and was glowering.

I got the idea she was in a big hurry, so I picked up the scrubbing tempo. I was almost clean when she stepped back up.

"Ja, vu half der blue." Pointing, "Here!" Then again, "There!" She grabbed my right hand and furiously scrubbed at the remaining spots.

Gertrude may have had the body of a goddess with beautiful hair and teeth but her voice and mannerisms turned me totally off.

Gertrude whipped a towel from a tray pack and jammed it at me. "Vry!" she commanded.

She commanded, "Hold yer hanks like thees!" Her hands were up extended out from the body at about fifteen degrees.

"Vu com!"

We marched out of that tent into another where we met three Korean nurses. One had a can of powder. A second held gloves open.

Gertrude commanded, "Like thees!" She stuck her hands out so the Korean gal could powder them, then she rubbed her hands together very briskly. I did the same. The powder smelled like baby powder. She stepped towards another Korean Nurse who was holding gloves wide open at their top. Gertrude jammed her hands into them. I copied but not as gruffly. My fingers did not quite get to the bottom of the gloves' fingertips.

Gertrude glared and commanded that I had to move my fingers to the end of the glove. She reached out and pulled a finger tight. "Dummkopf! Vu must go in to zee bottom like I vo!" The Korean gals tied facemasks over our mouths and noses.

"Yes Ma'am!"

"Von't get insoltinks wit der comments!"

I muttered, "Aye." We went next to an open service area and had taken a few steps toward a lady doctor working on a patient between two drawn curtains.

"Vatch!"

I looked at her wide-eyed.

"Dummkopf! Not me, her!" She pointed to the female doctor fixing a ligament to a bone of a hand.

Gertrude snarled, "Vu missed der important part!" She spit out the word, "Dummkopf! Ver too late. Vo scrubbin too slow!" Gertrude then stalked out.

The lady doctor looked up at me. I think she was smiling. Her blue eyes were twinkling and there were a few lines at their edge.

"I softly said, "I am Dummkopf."

Her head went back as she laughed. "Will you take this and pull up on it that way?" She pointed up the patient's arm and was handing me a hemostat.

She spoke excellent English with a nice soft voice. *What a difference!*

I took it and put some pressure on the part.

"Pull harder." She paused, - "Pull harder! This part has receded."

I pulled much harder. The part moved a little further up the patient's arm.

"That's good, hold it right there."

She inserted a small thin wire through a small hole in the bone and bent the wire about forty-five degrees. Then she pushed the wire through a tendon to hold it in place. She called it an aponeurosis tendon, a flat tendon. She closed the wound leaving a tail of wire protruding.

I said, "That is a clever way to do that. I guess you just pull the wire out in a week or so.

"That is right." She had lowered her mask, and was smiling broadly. *Wow, did she look good!*

"I see that Gertrude has departed."

"I'm Eva." Her voice had such a nice sound. "Gertrude doesn't quite have the stomach to do this work, however she is good at teaching scrubbing technique. She is on rest leave for the next three days. Dr. Green said you probably could do anything I asked."

"Just ask and I will work at it until I get it right."

"Good! Now stay close to me."

Eva was an Orthopedic Surgeon. I would follow her very closely in the operating room. She had me do many of the procedures. I followed her on rounds while reviewing patients, and examining their progress for the next three days. After she was finished, which was usually late afternoon, I was put to work in the Orthopedic Wards where I could watch and track her patients' recovery by making notes in charts. That forced me to look hard to see any change that was there. We met afterward to review the day over a drink.

There were a few nursing complications to learn about also. Some were unusual. One of our guys had a malaria relapse. His temp soared up very high. Quinine was given. We cooled him down with damp towels and some ice packs. Here they had an ice-making machine.

A US Army soldier got very dirty while helping to pull a buddy out of a cesspool he accidently slid into. His hands went up to his face. He had meningitis and was the only survivor of three who were involved in that incident. He was super sensitive to noise and light. We put earphones on him to keep the sound down and a tent over his head to dim the light.

There was a necessary test concerning the patients' internal organs being in proper working order that all patients had to perform. It concerned the kidneys and proof of their function. Simply put, did they pass water? On this surgical ward the staff had used a mild technique of placing a hand or foot in warm water. Often that would work. On this ward and with this group of patients that method had been tried with no results. The next trick was pouring water into a bedpan. A nurse asked, "Can vu do that?" As she departed she said something like, "It gets to me."

"Of course, I can do that!"

This was a group of six who were for the most part British and Australian non commissioned officers. Some had reading glasses, several had bushy mustaches, and all were rather burly. They all had their arms across their chests. They looked like tough hardboiled owls sitting in their bunks looking like "You can't make me do **that** here!" There was no way on earth they were going to use that tin tube in a bed in front of all these other guys! I started by standing in the middle of the passageway between two rows of beds. I took a half-gallon pitcher and slowly poured water into a clean empty metal bedpan. The falling water sound had some resonance. The patients had their metal johns close by to catch any release they may make. None were fazed. They continued to look like owls all perched on a line blinking their eyes. Nothing hoped for was happening. I sure got the message! My water master had opened the water valve and the water was on its way. *I have to finish this job!* I crossed my legs and hunched over and poured water faster, raising the container higher. I wiggled and squirmed. I carefully placed the items on a bed-stand. Holding my legs close together I desperately ran to the bathroom in a crouched over position. Perhaps I looked like Jerry Lewis in the *Disorderly Orderly*. They all laughed so hard some of them wet their bed. I know that because I got to change their beds.

On our last day at the Swedish Hospital it was celebrating something about the number of patients it had served. There was to be a party after dinner. A grateful former patient who wanted to remain anonymous paid for drinks. We would toast him several times and in several ways.

When Gertrude returned from rest leave she sent me a note saying I was to be her escort for this evening. She wanted me to meet her at that party at a particular time and a certain place. She gave me details regarding my appearance, which included a haircut. Also she wanted me to call her "Gertie." That really surprised me.

There were many tall thin thunderstorms, pencils, all around that afternoon and all evening. It would rain hard for a while then quit. The patio door was open but everyone crammed into the smaller area inside where it was warm and dry.

Properly attired and scrubbed up I arrived at the appointed place several minutes early. I picked up a beer and was waiting. I was looking for her to enter at the main entrance. By looking at a reflection in a window I could also see the length of the bar and was not looking directly at anyone.

Some of the popular songs of the year were being played on a wind up Victrola. Some were dancing to: "Wish You Were Here," by Eddie Fisher, "You Belong to Me," by Jo Stafford, "A Guy Is A Guy," by Doris Day, and many others.

Gertie had taken her time putting on her makeup, earrings on and other such. When she entered she really was a knockout! I was astounded by the change! She had her blond hair done up with low braids an inch or so behind her hairline. It was quite northern European. She wore a blue cocktail dress with some decoration on the wide straps. She took her time strolling past the many guys lined up along the bar. She spoke to most.

"You look absolutely stunning tonight!"

"Danke schr." She gave me a light cheek kiss.

"Would you like a drink?"

"Yah." She ordered a Ballet Russe.

"Would you like to dance?"

"Ya. Vin a fu meinites." We carried our drinks to a large low coffee table surrounded by about a dozen or so other guests. The table was very full of empty cocktail glasses and beer bottles.

Gertie knew everyone. Most of the gals were having exotic drinks in a wide variety of glasses including Gertie. She had hers and I held onto a 16-ounce beer mug. We mingled with the others easily. She was quite chatty. Gertie's voice remained high pitched but it was so much smoother.

We found a place to squeeze onto a bench. Gertie sat on my lap. She wiggled back and forth and around. That had sure had me stirring and my interest was increasing.

I had finished my mug of beer and was using the empty mug to gesture with as I was talking to Tom a wounded flight officer about flying maneuvers and tactics.

Gertie said, "I vill fill thesis vup foe vo." Her hand pressed on my groin as she rose up. She cooed in my ear, "Das goo-ten."

On the way back Gertie tripped on a throw rug and fell headlong forward, right arm out, face down on top of that coffee table that was stacked high with empty cocktail glasses. Glass went flying everywhere.

Broken glass cut her from head to mid thigh. Several of us guys jumped to lift her up. She was bleeding from head to toe. Someone brought in some paper towels to cover some of the worst bleeders. Another brought a litter and six of us quickly carried her out a side door to an attached building where there was a receiving room.

Gertie had a cocktail glass base and stem poking out of her lower abdomen's right quadrant. One guy accidently pressed it further in as we were moving her onto an examining table by pressing it with his gut. He had bent over much too hard. It seemed to have been pressed in about another inch. He was stone drunk and was staggering and swaying a lot. He was quickly helped out by few of those who had helped carry her in. They all departed.

Three Korean nurses were on duty. The one in charge, Kyung-Hee, was a Korean anesthesiologist, and spoke English quite well. She sent a Korean nurse's aid for the duty doctor.

"What was she drinking and how much has she had to drink?"

"We had just started. Gertie definitely had one maybe a sip or two of a second Ballet Russe. She is my date for this evening."

"I know you! You do study good with Eva." Kyung-Hee said, "You called yourself 'Dummkopf' I have worked with you and Eva. Please, you help us here, yes!"

"Sure, I remember you. I guess I can do something. I get in the way very well."

There was a duty nurse, Yong-chi, who promptly went into an assist mode. Working together we promptly stopped the large bleeders with hemostats and tied most off. There were many smaller bleeders, which we also clamped. All received gauze and some were taped. We discussed what to do with so many wounds, some being quite deep. I was concerned about scarring. Kyung-Hee agreed. She said, "I can keep her under with a general anesthetic quite some time."

Kyung-Hee put Gertie under as she was moving around and some glass was being ground in deeper on her left side. We cut away her clothing at that time. Such a nice dress, but we needed to work on her skin. I helped nurse Yong-chi debride from top to bottom. I asked, "Is there any Yunnan powder so we could sprinkle some in Gertie's wounds? It would stop the bleeding, prevent bruises, and promote healing."

Yong-chi said, "I know where. I bring more ice, yes?"

"Yes please do and some hand cloths too." She trotted off on her errand.

At that request Kyung-Hee became a little blurry eyed and choked up, as she said, "That is such good medicine! Why don't more of you American Doctors use it?"

"Sorry, but, I am not a Medical Doctor. I'm a medic trainee now temporarily serving with the Aussies. In my short training experience I have been taught about and have seen that Yunnan does a whole lot of good. There were so many wounds here. I think this will be another good place to use it, if you agree."

"Yes, yes! We have some here." As she nodded her assent her eyes swelled with moisture. She turned her head to one side.

Yong-chi quickly returned. We draped the wounds with a towel that had been dipped in a pan of ice water as cool would do a lot to lessen the swelling. The underside of her outstretched right arm did receive much of the glass that would have cut into her neck and face. Ice worked wonders to slow bleeding and preventing bruises by reducing the size of the capillaries and prevent swelling. It also helped lower pain. We used Yunnan and sutured all of Gertie's wounds.

Kyung-Hee removed much of her makeup. I started suturing Gertie's head, face and neck using a fine gut thread. The morgue work of placing and stitching tissue into its exact place sure came in handy here!

An hour or so later our scout for the duty doctor returned. The duty doctor could not be found. She was told that he went into town with many other officers. Kyung-Hee asked, "Please go to town and bring him back! We're suturing many serious wounds and there is a very bad abdominal wound that needs his attention." The scout scurried along on her mission.

I continued to suture wounds. There must have been a hundred of them. We had worked the remainder of the night and did all but the cocktail glass stem. I taped a cooking pot over the protruding cocktail glass stem to prevent it from being bumped or being pressed any further inward. Gertie was covered with bandages and now a blanket finally reached her lower thigh.

It was becoming daylight. Gertie was waking up. I stood up to stretch and walked around a bit.

Kyung-Hee said, "You not a doctor, but you do good work."

"Thank you. This patient has such good skin."

More nurses were arriving. One had a cup of coffee for me. I thanked her and went outside. Clouds were clearing. The duty doctor came in stone drunk and demanded. "Who did this?"

"I did."

On his heels was Dr. Green. He looked a bit tired and ragged, but perfectly capable. I removed the pot, "This cocktail glass is too deep for me to extract. There could be bleeding down there. It needs your attention."

Kyung-Hee gave him Gertie's vital signs, which were stable. Doctor Green ordered the drunken doctor out, scrubbed up, and took over.

A jeep driver from the US Army Transportation Department was looking for me. I was wanted to help locate a plane that went down in one of last night's thunderstorms. *I wonder how they always know where I am?*

Doctor Green quickly inspected Gertie's wounds.

"I used Yunnan and cool cloth on all them, some got ice."

"Okay Zak, I will take it from here. See ya later."

I slept while being driven to the search headquarters tent where I promptly received my search grid assignment and departed with a ten-man search team in five jeeps. Three of the Korean team spoke English. Each team had a walkie-talkie.

Our assigned area was a high valley with some hills to the west. The area was a quarter of a fifteen-minute chart, or an area fifteen miles square. We had to report to the base every hour on a crank for power radio and smaller battery powered ones to communicate within our group. As soon as we got there we fanned out to see if any of the farmers or other locals had seen or heard of an airplane. My driver took me up to the hills where we surveyed a wide grassy area with field glasses.

A small observation plane was seen flying the whole area in our grid earlier. At the end of each hour I called the search team to talk about our findings. No one had any information for us, other than seeing the spotter plane. It was mid morning when we were told that the aircraft had a visual sighting on a grid just east of ours and that a ground team was en route to that location. Our orders were to return to base. Later we learned the sighting was confirmed. The perished and equipment were retrieved. It was a little before noon when I was able to get a ride back to the Aussie base.

There had been another several day delay of our going up to the front line. There was a communication glitch of some kind. I returned to the hospital and continued training.

The following week I was sent to a Korean receiving unit well to the east for a few days.

Chapter Twenty-Five

ORIENTAL WAYS AND MULES

Again traveling was a slow drive with a lot of waiting to go around shell holes and using lower gears to the Korean unit. In the 21st Century we would call it off road driving, but in 1952 this was the main road. This South Korean receiving center was close to the presently marked line on the demilitarized map and somewhat north of a village.

I was to work at their receiving station assisting Doctor Blu. Doctor Blu was a proponent of Oriental and Holistic Medicine. He also used acupuncture and meditation. He said the body would heal its self when put at rest and fed correctly. For example broken bones must be kept from moving in order to heal and so does everything else. He said that tissue quivers when cut. Pain causes it to do that. He used several small pins to keep the tissue quiet. Those made the tissue lie quiet and the pain went away. When tissue could lie quiet it would heal. We use pain pills and shots to do the same thing. He was as adamant about using Yunnan as Jane was. He told me the many things it could do. He knew the US Army Supply section would not pay for my use of Yunnan. A funny thing, they paid for everything he ordered, but then his orders were written in Korean. He was very happy when I told him I knew of it and had used it recently. Later he would introduce me to a black market vendor, Kala Ku. I paid strict attention to his teachings.

Dr. Blu taught that meditation was very useful in quieting the disturbed mind. It was especially useful in treating anxiety. A mind, if watered and quiet will heal. Also he used hypnosis on the female staff, as they got very uptight in the war zone. Meditation focused on breathing and relaxation as its basic technique. He insisted on using the nose. Again it was the calm and quiet that healed. Well, it was not quiet at all here on the line, but we worked at it. Neither he nor I had anything special to offer. We worked together quite well.

Here you could see the power of Yunnan. Some wounds seemed to heal overnight. I tested a few to see if they would pull apart like ours could do. The adhesion was quite good! Many patients were able to return to the line very quickly when Yunnan was used. I was amazed at their fast recovery. Some went back to the outpost on the following day, of course they carried some supplies with them.

Mules were used to pack supplies to the outpost, as this terrain was far too rugged for any kind of machinery. There was low brush and huge rocks lying close together piled every which direction. Most boulders were the size of motorcycles up to bus size. This outpost had well developed deep trenches, which were lined with sand bags and had thick wood siding and wood flooring. This was one place where the line did not move. They said that the enemy was dug in as well. The gooks also used mules to carry supplies in. We had captured some of the Chinese mules. One had a US brand on it. This outpost was too exposed to enemy fire for helicopters. There was little cover or places for helicopters to land and unload supplies safely and we were far away from any air base.

Mules and men were used to provide supplies, as the outpost was several miles up a mountain.

On my second day an Army muleskinner broke his leg and was sent by ambulance to a rear hospital. His assistant was on annual leave. A message was sent for a muleskinner replacement but it would take several days for him to arrive. Very early in the morning word came that the fighting was intense and they were running out of ammunition and more supplies were needed on the line. I was ordered to carry med supplies up to the line with a fresh company of Korean troops. We carried ammunition, food and water on our backs. There was enough moonlight to see the well-trodden trail.

WAR WOUNDS

On our return all the pack train gear and supplies for the troops were set out and the mules were standing by. The packs were stuffed. None of the Koreans seemed to know much about how to put the packsaddles on. I started to show them how it was done. *I guess I had just volunteered to make another trip up to the outpost.* At home I had used a neighbor's mules to work a bean field. There I had learned how to use and command mules. All mules worldwide understood the basic terms and mules responded very well to vocal commands. Gee meant turn right. Haw was said to make a turn left, whoa was stop, ya start, and thank you was cha cha.

Mules are much larger than donkeys and can carry three times as much, which was close to three hundred pounds. The general rule for mules was if you could pick it up that was a load for one side. The trail was steep and I was not going to load all that much on any one animal. The South Korean troops had filled the packs up to the limit. One side would be held up until the other side pack was lifted up and its hitch line placed over the crossed braces of the pack rack. Three mules made the train. I would lead them. No commands were needed. My picking the halter line up did the trick. We were on our way up. In about an hour or so we stopped for a rest. I had not noticed, but the rear mule had stepped back into a bush. When he moved out a limb on that bush hit him in the rear quarters. He broke away and galloped up the hill. I reached to grab his line and was dragged along a little way. I got skinned up a little bit. Considerable gear was tossed out of the packs, which I had to pick up. Here the terrain was steep and clear. A lot of things had rolled down hill. It all had to go back in its correct place. There was a weight and balance issue for each mule.

It was daylight for the return trip. The pack train was empty and the lead mare was nudging me to go faster by lowering her head and nudging my back. This was my second trip up the hill today and it had wiped me out. I just wasn't able to walk any faster.

The lead mare stopped by a large rock and was tossing her head. The others had closed the gap and were almost nose to tail. They too were tossing their heads up and down. I wandered back up to the lead mare slowly coiling the lead line. She stepped closer to a large rock. She looked back. I am getting the idea that if I were to ride this trip would be faster. After all they knew where the barn was and they wanted to get back. The grade was fairly steep and I had never ridden on a pack rack or for that matter on top of a mule. A blanket would have been good. None of those nice to have items were here. *What if I put a loop of this line on both sides of this saw buck saddle? It is well understood that all mules respond well to vocal commands.* I unfastened the lead line, ran that line out two arms lengths. I made a square knot close to the center. Then I took one turn around the sawbuck horns like the horns of a boat's cleat so they could serve as stirrups. I swung aboard from the left side. My feet went in the loops and we were instantly moving. I had not said 'ya' or anything. Did those long legged mules ever want to move! We were moving four times as fast as I was able to walk when I felt fresh and good.

My legs were fairly well bent because the loops were smaller than I thought they would be. In some distance the trail crossed a shale slide area and the trail went across to the left. My mule stopped dead in her tracks, right in the middle of that cut and turned her head right and tossed it up and down. I called out, "Haw Haw! Turn left! Left!" I bellowed, "Haw!" I leaned left and tapped her left flank with my heel. Nothing doing! She totally ignored me.

That mare mule had made the turn and taken the first step. There was no going back. The other mules had turned at the same time and all three were moving down an extremely steep slope in deep loose small particles of shale like material. I slid forward into the cross hitch. My legs shot forward and were well bent. I leaned back and hung onto the saddle fore and aft. I tried to keep my weight in the middle and my body vertical and from jerking around. The mules hunkered down some on their hind legs. Their fore legs were churning the dirt in front creating a huge cloud of dust. They had their head. I had no reins to use. All my commands went unnoticed. They had done this before. I had not!

I would like to say that slide was a mile long and straight down. It was not. It just seemed that way, but we went down a good seventy yards. At the bottom the mules stopped momentarily and turned left. I said, "Haw," then in a lower voice, "Whoa." The mare stayed there almost one full minute. Then she walked a short way, as the incline was rather rocky and steep but on a trail. When the trail flattened out they started to trot. I raised up in my make shift stirrups to lessen the jolting movement of the trot. My legs were not use to this. In a few minutes they were burning with pain. I bellowed, "Whoa," several times to no avail. I pulled on my mare's mane and she slowed to a walk. I said, "Cha cha," reached down and gave her a pat. She paid no attention. My legs did dangle for almost one minute. I was ready to get off and walk slowly, very slowly. If I got off and walked I would never be able to get back up. I was so beat I would not be able to walk back to the med center.

The lead mare went into a canter. I was better able to handle that movement. It was certainly a different gate than I had ever ridden! It seemed like an hour before we entered the barn area in a cloud of dust. The regular muleskinner was in the yard, his leg in a cast and was sitting in a wheel chair with his leg up. He had been watching with binoculars. He was shaking with laughter.

"Took the short cut I see!"

I slid down to the ground as soon as possible, "Not me! They did! I was calling haw and whoa and was totally ignored! Once going down there was no turning back!"

"These mules were captured from the Chinese. They are accustomed to Chinese commands. You were using a foreign language to them! I'm trying to teach them English. You look like hell! I'll see that they get cared for. You go in and take care of yourself."

"Thanks." I went to a tent and bathed in a tub of warm water, then went to bed.

It started to rain steadily the last two days before my departure. Several mudslides had closed the main road to the east and to the west. My relief had arrived by horseback. I had a horse with a saddle and reins. There was a muddy trail that was easy to follow. This was much faster than by jeep.

Chapter Twenty-Six

ENGAGEMENT

When I arrived at our command center a Korean jeep driver was waiting for me. My company had already departed to the line. The driver said, "We must leave now. I catch up, drive very fast!" He also knew a less traveled route further south. The unit was stopping at a command center and we arrived just as they were starting evening chow.

Orders had arrived to stay put. We bivouacked around that center. It seems that our attack notice had not yet passed through the United Nations command. *That seems to be rather odd but that is what we did. The gooks rarely used those channels!*

Master Sergeant Adams introduced me to John a seasoned Aussie Medic from another Australian Company. He gave me a very valuable lesson in crawling, "Kee' yur 'ead d'on." He wanted me several inches lower, not up on my elbows. "Put yur helmet flat on the ground with yur head strapped in it, and never, never rise up! If you need to look up or ahead move yer chin up'n swing yer body around. Keep flat on the ground. Never rise any part up for any reason. Put yer feet out to the side 'n yer heels down 'n toes out. Arms flat on the ground, elbows on the ground, nothing is sticking up. Be as flat as a cat ran over on a highway. That white patch with a red cross is a target. Rub it off as you crawl!" He had me crawling on the ground correctly before we got chow. Often that lesson would be extremely valuable. I am sure it is the main reason I am still alive! "Thanks John!"

WAR WOUNDS

There were thunderstorms in the region all night. Some spots got a lot of water, others nothing. Next morning we loaded into trucks and ground our way along a muddy road. Our truck lagged well behind as the trucks ahead had churned the road we were on into a quagmire.

A farmer saw the gap and was crossing the road up ahead of us. A wheel of his wagon got stuck in a deep rut. He tried to move quickly but the movement forced a wheel to come off. There he was right in the middle of the road. Our truck had to stop. All of us piled out to help. Some of us unhooked his donkey. No matter how much coaxing, pulling, or begging it refused to move. The guys got gruffer and pulled and shoved to no avail. We would let the farmer deal with him. We turned to the stuck wagon and centered our attention on that wheel. Its holding pin had sheered. In a few minutes someone came up with a nail to substitute for the pin. Everyone surrounded the wagon. We picked it up and carried it to the side of the road where the wheel was soon mounted.

The ignored donkey had walked across the road and was standing there waiting looking at us.

The farmer hitched up his donkey and moved onto a side road. We all clambered back into the truck with mud caked on our feet. We waved to the farmer as the truck started slogging along.

Later I was told this story: On this attack our unit was to follow a Scottish Brigade who managed to finagle the lead. They had arrived a bit early and were anxious to charge. A United Nations Commanding Officer was on station on a hillside. He had to sneeze. His hand went promptly up to his nose and he raised his other for balance so he would not spill his coffee, tea or whatever. The watching very anxious Scots saw two hands up as their prearranged signal to charge. Bagpipes had been puffed full and now blew their tune. Drums were booming and the charge was off! The main point is that it was a tad early for the gooks. They were only setting themselves up. Such a pity! The gooks thought the Scotts were demons. They hated the sound of bagpipes. The drums sounded like cannon. They threw their guns down and ran like hell to the north, Scots in hot pursuit!

What I do know for sure is that we were some fifteen minutes late getting around the wagon obstruction. When we finally arrived, an irate officer told us in uncomplimentary terms to clear the west side of that hill and be quick about it. We were to capture all the gooks we could.

Our truck had stopped on the steepest hill we had been on. The first guys just jumped out and ran in the pointed direction. All the others stepped on their mud. I was last off. I slipped and lost my balance. I had a nice slick slide most of the way down. The truck took off! I landed sprawled out down in the mud, some of my gear was strewn out. We carried several days of supplies. I lost several valuable minutes picking it all up then I ran as fast as I could in the pointed direction. They had been doing physical training while I had been training and practicing how to do my med stuff most of the time. The first part was uphill and I had some energy that soon waned. On the flats I was many yards behind and not gaining. I was out of breath, but pushed on. I would get a second wind. I could see the last three guys ahead and ran after them. Up ahead two of our lads were running hard side by side and a third was several yards behind. The first two hit a mine and were blown sky high. Some debris hit a large long limb and it slowly fell setting off more mines. The third lad got hit. The impact spun him around. I was upon him in about a minute. The first two were obviously dead as their middles were blasted wide open and there was a huge amount of blood splattered all around both.

The last guy had his left arm completely severed. It had a clean cut below the biceps. I quickly applied tourniquets to his arm and to his left leg, which had a great gash in his thigh. There were smaller ones below that. I had to catch my breath.

I saw no one. I hollered loudly for help. I listened. There was some sound of shots quite a distance away. No answer.

I went to look at what was left of the other two. There was nothing that I could do as both men had their legs completely blown off, one well above his hips. Both had their trunks split wide open. It was a ghastly sight! I'm sure they died instantly and were drained in seconds. The large amount of blood on the path testified to that. I thought that here they looked worse than they would have in the morgue. On seeing that horrible mess, I stepped a few yards back and saw a dark object. *This is a minefield!* I carefully retraced my steps feeling very anxious. This was next to a marshy area that was swarming with all sorts of bugs.

I returned to the lad I could help. I tied the visible larger vessels off with catgut. I released the tourniquets. That stopped the massive bleeding. I lit a cigarillo and cauterized the smaller ones and then I checked his vital signs. He had a strong but rapid pulse. I put Yunnan on the stump and on the leg cuts. The blood was attracting bugs. I picked up his forearm and propped it against his good leg, then cleaned the lower thigh wound with hydrogen peroxide. I applied more Yunnan and used a cigarillo to cauterize several smaller bleeders and then I closed the leg wounds with tape.

Again I bellowed for help as loud as I could. No answer. There was no sound at all, just silence. My ears were ringing. The sounds of battle were faint. There were only occasional small arms sounds. The bugs were swarming all around.

I needed to get rid of some water. I found some bushes that needed water. My stream washed away soft dirt slowly uncovering another black surface that was becoming visible. Water off. *This is a big minefield! I am very alone!* It was dreadful feeling! The hair rose on my neck. I was sweating profusely. I stepped back and looked hard for freshly disturbed dirt. I saw a few possible places for mines close by. I carefully looked over the ground around and further up the small hill, and then I very carefully retraced my steps. The thought of being blown wide open was horrifying! I shook for a moment. I looked at the ground and then carefully pulled my patient several yards further from that swampy place and more on the level. There was no evidence of the earth being messed with here. I prayed for His help and guidance.

I felt that I should not work on his stump. That was for a doctor. On the other hand, I had assisted and done that several times while training with Eva and I had sawed several bones every day.

I lamented some more about proceeding. There were fewer bugs here. If I left his arm wound open or lightly bandaged surely dirt, flies and bugs would contaminate it. There were a great variety of bugs and

I didn't know what they might carry. He could be worse off if they were carrying something awful.

I hollered again in four directions with cupped hands around my mouth loudly calling for help. There was no answer, no sound - - dead silence.

Again, I got the thought from that Marine Weapons Drill Sergeant, "SEE IT - DO IT!" Also I recalled doctor Green saying, "We should not put our work off." I agonized over what to do.

My suture kit came out and I closed the leg wounds and used double bandages and tape on all his wounds. Using some canteen water I washed off some of the blood that was on his body and clothes trying to leave less to attract bugs.

I thought of carrying him but he was too big for me to carry him all that far. I carefully went down to the broken tree limb and used the teeth on the backside of my knife to cut off the remaining few strands of wood and bark to finish the cut. Then I heaved the branch onto a vehicle track. I let more of my water off and uncovered another black object! I sent thanks up for making me toss the limb out and away and not letting it fall straight down onto that other mine, which would have ripped me up my middle. I stood there shaking from fear for a few moments.

A few minutes later I carried the limb up close to the patient. There I peeled bark strips to be used as ties. Then cut some branches and used some of the broken ones to weave a nest between the forks of the limbs for the patient. I pulled my patient onto the limb, which I would use as a drag to carry him on. I used some bark strips to tie him on. I took a drink of water and left my pack and med kit, as I should soon be coming back for the other two bodies a little later. I picked up the limb butt and put it over my shoulder and started my drag with patient back towards the main road. To be safe I stayed on the tracks made by tanks and trucks. *Okay, it is a longer way but it's a lot safer. No one will find us. I need to get out of here! I have to do this.*

Along the way I trudged over a large flat rock that was angled some down to my right. The branch end slid down off the tank track to the right. A mine exploded. It was startling! It blew straight up and removed many of the trailing small branches. Some small pieces fell on my patient but most fell behind us. The flying trash caused little harm, nothing that required attention. I was shaking hard from fear, enough to go down to my knees where I quivered. While there I gave more thanks to God.

The day was muggy and hot with no wind. Within a short time I stopped and got rid of some runny bowels and would do that again in a few minutes. I had to stop a third time for the same reason. I was sweating profusely. I checked my patient. He was starting to move and wake up. I gave him half a tube of morphine. I waited several minutes for both of us to become calmer.

The soil went from sand to mud and back to mostly loose sand. The branches sunk into the sand creating lots of drag. Pulling was hard. I turned around and pulled backwards to better use my legs and weight.

After what seemed to be hours we made it to the road. There were another three or four more miles of mud to the command post, which had a moderate sized receiving center.

I checked my patient. He was stable. I was getting quite hot and tired. There was no shade. My sweating had slowed. I had slowed my pace down to a steady tug with shorter steps. Pulling was a little easier on a road of packed dirt. There were no mines to worry about. I doggedly drug my patient.

I came to a long upgrade. I stopped to rest at the bottom. I was not sweating. I was hot but not very thirsty any more, but I drank the remainder of his water. I felt light headed. My ears were ringing very loudly. The grade was not all that steep but I had to stop several times on the way up. I started weaving a little. My head started to swirl. I hung onto the tree limb I was dragging and moved along with more determination. I stumbled a few times. Several minutes later I again became light headed and dizzy. I fell down. I felt as if the world was turning upside down. I was not able to stop the turning motion.

A South Korean Army patrol was on a trail some twenty yards to the south. They spotted me as I was staggering. They saw me fall. I had picked up my tree limb and started pulling my patient again. They came over to me as I was struggling to get up and were talking on a walkie-talkie. Everything went dark.

I woke up in a front line tent with a nearly empty bottle of water hanging above me. A very sweet young Korean nurse was standing by my cot.

"My name is Bong Cha, I am your number one nurse. How do they call you?"

"My name is Zak."

She put her hand on my forehead. "Plenty hot now." She removed a light blanket as the day's temperature and humidity was increasing. It was an hour or so before noon. "You pretty bad! You have one more bottle before you get up. You pee in this. I will be back soon." She presented a male 'John,' a container, so I would not have to get up to pee. She quickly departed.

I fell asleep. When I awoke there was a half full bottle of water dripping into me. Bong Cha was now shaking down a mercury thermometer. She held it between her forefinger and the middle finger with thumb between them, and then she raised her arm and then quickly lowered it with a smart wrist snap at the bottom. She did that several times. She looked at me and smiled a lovely smile, reached over and placed it under my tongue. "Hold it there for two minutes." She held up two fingers, and seemed to float out of the tent.

She returned and removed the thermometer and looked at it. "Too high." She held my wrist with her middle finger and the third finger and placed my wrist over my chest to count my respirations, all correct methods. Then she took my blood pressure. "First, you must pee. Have you done pee?"

"No, I just can't pee right now.

She was not pleased, "Not good! You know how important it is to pee." She was holding my shirt. It had been hanging over a metal folding chair at the foot of the bed and she was pointing to the medical symbol, a Rod of Asclepius imprinted on my shirt.

"I am a medical technician working with the Aussies."

"Aha so, then you know how important it is to pee!"

"Sure I do, but I just can't do that now. I need to tell you about two bodies close to where I found my patient. I need to get back there. They need to be removed!"

She firmly said, "You are not going any place! I will tell command about them. First I must speak to doctor about you." She hurried out with the container in hand.

She spoke to the South Korean Army doctor. He wanted to know if I could get up and how well I walked. Her report was not good. An ambulance had delivered the last of their night's wounded and was currently taking patients to a rear hospital. The doctor ordered me onto the ambulance and then he ordered the driver to a hospital.

While waiting to get in I noticed that the ambulance had headlight deflectors to keep the lamps from shining up or sideways and making a good target while directing light onto the road ahead. Six men were stuffed in it. I sat on a three-legged folding stool with a bottle of water hanging from the top of the rear compartment. The ambulance had no side windows but it was cooler than a tent. We jerked, rocked and swayed along.

On arrival at the hospital they evaluated me, I was given a bed and took a shower. The falling water made me pee. I was still light headed, but able to walk and talk.

This has been an event that I would not soon get over. In four or five days I would rejoin my Aussie company.

Chapter Twenty-Seven

◆◆◆

DIFFICULT WOUNDS

My temporary Aussie company had to hike a few miles up to hill something or other. All the hills had numbers and names but they changed numbers and names from time to time, so did it matter to me? It kept the enemy confused and me also. The hike was a regular grind. It was another very hot humid day and our clothes were wet with sweat.

Here I was told to get into a bunker. I was ordered to sit, stay, and come running when called. Well, I sure felt like the company's St. Bernard!

They had us fairly well pinned down. I did the 'fetch' on my belly using the Aussie ground crawl method taught by John last week. I think I went along as fast as when I was up on my elbows.

Both sides were taking shots at every opportunity. Several of our guys were wounded. They probably rose up too high, anxious to take a look and get an accurate shot. We were able to return most of the wounded back to the line as most were hit on their arms or sides with rifle fire.

Artillery was hitting close by, which was a worry. I was told, "Ya never know if you will get hit. Ya'll never hear it coming. It takes some getting used to."

A patient walked into the bunker during a lull. He had a cyst.

"What can you do for me? It's quite a bother."

WAR WOUNDS

He has too much confidence in what I can do. "I will get you cared for by a doctor when we get back to the rear area. That is the proper person, time and place for something like that. I can't get started with something that can be put off. I have to be ready in case an injury comes up." One did just then and he helped move that casualty into the bunker.

This was an emotional breakdown. He was resisting us. My treatment was an aspirin and water. I talked it up as a special remedy just for his particular condition. It is amazing what an aspirin, some water and some small talk did. I paid attention to him as a living individual. The military is very good about keeping a unit and a person as a faceless number.

Daily there were several patients showing a variety of confusing symptoms that I could do nothing about. That caused me inner stress because not all showed the same symptom mix. These were the guys who were disoriented, anxious, nauseated. Often they had balance, speech or visual problems. They were exhausted, lethargic, listless, dizzy and confused. They could have concussions, a stroke, seizure, heat stroke or low blood sugar. *I wish I knew more!* I wrote up what I saw, gave them water and aspirin, then tried to send them to the rear. That was most often disregarded, as there was nothing visual for them to see.

Korea had four varieties of poisonous snakes, two belonging to the viper family. One lad shot a snake that had slithered into his foxhole and was parading around with it. A little later he became a patient. He was out like a light. I was not seeing any wounds or bite holes, but it was pitch dark. I did have a small pencil flashlight. He was dirty and his pulse was rapid and his mouth dry. I wrote 'urgent' in my notes and had him sent to a rear hospital. That was postponed. I was miffed at that.

When we left the area I was sent to a South Korean med unit that was next to us who needed help. I pitched in assisting getting their casualties off a truck and onto gurneys and I assisted their doctors. The Korean unit was rotating back the next day and I was returned to my Aussie unit.

My cyst patient was waiting for my return. He thought I had ditched the unit because of him. "No! I was sent to where work was needed to be done and stepped up and did it."

I picked up a corporal's cloth cap and took him to the hospital and arranged for a doctor to see him. I did not mention that I was a medic.

I was transferred to another company that was going up to the line. The night was dark as the moon was late to rise. Some of the guys told me they looked up and had many differing thoughts. After midnight we packed more ammo up the hill. It was just two thirds of what the Sergeant ordered. On arrival the Sergeant didn't like this place or the skimpy supplies. He pointed out how they could swarm us easily. He ordered more ammo and mortars. We had a massive attack before daylight. The machine gunners fired until their guns were glowing red. I packed tins of ammo up to them. We were swamped by hoards of onrushing gooks, wave after wave. Sergeant called for more ammo and asked for a napalm drop as daylight was approaching.

The Navy soon gave us a favorable reply. AD dive-bombers with rockets and napalm were diving on the gooks. They came in very close to us while they made two passes. They wiped the gooks out completely. We cheered when an ammo dump was hit on that last run by the last plane.

Debris from a ground explosion rose up and hit a Navy AD dive-bomber in its tail section. The pilot bailed out and landed a short mile away. His parachute had opened, but he didn't have much time to maneuver and landed hard on large rocks and burnt brush.

When I had finished taping a bandage on my latest patient I called to the Sergeant, "I think that pilot could be hurt. Do you want me to run over and see?"

"Go!"

I grabbed my kit and a bottle of water and started running downhill, and then up a steep slope to where he had landed.

It was obvious that he had a compound break as his leg was at an odd angle and he had some other cuts from his landing. I tied a tourniquet above the break. Then I applied a bandage to keep more dirt from doing more damage to the open wound and gave him a shot of morphine. I took the time from his watch and put the time and MS on his forehead, using his blood to do that. Then I patched his smaller wounds. I got an Aussie chap to help move him to a flat rock nearby. There I tied off a large bleeder, and then released the tourniquet. I taped both legs together to prevent the parts from rubbing during transportation. One lad had a radio. I asked him to call for an airlift, as I did not have a splint for a compound fracture. He quickly made the call. The pilot had unequal pupils. I suspected a head injury. I think he was stable enough to transport. I thanked the lad for his help and then I wrote up notes on the pilot.

In a while the blades from a helicopter could be heard approaching. It was a dark blue dragonfly. It landed in a flat place just below the crash site. Its nose was pointed right towards us as two of our lads went down to get a basket out of it for the wounded pilot, then we strapped him in and carried him to the chopper.

The Helicopter was from my ship! The pilot was Lt. Gardner. He had a new crewman. He pointed his finger at me in recognition. I pointed right back smiling, and then went to tell Lt. Gardner that the injured pilot was stable and secure. I gave him the medical notes about the patient.

"Hey Doc! We went looking for you and couldn't find you anywhere."

"I faintly heard you and later heard some planes. I swam to shore because the gooks shot up my raft. I was frozen nearly to death so I went inland a bit to warm up. I think I lost my identification in the waves."

"No shit!"

"So, I have to be re-certified. That takes about six weeks or longer. Since I had nothing and the Aussies needed a medic I threw in with them for a time. I was able to pass their warrant specialty tests for medic."

"That is good news! Baker was worried about you. Hell, everyone was including me! I hate it when we can't find our guys!"

I stepped back from the rotors and gave him thumb up. He returned a thumb up. Quickly they were off.

We climbed the hill and ate 'C' rations, then slept some that afternoon. Warfare was conducted mostly at night and on patrols. Both sides did that. Guards were posted. At twilight I made the rounds to give everyone some eye drops. Their eyes became sun burned and that affected their ability to be effective. We depended heavily on each other. The short-billed helmet may look good but provided little protection for the eyes on sunny days. Sunglasses would have been helpful.

Again the night started out quietly and many men were lying looking at the stars, most were probably thinking of home or a gal, no telling. It gets very lonely on the line. It is so much worse when they are alone in a hole. A large shell burst overhead, I'm sure that everyone jerked. It was luminous and had phosphorous which sprayed all over the troops in their foxholes. Explosions take a lot of oxygen out of the air and make breathing difficult. Also they create great drying and often cracking and bleeding of the skin. I treated burns and made the rounds with burn ointment, skin lotion and more eye drops.

The exchange of shells continued for hours. You flinch with every close explosion. They were aimed at us with intent to kill and ours to them had the same message. This was not a game, target practice or a war drill as many back home were thinking, and still do.

In the early morning hours we were attacked by a large patrol of gooks from the side. We sent a lot of lead down the hill. The rest of the night was quiet. I'm sure we killed every one of them, as in the morning I had a lot of bodies to move.

Sometime after daylight two very anxious mates called me to look at another lad who was close to them. They didn't see any injury, he just failed to answer or respond. He seemed to be dead for no apparent reason. I was not able to get a pulse and unable to tell if he was breathing. I had no stethoscope or mirror to use. The pupils of his eyes did not respond to light. The pinch skin test failed to return. That showed dehydration, or did it not? Was he dead? I started a bottle of water in his right arm and fixed the needle in place. The needle puncture went very well into the vein unlike the guys in the morgue and then I taped a wood scrap as a splint on it so his arm would not bend. His body temp was lower than normal but he was not all that cool to the touch. It was a hot humid night. This was a recent causality. He definitely had crapped in his pants. I did not know what to do. I was exasperated, prayed and lamented. It came to me that dehydration could do that. I wrote patient notes of what I saw and the tests, I added 'a possible sleeper.' I told the Sergeant. "I'm stumped! He needs a doctor and a hospital very soon." Sergeant got four mates to carry his litter downhill. He was also stressed.

In the next round of firing one of the guys received a bullet wound in his leg. It was a small caliber and in a fleshy place. There was little bleeding as the hot missile had cauterized the tissues. He had the use of his limbs. I put some salve and a bandage on the wound, gave him two aspirin and sent him back to the line.

Later a lad went berserk and started running towards the enemy. Some company mates tackled him. He put up a bit of a scuffle. They brought him to me. There was less noise in the med bunker and it was a bit cooler. This lad got lots of water and conversation. I continued attending to other patients while talking to him. He said that he was more nervous when it was quiet than when the shells were bursting. We talked about his future, about his hometown, a place in Australia that sounded like west Texas. I told him that. He wanted to know, "Why do Yanks compare so much to Texas?"

"It's a big place and has great variety, so, almost anything fits and most people know where it is. Like everyone knows that Melbourne is down south." I thought he was scared shitless, so, he was probably a bit clogged up. That was the other extreme and was rarely an issue that I saw. There was no tube for an enema. I told him that I would take care of that when we got back to the rest area. I told him, "You may have weird chemicals and such in your waste and they are probably doing a dance all through your body." Water, attention and conversation were a huge help to him. He was still shaky but he got up and returned to his post.

About midday we were relieved and told to return to the rear. We never got the extra water or other supplies that were requested. The few miles back to base seemed to be an eternity. We stopped several times. We were all really dragging.

One lad said, "I'm just out of gas." Translation, gas to humans is water. I was surprised how much water they had carried back and still refused to drink. I begged, "Finish off your canteens now!"

Sergeant gathered us up and we marched as a unit the last bit of a mile. Some of the lads puckered up enough to whistle a popular tune. Our cloth slouch hats were pinned up and the metal helmets hanging on our packs. We brightly marched through the gates. It felt so very good to slide under a shower, drink some cool water and eat all the good hot food we wanted!

In the afternoon the second day an entertainment group was in camp with a variety show. That was a great boost for our morale! Everyone sat on the ground. Our company had a close up view.

The performers used a flat bed truck as their stage. It was parked in front of a Quonset hut off a runway. All events started with a recording of the Star Spangled Banner that was played on a crank up Victrola. Everyone stood up and we all removed our hats and other head wear and then held our right hand over our hearts.

Towards the last few phrases the record hit a crack or something and started repeating several times. No one made a sound. No one moved.

The Victrola was started again after a second winding up. It got hung up at that same spot. No one made a sound. A third time is the charm. Again it was started and again it hit that same crack. No one made a sound.

The Master of Ceremonies started off by singing the remainder and waving his hands for us to join in starting with: "Oh, say does that," We all joined in. "Star Spangled Banner yet wave, o'er the land of the free and the home of the brave!" Everyone seemed to know the words, the French, Turks, English and the Aussies. Quietly, we all sat down.

The show went on with an abundance of enthusiasm and applause. Singers and dancers of the day who were starting up the ladder to stardom entertained us. There were two comedians.

The hypnotist was about in the middle of the show. He told us that he could hypnotize all of us at once. We all gave a 'guffaw' at that! Then he would tell us how good the chow was and how much we liked being here in Korea holding the North Koreans at bay. We gave him a bigger laugh. He held up a family heirloom. He said his grandfather gave it him. It was a golden watch that was engraved on the front and back.

"I want every one of you to keep your eyes on this watch." He started to swing it back and forth saying, "Watch the watch - Watch the watch. - Watch the watch. - Watch the watch."

It was mesmerizing watching the watch swing back and forth on the long golden chain. A sudden gust of wind came from behind him. He strode forward and tripped on a wire holding the microphone in place. The watch slammed onto the truck bed breaking the face and its cover flew off.

He bellowed, "SHIT!"

The Master of Ceremonies called a recess. The show would continue in an hour.

Chapter Twenty-Eight

US MARINE ON A FENCE

I had just sat down to bask in the sun when I was called to the command tent. They had an important job that they wanted done at once. Last night a US Marine was with a scouting patrol when he was cut off, and then captured but he soon got away. He was shot in the back and was killed as he was hurdling a barbed wire fence in no-man's-land in full view of his outpost. The Corpsman who went out to bring him back was killed and they also wanted him to be picked up.

"Lieutenant Cook of the United States Marine Corps wants both bodies returned promptly."

Hello self, I'm from a foreign unit. I could refuse and not lose face, right? Wrong! I had prayed for life and to be of service, better not say no to anything! After all I am here for some reason."

"Sure, I would be delighted to do that." I started to leave without my med bag as I would not need that to retrieve two bodies. *Hello self. That Corpsman and his kit are out of service. Better take mine! Someone gets injured every few minutes.*

I was whisked off in a jeep driven by a Korean driver. We bounced and jolted right up to the outpost. Thunderstorms were rapidly developing clearly showing their magnificence and awesome power.

This hill had an eerie feeling about it. The air had a gun powdery smell to it mixed with a garlic odor, like phosphorus. Lieutenant Cook came up towards the jeep as we were easily heard grinding up this steep hill. He took me right up to the north side of this hill and pointed out the problem. There was a body on a huge moderately sloping rock on the right side of the outpost. Over much further and fairly close to the gooks there was a second body also in plain view. That body was entangled in a barbed wire fence and was very mutilated, a horrifying sight!

"We are very distraught seeing both dead bodies stranded and especially the one they are using as a practice target. Take a look through these glasses."

I took a look using his field glasses. His arms had been shot off, as had a leg.

"I want both of them back!"

I nodded my head, "I can certainly understand that!" We surveyed the area for a few minutes and discussed some details. There were three sections of about twenty yards each. First there was some brush, then a smaller very bare section and over much further the larger area with some fair size rocks around the body and some scattered brush.

"Can you provide some cover?"

"We can!" Cook pointed out two tanks that were just then grinding into position. Behind them a large group of papa-sans had arrived with cases of ammo. I nodded my understanding.

We discussed the most likely route to take advantage of the varied terrain.

"Give me a signal when you are ready to make the dash over the bare section and we will provide enough fire to keep their heads down. We can provide five or six minutes for your cover."

"Jolly good! It shouldn't take me all that long to waltz over there, eh mate?" I gave him a thumb up. "This will be the signal that I am ready to make that final dash!" Not wanting to attract the gooks attention by strutting about I started right then by using the Aussie ground crawl down a path that had some rocks to the north side. I was out of the gooks' sight. At the edge of the large flat rock the path stopped. I had my helmet scraping on the ground. Just as I turned to go out on the large flat sloping rock the outpost hill came alive with rifle fire. What a stupendous amount of fire cover!

I crawled hastily up slope to the first body, their Corpsman, and drug him south to a lower part of this huge rock, out of the gooks view. There was some fine gravel on the top of that huge slab of rock. It worked a little like ball bearings. There I was able to turn his body belly down to go over the edge feet first. I slid over and carefully pulled him down and then around to a flat place behind the huge rock. Marines ceased firing while I was behind the rock. I was quite up tight.

Lightening flashed, thunder crashed and rain came pouring down. I took a few deep breaths and was almost ready. Why wait? Nothing will improve. I gave the Lieutenant a thumb up. The Marines responded with another huge barrage of fire cover. I sprinted across the open section to the body on the wire and landed on my belly. I used wire cutters to remove the shredded remains from the twisted barbed wire and pulled his trunk back and then placed it in a body bag while remaining as low as possible. There were some rocks that provided a little shielding from the gooks. The gooks started firing at me. I heard cannon fire and some explosions on the gook side. Then by keeping very flat I moved left sideways a bit to grab the lower part of an arm. A little up and over to the right was a wrist and hand. I slid up to pick those parts and placed them in the bag. A lower leg had been shot off. It was entangled in barbed wire in a good size shell or bomb hole. I stretched down to get it. It was stuck. I slid down into the depression and put my foot down on the barbed wire so I could tug on the leg. It moved but it was tightly held. I reached down to cut more wire and then put my foot on some wire and tugged some more. The leg came loose all of a sudden. I jerked up and fell backwards and was fully exposed. That was scary! My leg was stuck. I pulled my leg up quickly and got a few good wire gashes on it.

I saw that there were a few more pieces of tissue here and there and wiggled over to them. All went in the bag. His dog tags were near. I put them in my back pocket. For a minute I lay flat and looked for any other parts. There was another body part, a foot in a shoe. I slid through puddles that were dancing with large raindrops, so I could grab it.

It was creepy being out front and so close to the gooks. I was able to faintly see a few of their faces. They were diffused due to the very heavy rain. I think they were whispering to each other as they looked to be talking behind the back of their hands. *Well, okay. Yeah, we do this for our guys. You guys won't.*

All this time the Marines had provided a lot of fire cover. It was so very different being out in front. It sounded like nothing I had never heard before or since.

I crawled through mud and puddles low to the ground for my return trip. Our guys ceased firing only when I was well behind the large rock and out of the gooks line of fire. I continued over to the first body and pulled both bodies well behind that huge rock. I had reached a spot where I could sit up. There I removed the remaining pieces of barbed wire from the mutilated body. That would keep the bag intact. I labeled each with their name and service number from their dog tags, and then I replaced the dog tags around the very mangled neck. *Rats, the ink is smearing in this rain! I will have to do it again later.* Four marines with grim faces came around this huge rock with rifles and litters in hand. I put the bags containing the remains on separate stretchers. They quickly carried the litters up to the top. I started to fix my cuts.

Somebody hollered, "Doc come on up. You are needed up here."

"Okay! In one minute. Let me stop my bleeding." I applied Yunnan to my barbed wire cuts and hurried up to the outpost.

It was only about thirty feet up. I was uptight from being under that much fire! I had a great need to use the latrine so I ran directly over to it. I just made it! Heat, tension and exertion can loosen one up quite quickly.

"Hey look! They have toilet paper!" I used some, and then washed my hands in some mud and rinsed in a puddle, and then wiped them on my behind.

The rain had stopped. I walked over to where the Lieutenant and Sergeant were working on some papers. I gave them my runny notes and asked for more forms "Do you have any wounded that need my attention?"

The Lieutenant answered, "A couple." He paused. "Doc. Can you say a few words over them?" He was pointing to the dead by leaning his head. They had been laid side by side on stretchers on a flat place in a depression between two arms of this mountain. In front of them was a semi circle of rock that was stepped up in several rows, somewhat like an outdoor theater.

"Sure! I'd be honored!" *Holy Cow, what am I getting myself into now?*

In a lowered voice he said, "It's Sunday. Some of the guys usually try to attend a service. It would be best if it were a short service."

"I'm not a preacher, but I have a vague idea." *Now, **this is scary**! Hello self. I'm going to be a representative for **Him**! So, just what are those ideas?*

"Very good. I'll introduce you to the guys. Tell me where are you from? You don't sound like an Australian, more like trying to act like one. Are you possibly a Californian?" He was looking directly in my eyes. *Rats! I've been caught.*

"I am from the Central California Coast." I told him the shortest version. He laid his hand on my back and then called the troops together in the center of the outpost. They crawled out of their foxholes and the sand bagged trench. They all looked very exhausted and drawn. A few stood watch at the rim. He clearly boomed, "Doc will be saying a few words for us after he looks at our wounded. Police the area and yourselves. Our relief will be here soon."

He took me to where his wounded were. There were two wounded men who did need some attention. They were leaking quite a bit of blood. "Hello lads, I'll treat you like Aussie chaps, eh?"

Hello self. You are still faking it!

I used Yunnan and that promptly stopped all the bleeding and then I bandaged them. There were no bottles of water for them and that was needed. I felt so inadequate.

I went promptly up to the rock stage. I had no time to prepare any thoughts. The area was large. *I must project my voice.* I was in a play and they had taught me how to whisper to the back of the theater. *I have to do this! I had promised to do this.* I prayed for guidance and help. *I'm so damn pathetic!*

I heard a bellow that had no rival on this earth, a Marine Sergeant calling his troops together. They gathered in the bowl. *I would have rather been standing in front of their pointed guns!*

I took a place on an elevated rock and took my helmet off as the Sergeant introduced me, "Doc is a Navy Corpsman off an aircraft carrier. He is now serving with the Australian Army as a medical technician; Doc!"

He stepped off the rock. I put my helmet at my feet. They all took their helmets off and remained standing and silent. The relief column was moving up. They were along the ridge up to my right several yards or so. They also stopped and removed their helmets.

"Thank you Sergeant. - I am truly sorry for your losses. I am not a preacher, nor do I have a bible to read from. We all know that these men could be any of us on any day, at any time. I wonder if they had a chance to speak to their maker? Not likely. We can do that for them now.

"Repeat after me, if you will." I spoke clearly and slowly, "Lord, please provide these fallen men a chance to ask for your forgiveness through us now. You want us to ask. May I ask for that at this time? If we don't ask, we cannot receive."

"Services of all kinds ask for a sacrifice of some sort. Our custom is to give money. Not today! I ask that you do something different. Take your canteen out and remove its cap." I pulled mine out of its holder and removed the cap. I held it up and out and turned a little to better address the relief column. "Take a swig and swallow." - I took a swig. - "That is the bread. Take one more swig and swallow." I took another swig and they did too. "That is the wine. Since we have no bread or wine this is the best we can do. Forgiveness is the best we can ask. You now have God's most important gift inside you, water. Without water there is no life. We cherish life. May His will be done. Amen."

Without a sound the troops picked up the litters and moved quietly down a trail to the right. I waited for the last man before I moved to join the departure. It started to rain again.

We went to a reserve camp where I filled out forms and I was returned to my Australian unit later that day.

Chapter Twenty-Nine

———◆———

MINE FIELDS

Captain Bass asked, "Zak, would you like to do something a bit different and take a walkabout with another Australian company a little north of the demarcation line? This area has been rather inactive for a while so there may be mine fields and such to chart. Would you like to stroll along and perhaps take a few photos? It would be bit of a change for you." *How did he find out about that? I haven't mentioned my interest in photography to anyone around here.*

"Right, that's something I haven't done for quite a while." I took along a second pack of cigarillos to cauterize with and a few extra bags of Yunnan, just in case. I've had several exposures to the results of mine fields.

When I arrived at the command tent, Sergeant Alan Plumber, a huge man with a bushy mustache, was memorizing details of a topographical map of where we were to go. There were ten of us. Our briefing included some information from laborers who worked on that hill. That digging project had created a lot of employment for the locals and they pointed out an abandoned farmhouse on the chart that was fairly close to the place of interest. We were to find out as much as we could about those minefields and caves.

There were two other photographers. One lad was an expert on infrared film and its use. He gave us a good briefing on the Kodak film, the difference in light settings and red filters. It was an interesting film because it would clearly distinguish between foliage and camouflage.

They wanted us to shoot the same subject, each one standing quite some distance apart. We were trucked off for a few miles. We started our hike alongside a stream. It was an easy walk on a trodden path along the stream, which we followed for quite some distance north. Here on this trail our walking created quite a bit of dust. In a while someone saw a rock marker up hill. That was how the gooks marked their minefields. Plumber told us to step exactly where another had put their foot down, as this area was 'hot.' Two lads had mine detectors. They carefully surveyed the area we would walk on. We took photos of those markers and all around from the cleared areas. It took hours to go the next few miles. The late afternoon sun was hot. We came to a stop. I was glad to sit on a rock and take a swig of water. I sat there just looking around and spotted a wire and pointed it out. One of the three mine specialists found that wire was attached to a mine, and then others were located off towards the stream. The lads disabled all that were found. Sergeant and another mate marked the place on our map by taking compass bearings on landmarks. He also had a sextant. Each mine find raised a huge level of personal concern. It was a slow process to discover, make notes and clear the mines during the day and much longer at night.

This would be a good time to mention the mine process. I think they were planted every day, found, removed or exploded, and crews cleared and repaired those holes with dirt. Both sides used patrols to plant mines.

When the path was passable along we went. The mine monitor led with his detector on. It had taken all night but we had made it to the north face and took photos of it then and again at daybreak.

The mountain stood out quite well. It was probably three miles east to west, maybe one or so north to south, and about six to eight hundred feet high. One lad said it reminded him of Ayers Rock in central Australia.

Nah, first it's not red, but it does stick right up. He is homesick.

We found the abandoned farmhouse and a village about a mile to the north of it. We took photos of those and the hill from a high rock outcropping. We discovered more mine markers, so we had to clear those.

Sergeant Plumber wanted to get closer and get better shots of the north side. He selected the farmhouse as daylight cover as we would not likely get back to base without being discovered and possibly wiped out. There was a stream nearby and there were lots of mosquitoes and gnats here. We took turns watching and sleeping. A few of us climbed up on the roof and could see over a rise. The house had a vent near the peak. A few of us went up and removed two louvers to make a slot window. One of the photographers, Pat, came up and we looked to see what we could see. Others took turns from that place too. On our second watch we were looking and Pat saw what looked like some bent over grass. There it was every so often, some bent grass. The light was now reflecting off the bent over part. Plumber came up to see. He sent us out to take a closer look. Sure enough we found footsteps where someone had walked up the hill.

"Should we follow those tracks?"

"Good on ya lads. Off ya go! Keep your ead don."

With cameras in hand Pat and I started out hunched over and on our hands and knees as we neared the ridge where the grass was shorter. That is where the walker had turned to go east. We continued to follow his footprints. From another rise we saw a small path down below. There was a very narrow gauge track running along the bottom of that canyon. It looked smaller than what I had seen in a museum mine exhibition. These were not shiny recently used rails as they were wood and had been painted flat black. We crawled beside the tracks and got up much closer, separated and took several shots. On the way back we were better aware of the places where the ground had sharp rocks. We stopped before we got to the ridge top and looked back. Good thing we did! Up a canyon a short way there was a gook standing at an entrance looking around. He would have seen us if we had continued moving along. We hadn't noticed that small shelf before. There were quite a few good size bushes in front of it. Pat wanted to take a shot of it right then. I convinced him that a little later would be better. The surrounding grass was six or eight inches above our backs. We inched closer toward the grass on the mountainside. We were well within his shooting range. The sun was getting lower and was casting longer shadows now. He was looking straight at us. He just stood there. He lit a cigarette and slowly smoked it. He was pacing back and forth in a small area. He looked all around and looked right at us again, and then he looked away. *If we can see him he can see us.* That was not a comforting thought. After what seemed to be a very long time he squashed his cigarette and went out of sight.

We crawled up closer to the hole, and then spread out some distance and both took some photos. *That was very likely the place we are looking for!*

We crawled back slowly over the hillcrest. Then we rose up higher and hunched over in a very quick walk back to the farmhouse. It felt good to stand up straight again.

We told Sergeant Plumber and our mates what we saw and photographed.

"Good on you lads! We will know more when the film is developed and reviewed."

I took two aspirin and a few long swigs of water and tried to get Pat to do the same. He refused the aspirin, but took one little sip from his canteen. "Pat, I want to go down to the stream to soak my knees in some cool water. They hurt. Want to come along?"

"No I'm fine."

I found a pool that had a limb sticking out over the water. I was able to lay over it on my belly and hang over the limb with my knees off the bottom. There was sand to dig my toes into. The water was cool and felt good. Cool water would reduce some knee swelling.

When I returned I stretched out on the cool dirt floor of the farmhouse to take a nap. We would be going back in an hour or so. The trip back would likely take several hours. Our pace would be steady and quiet. Walking quietly takes more strength then a normal walk.

It was dusk when Sergeant tapped on my boot to wake me up. We ate the K rations we packed. Again I encouraged the guys to drink water. A few took some small sips. *I don't get it. They carry their water all over creation and never take a drink.*

We started back when it was dark. We all had a pencil flashlight with a sleeve. There was quite a bit of ambient light from the stars with only an occasional cloud. The start was a rather normal walk but it didn't take long before we got the hold up sign.

We moved up the hill as most of the minefields were on the side towards the stream. The warning was none too soon as a patrol of what looked like Korean troops came by. We couldn't tell if they were North or South. We held our breath as they quietly moved past. By holding our breath we could not smell if they had garlic breath. If we tried to speak to them we would have had a huge language issue. Their reputation was to shoot first and ask questions later. We let them pass and move along a considerable distance before we moved out.

Again we were on a steady quiet walk back down the trail. After an hour or so we were on a straight stretch where we got another hold up signal. We froze in our tracks as another group was heard. We got a signal to move for cover this time down towards the stream as we had found and mapped scattered mines on the high side all along this section. The other group moved to the higher ground. One of their guys was unlucky and hit a mine. He loudly uttered a few words that indicated he was an American and had suffered an injury.

Sergeant Mac Pearson stood up and called out a password, paused and asked, "Do you mates need a medic?"

The reply was, "Got cha Aussie! Yeah, 'n a hell of a hurry. E' got his ass blown all to hell!"

We tried to keep quiet and still hustle down the path. It seemed to be a considerable distance before we came to them. They were US Marines who were sent out to look for us when we didn't come back on time.

The guy had been hit up his backside. His buddies said he dislodged a rock and it rolled down on the mine. It blew straight up. Shrapnel hit him. He had two fairly deep wounds on his backside and a smaller one on his hamstring. I pulled metal and rock out of both wounds and used Yunnan on all his wounds and then taped gauze tightly over them. His hamstring was not working well. I ran tape over the knee to make that stiffer, and then taped a green stick on top to keep it from moving too much.

WAR WOUNDS

All the guys would take turns helping the wounded man back. We were back at base in two or three hours. We took the wounded Marine straight to the Med Center.

Chow was over several hours ago, but the cooks tossed sliced Spam and grated potatoes on the griddle. Now aren't these guys great?

Chapter Thirty

---◆---

THE MAIN LINE

*I*t is quite nice to be needed and appreciated. The next day I was sent to help the British and I was told to take extra bug ointment and A & D ointment for burns, and not any Yunnan as they may object to its use. After all it is the enemy's product. No worries, I can apply pressure dressings. What the British meds did on their routine was to give most patients morphine and a cup of tea. *I wondered how that would play out in an early surgery as the morphine could interfere with anesthesia and the tea could come up?*

This place was well to the west in the lower flat land. It was very hot and humid. There were insects by the mega ton. Insects seemed to suck our blood like there was no tomorrow for them. You couldn't open your mouth to take a deeper breath without inhaling a nasty bug. I taped some gauze over my mouth and nose and made a little mud to smear on it to soften its white glare. Bug ointment was liberally applied to all exposed areas and everyone took it with out stretched hands.

All summer our shirts were wet with sweat. There was a huge dehydration issue for everyone. I was unable to convince anyone that they sweat a ton of water every day. So, in 1952 what was understood about dehydration or the value of water? Not much! They seemed to think drinking water was a sissy thing. Most would say, "It would just make me pee more."

On many outposts we were often close enough to see the gooks, hear some of their chatter and also smell their cooking. They stunk.

Both sides took shots of opportunity all day every day. There was never a safe moment. A few of our guys removed their helmets during the day. *Yeah, they get heavy.* My collar size would expand two inches this summer. Several had their brains blown out because of that or got a bad chest wound. That devastated everyone. *There is another lifetime scar for every one of us.*

There was constant fire from cannon from both sides. We admit to firing an average of a thousand rounds a day and they more than doubled that our way. That heavy stuff caused shock waves and an unimaginable amount of noise. The ground seemed to shake incessantly. Every shell rattled everyone everywhere to their inner core and being. It caused emotional tension and deep physical and psychological issues to otherwise normal men. Someone said it bent our brains. If you were close, your body would jerk from the shells' explosion and impact. What debris went up came back down flying in every which direction. It really hurt when it hit. Artillery was firing so often some rounds collided midair and that hot debris rained down on us. That caused burning wounds of various sizes. I used A&D ointment on those.

Most heart rates were very high. I think they averaged close to 130 heart beats a minute as a 'normal' while on the line under this kind of fire. Everyone had a very high level of tension.

Constantly we had wave after wave of gooks attacking. Our machine guns were red hot almost all the time. We must have shot five hundred rounds a minute. We fired right back when they shot at us. It seemed to be at a little longer distance here than at some other outposts, but they were not real long shots either. I could not see the whites of their eyes. Some of the guys carried the more seriously wounded back to a med center. Here from far off I heard helicopters coming and going during the day.

Some of the shells contained phosphorous and in many places the terrain was covered with a powdery white from it. It was stirred up from new explosions that picked up dust causing our mouth and eyes to get dry and the skin to crack. I applied lots of ointment. Also it got into their eyes making them red and itchy. I used lots of eye drops. Do you think now they would stop for a drink? Perish the thought! They turned away, took aim and pulled the trigger.

Living in the unnatural confines of a foxhole under the constant fear from bombardment and being blasted was extremely fearful and raked our innards. I'm sure that the top brass sitting comfortably in Japan had no idea of what we were actually going through in Korea. They were WWII hero's who had been on the move and making the news and progress. Not us! We were stuck in a stinking hole! Where is the news story here? The report writing of field officers was quite sterile. They were mainly interested in units, time, movements and numbers. The top brass only wanted a short version and that is what the press got also. It was the same thing, just another day.

Never would they write a word about feelings of being stuck in a hole and in one place on a constant basis. There was little news of interest for the folks back home about our patrols or in holding a line. The news reporters and Americans comfortable at home became calloused to the numbers. Every month we averaged nine hundred dead and over three thousand wounded, greater numbers than most of the other wars. At home they were most interested in the snappy new cars, music and dances. They certainly were not interested in what we were doing in Korea, and still are not.

Heavy shelling was tough and I was fairly safe in a bunker much of the time. Sure, I crawled out to the guy that just got hit. That's my job. Also I made foxhole calls where I was very often hit hard and bruised by flying rocks, dirt and other stuff.

Sure our bodies took a beating. Sometimes it was rather hard to walk! *We walked like very old men*. It was much harder on those who were confined to their holes dug into the dirt and continuously shaking in fear and alone with no way to escape. Fear and loneliness was a huge negative factor that would smolder in our guts forever.

Are these guys getting concussions from the shelling? I notice some are correcting their walk often. That may mean a balance problem. Some seem to be dizzy and others have their speech slurred. Some others are confused. Many are wiping their eyes often trying to see. Many are complaining of headaches and aspirin did little for that. All those are symptoms of concussions. That bothered me a whole lot. Do you think for one moment that any of that would ever get into a report or make news back home? Would it get in a letter going home? Perish the thought. Just now well over sixty years later we are recognizing concussions, sometimes. Rarely was, or is there positive or constructive action for those injuries.

I was called to a patient who had a small chest hole. As I got to him he was calling, "Mamma, Mamma." Another guy was screaming medic! The first guy waved me over to the other screaming guy. He had a small leg wound which I patched up quickly. I went back to the first guy. He was dead. I rolled him over and saw a huge gaping wound on his backside. Large vessels had been torn to smithereens. He had drained quite quickly. I felt extremely bad for not trying to do something for him and going over to the screamer. I didn't give morphine to that second guy although he had begged for it. Two APC's is what he got, aspirin, phenacetin with caffeine. That mix will relieve more pain than aspirin alone. He rewarded me with some crude and cutting personal comments.

That evening the weather had turned rainy and blustery. Everyone bailed water out of their foxholes. The mud felt very heavy, tar like. I was crawling, but it felt like I was swimming through mud to get to the wounded.

Before we left that hill we pitched in and picked up around the area and all casualties were taken back. It was well into the afternoon before we were relieved. We slogged back in mud, wet and shivering from cold and exhaustion. So, this is what it would be like on many summer trips we made to the front line. *Thank God it is not snow!* We longed for some decent food, quiet and a shower. Now we had mud clinging to our clothing. We didn't have enough energy to flip it off or to avoid stepping in the many mud puddles. *Thank God for good boots!* My ears were still ringing very loudly from all the shelling. *Why are my ears doing this? I can't hear a thing! Is it something the body is doing to shield me from all the noise? Thank God I'm walking and can hear!*

By the time we reached the main road the rain had stopped. I looked west and saw a huge wall of very dark clouds. The clearing would not last long.

Ahead a few yards on a cross road there were several high ranking staff officers who came up to the front to look things over, but from a very safe place several miles from the nearest outpost. They had arrived in a new Sikorsky helicopter that was much larger than I had seen before. Its pilot was perched up high. That looked quite different, but it had a lot more room under and behind the pilot.

The officers were posing for photos. When we halted, most of us just dropped to the ground and sat there. Some of the troops had enough energy and gumption to get in the photos. Some of the nice clean and tidy officers objected to our guys being unshaven, having dirty faces and clothes. Our guys just glommed onto them and grinned for the photographer. His four by five camera's flash went off. He encouraged more of us to get in the photo. A few more of our lads joined the group. The photographer pulled the film out and put another holder in and was stepping back without looking. He was concentrating on getting the framing just right. One more step. He was unaware but he was very close to that helicopter's rear rotor and no one noticed or called out.

The chopper had started up. The wind had increased and changed direction. It now carried the chopper's sound away. The pilot moved its rear rotor a bit on a normal control test. Its small aft rotor reacted to the pilot's testing movement properly by waggling a little. It made contact with the photographer's head. Part of his skull wound up being severed and tossed onto the chest of one of the officers. That officer gasped, his eyes bulged, and he had what looked like a heart attack. He was holding the skull piece against his chest. Many others surrounded him. I jumped up and ran over to him and took the skull piece, almost hand size that he was still holding in his hands and quickly took it over to the photographer.

Two Brits helped me get the photographer into the helicopter in the far seat. He had blood squirting from his wound in regular impulses. I slapped a large gauze pad on the wound and pressed on it. From my med bag I grabbed several hemostats and clamped some arteries off.

The pilot was angry that I invaded his plane, "What in hell are you doing?"

"I'm trying to stop his bleeding! We need a complete hospital! Hell! This guy needs a brain surgeon right now!"

Others were helping the officer in the door seat and strapped him in it. The helicopter sat there turning up. Again I shouted to the crewman, "We need a Brain Surgeon NOW!"

"Roger, Doc." He started talking to someone on the radio. In what seemed like a long time my two patients and I were taken off to some place. I had used all my clamps on his major arteries. I applied pressure to a few compresses on the profusely bleeding head wound. I picked out some catgut from my kit and started tying off the larger clamped bleeders. I used those clamps on smaller arteries. That slowed the flow. There was lots of blood on the chopper's deck. I was so afraid of this guy bleeding to death while I'm trying to stop the bleeding. It was welling up like an artesian spring. I was afraid to use Yunnan because I had not been told that the brain was a proper place for its use. *I shall do no harm!*

Then I turned my full attention to the Army Officer with a chest full of decorations. He looked and sounded familiar. He was grimacing with pain. His chest was heaving, his breath was short and he was holding his left shoulder. He bent over and puked right in the middle of the chopper's deck. *He could have turned his head and have it go overboard. He could be having a heart or stress attack.* I dug into the med kit and removed a metal tin, which now had three regular aspirin in it. I squeezed the backside to open the tin and shook one pill out. I offered it to the now profusely cursing officer. He knocked it out of my hand. I picked another pill out of my tin and presented it. He took a swipe at my hand. This time I was able to move under and away from his swing.

He ranted, "I want a fucking doctor not a God damned mother fucking nincompoop! I don't need some God damned fucking pill!"

I have seen this guy before. His voice is familiar. - Yeah, now I remember him. He is the most cursing officer within the gout group.

"Didn't I treat you several weeks ago for gout? Then you thought I was a fucking genius. Am I correct?"

"You were with the fucking Dutch?"

"Nah, I was sent there by the Turks to replace the Dutch doctor who you ordered out. Now, I am qualified as a Medical Specialist and a Warrant Officer with the Australian Army."

"Take this!" I presented a second pill a second time. I looked him straight in his eye and firmly said, "Swallow this fucking pill now or I will put you on report for disobeying a certified United Nations medical representative offering what appears to be needed medical assistance! Maybe I can get you a court martial or perhaps you would rather just die. Don't do that because I would have to write up your fucking report!" He swallowed the pill and continued his cursing rant of me, the situation and of everyone and the world in general.

A few minutes later the crewman stuck his head in the cabin from the cockpit. He had to shout over the engine and blade noise saying, "We are heading for a hospital ship off the west coast in the Yellow Sea maybe thirty miles away from where we are. It will take maybe ten or twelve minutes. We have a good tail wind. There are other hospitals closer but they don't have any brain surgeons. Does that matter?"

"Hell yes it does! This guy has brain matter in his severed cap! This is not a simple head cut injury. He needs proper immediate attention!" Hospital Ships have brain surgeons aboard and fully equipped operating rooms with very well trained staff.

The officer continued his pointless ranting. *Perhaps this is a stress attack, which I had read about. I suppose the skull hit could set off something like this. It was rather sudden and shocking.*

I returned my attention to the head injury. It seemed that more bleeders had popped up. There must be thousands of arteries in the brain. The whole area was flooded with blood. I sponged and tied them off. *Ee gads! I'm out of gauze!*

It seemed like an hour but I finally got the bleeders tied and the skull piece replaced. I needed gauze. I cut my patient's sleeve off to cover a now single dressing in place and his web belt to hold it on strapping it from under his chin up over the wound. The officer was cursing me for not paying attention to him and his extremely serious condition.

"If you calm down the pill will work."

WAR WOUNDS

Downwash of the choppers blades did little to rid the puke stink. It seemed to just move it around and around. This flight was getting very bumpy. My head wound patient complained of being nauseated. With my scissors I cut the officer's pant leg from bottom up to his knee, and ripped it into four squares.

The officer glowered intensely and loudly regurgitated tons of verbal filth. Now, his cursing rant was directed at my actions for cutting his pants.

"It's for your puke. You could have turned your head." I tossed one piece over the closest part of his puke and swiped it out of the door. I did the same to the other splatters. The rancid smell was much less after a few moments. It was still a bother so I dribbled the last of my canteen water on the deck and gave it a final wipe. In a few moments the compartment smelled better. I wiped my hands on my butt. *This trip seems to be taking hours.* In a moment the crewman poked his head back into the cabin and said, "Doc, we will make it in a few minutes."

My reply was, "Good on you mate!"

We exchanged a thumb up. I looked at my head patient.

"Will my vision be damaged?"

"I don't know enough to say. This is in the vision section and this looks like the outer part. You will be talking to a brain surgeon soon, ask him. Okay?"

"Okay."

The Hospital Ship was now in sight. It was over 500 feet long. She was all white gleaming against the now gray and angry tossing ocean. It had three very large red crosses on its sides, with a narrow green stripe painted between the red crosses. It boasted of a newly installed helicopter flight deck. The ship was rolling and heaving in the now heavy sea. The sun was quite low.

Our chopper had to fly in a large crab angle due to high winds. It made my view of the ship much better. It was extremely bumpy. I was hanging tightly to my patient's chair. Waves had breaking rolling white caps. As we approached the landing deck a strong gust of wind caught us and shoved the chopper sideways. The pilot continued his approach straight into the sun. There was no one on deck to signal the deck's angle and ship's movement or provide any help for our landing approach. Our pilot was flying directly into the ship's stern and he had a flat white wall in front of him. Another gust suddenly hit us. The landing was very hard. One rotor blade struck the tail boom ahead of its rotor. Another blade hit the landing deck on the port downwind side and sent parts aft and over the side. The third blade hit the deck to starboard and forward. Many pieces hit the metal structure making loud sounds. The craft shuddered to a stop with a jerk creating a sideways motion. That forced the photographer and me out the open door. He landed on top of me on the ship's landing deck. The cursing officer was still strapped to his seat face down and was again clutching his chest.

Attendants cut the still cursing officer out of his seat. They had litters and were quick to lift both patients and carry them off. I promptly told a nurse what their problems were and what I did. She scurried off after the litters. The head wound was rushed into an operating room where brain surgeons would treat him. Heart specialists examined the officer. His cursing of everybody continued through that process. They found no evidence of a heart attack. They said it was a stress attack probably from the skull catch he made.

The crew was very happy to see that we were all right. *That only meant we were alive.* Many helped the pilot and crewman push the helicopter off to one side. The chopper's crewman secured the chopper to the in-deck fasteners. The ship's crew picked up pieces and put them in the copter.

About a dozen nurses were doing exercises to music being played on a wind up Victrola. They along with the ship's crew had quickly taken cover as we wallowed in the air trying to get square to the ship before landing. Now they surrounded us. They bet that we could not keep up with them. Several dangled their room keys tempting us as a reward if we could keep up with them.

The pilot said he had to call Headquarters about the accident and he hastily departed to do that. The crewman had mechanical problems to call about. He departed to do that. I was left alone in the midst of a bunch of scantly clad nurses. *Such a pity!*

I was quite willing to accept the nurses' challenge! I sat down to take my boots off. I asked, "Exercise on this deck in all this wind and spray?"

I got an enthusiastic reply. I saw one had started to wind up the Victrola again. As soon as I sat on the deck to take my boots off I fell asleep. I was a very dirty mess having been on the line for a few days and with all the mud, blood from the head wound and a touch of puke. I had been up all night and had walked back in the rain and mud. Nurses are very practical. "He's filthy!"

I was wakened, drug off, pushed into a shower, and all my clothes were sent to the laundry. I was then stuffed into a rack and told to go to sleep. I would be up and dressed in time for chow and given scrubs to wear. *Rats! I had flunked their challenge.*

At dinner I was placed in the middle of a long table full of nurses. Most were from European countries and they were full of questions. How was it that I an American was serving in the Australian Army?

"I'm an exchange."

They promised another chance to prove my worth at an exercise-to-music shortly. *It was so nice to be given a second chance! I had gone from Hell to Heaven in short order.*

The leader of the evening exercise group was from Ireland. She was petite with fiery red hair and limpid green eyes, in a word, dazzling! They started by stretching for a few minutes. Then the pace picked up with rotating and standard calisthenics. The fast part was an Irish Jig. It went along for several turns, and then the record hit a crack in the player. It repeated many times. Many of the gals quit after the second or third repeat. I had a bet to win and continued the jig until she stopped the music.

I got a shave and a haircut before my departure and signed a chit for my Aussie account to be charged for my keep while aboard. It was with reluctance that I left this ship.

I was returned by a series of Korean drivers. They did not know where to take me as the Australian Headquarters had been moved again.

Chapter Thirty-One

OCCUPIED FOXHOLE

On arrival at our headquarters I had a message from Captain Bass so I promptly went to see him. He was behind his desk. "I see you're back from the Brits in one piece?"

"Aye, I am."

"I heard about your delay. Is there any chance might you be willing to provide some assistance to the Scots? They are being served by a receiving station manned by a splendid Medical Unit from India."

"Why yes I would!"

Straight off I was on my way. The Scots did not wait for me as they had departed early, wouldn't you know. I was given a ride in a jeep driven by an experienced Korean driver. He dropped me off just below the Scottish company who was fighting their way up to the top of this hill that they were presently attacking.

A gook machine gun had pinned the Scots to the ground. It was making sweeps over the heads of the advancing Scots. It started again. I hit the deck. Their firing was only inches above the gulley area we were in. I hailed the Sergeant, "I finally got here."

He shouted, "Good to see ya Doc!" Then he pointed to a foxhole and commanded, "Get in that hole over there, NOW!"

While the bullets raked the other side of this gulley I took a few quick crouched over steps and dove for a larger than usual foxhole. Several rotting gook corpses occupied it. My hand was slowly oozing through the soft rotting flesh of several bodies. My face was nose to nose from a rotting gook's face. Its teeth were protruding. There were things crawling all around in his mouth. An eye was dangling out of its socket. Part of the flesh I had just jammed through emitted a stinky smelly dark rotting fluid oozing from the decaying flesh. The stench was horrendous! In one involuntary process I puked and instantly emptied all orifices. My hand was pushed through a second body. In an instant I somehow rose up and flung myself out of that horrific hole! I rolled over face down on the ground. Just then the machine gun made another raking, this time much closer. I laid still for an instant. I was glad that I had been taught the Australian ground crawl. I was flat as possible and I moved back down hill dragging my arms and hands wiping off the stinky flesh that had maggots moving everywhere in it. I shivered from the stench, sight and fright of that moment. I puked again.

The Scots tossed a few grenades at the machine gun nest. Their explosions created several more. A cheer rose up. I think they hit some ammunition.

All was suddenly quiet for the moment. A sharp command came from just behind me.

"Doc! Stay right where you are. I'm right behind ya." It was the Sergeant. "Sorry about all that. I didn't know it was occupied. You are one bloody mess! Go back down this hill and get cleaned up! Yer much too dirty to do your work don't you know!"

"Aye."

"I will give them a shout and tell them yer coming. I say, keep yer ead down now, n' stay on the ground. Tis right down along that path there." He pointed out the path and direction.

"Aye." I used the Australian land crawl staying very close to the ground. That way I could move and wipe slime off at the same time. There was a depression just ahead and the gooks' firing was well above me. The Scots were shooting back in reply. The weapons on each side made different sounds.

I continued wiping decayed flesh off my arms and body as I crawled down the trail. In a minute I got to a lower elevation and was able to stand and removed all my clothing. I found some loose clean dirt and rubbed it over all of my body. The stink was horrendous, worse than anything you can imagine! I was in my skivvies that were also dirty. I wiped them in the loose dirt and then continued carefully down the hill. In my dirty skivvies I shuffled into the Indian Med Receiving Center dragging my clothes behind by a clean pant leg end.

A young lad with a white cap politely spoke to me in English. "We know about your day, follow me." I was taken to an outside shower. He then took my boots and clothes saying, "I will clean these for you." He set up a folding screen. I did a thorough wash job. I was almost in a panic to get that rotten stuff off. When finished I was probably was the cleanest I had been since the formaldehyde spill. A folding chair appeared with towels and a scrub suit. Included were a pair of sandals and a robe made of khaki toweling which I put on over the scrubs. Then I started towards the receiving tent where I came in. The same young man trotted up, "Please follow me sir."

I was shown to a tent that was behind the receiving station. In it a beautiful young woman with long dark hair in brightly colored flowing robes was strumming a stringed instrument and humming. Something like incense was in the air. There were several large brightly colored pillows with some very fancy designs. The lad poured a brandy and water in a monster brandy glass. He handed it to me and pointed out a very large pillow. "Enjoy. I will come for you in an hour and take you to dinner." I thanked him. I remember taking a sip of the brandy, and then fell asleep. He woke me as promised. The woman had departed. He had my clean clothes neatly folded and my boots were cleansed.

"Thank you so very much!"

We arrived as soon as the chow hall opened. I picked some chicken curry over rice, a few other items and some tea. Indian food was very nice. It had spices but they were not nearly as strong as the Korean spices.

I departed back up that same hill in a jeep that had some supplies in a trailer. The Scots had moved up to the top of that hill. It had a bunker and several deep trenches, which they now controlled. There was a commanding view to the north. The firing was sporadic.

The Sergeant was quick to greet me, "There are a few lads who need your attention."

WAR WOUNDS

Three men were in the med bunker. They all had been bandaged. One had a leg that was bleeding with a tourniquet. He was the worst. I felt his leg. He had a broken lower leg bone that was protruding some, the fibula. He was withering in pain. There was blood dribbling out the bottom of his bandage. His lower leg was greatly enlarged. He was calling for "Mamma." I quickly checked the other patients. They had quite bloody bandages that were dripping and needed attention but seemed to be fairly stable. I went back to the first and gave him a shot of morphine. I thought the great swelling on the backside of his leg was rather odd looking. His abdomen was extended and taut. I didn't like that one bit, but I turned to the leg bleeders, tied them off, applied one packet of Yunnan, started a bottle of water, and bandaged him back up.

I found the Sergeant, "One lad is in very bad shape. We need to evacuate him as soon as possible. Can we call a chopper while there is still light? I'm not seeing any stretchers."

"It was used to take a man down a little while ago, and no we don't have another."

"Can we get this guy an air lift? I know he has a broken leg but there is something else that I can't put my finger on and I sure don't like it! He made the call and was told to stand by.

I returned to the patients and reviewed the serious guy for additional wounds and what I may have overlooked. He was repeatedly calling "Mama." That bothered me a whole lot. I was not seeing something. I was exasperated. I retied the tourniquet. I didn't like that either. I lit a cigarillo to cauterization the main bleeders. I felt so bad that my gut was hurting. *What was I overlooking! What?* I felt his abdomen again it was quite taut. *Aha ha! Internal bleeding!* I rushed out to the Sergeant and asked about the evacuation. "I was told that a broken leg is not an evacuation emergency and that I had made a frivolous call."

"Please call again! He has internal bleeding, which I overlooked and that is what was bothering me! At first I focused on stopping his bleeding and the obvious broken leg. I cannot do a thing about the internal bleeding. He needs an operating room and a surgeon. We could lose him!"

Sergeant shook his head and sadly said, "No."

I was exasperated, "Tell them it is internal bleeding which I can not stop!"

He called again and was told to stand by. I returned to the bunker. That patient was still repeatedly murmuring 'Mama.' I spoke to him in a projected whispered; "I think I have done everything I can for you. You may not make it. I called for an air lift."

He murmured, "Mama" again. I felt so helpless. I whispered but with projection, "Ask Jesus for forgiveness of your sins."

He weakly nodded his understanding.

I pulled him up onto my lap, and bent over and put my arms around him. I felt a flow of enlightenment and understanding as I finally realized what they meant when they were murmuring "Mama." They were dying.

I sat back, looked up, and asked, "Jesus, We need your help here, Your forgiveness of his sins and me for my incompetence."

He made no further sounds. I felt his carotid artery and got no pulse. I checked his breathing. There was nothing. I was totally numb.

"Doc. - He just checked out. - You did your best. You are not Jesus Christ!" That was from one of the other patients. I nodded my understanding as I lay this patient horizontal and then sadly I covered him up. I resolved that I would check every belly and would tell every patient calling for "Mama" that they should ask for forgiveness if I even slightly felt they might not make it. There would be many more in the near future.

I went out and told Sergeant, "We no longer need an emergency evacuation. We do need a stretcher." He looked at my face and nodded his understanding. The radio responded. It was the Seventh Air force in charge of evacuations. He turned to speak to them. I returned to the other patients. The first two in the bunker had bandages that were sopping with blood. They got Yunnan and fresh gauze and were wrapped up properly. I thought they had lost too much blood to continue on the line. I wanted those two to go down to the receiving station.

The Sergeant said, "You seem to be quite quick to send lads down the hill."

WAR WOUNDS

"These guys have lost a whole lot of blood." I showed him their very bloody dressings. "They will be too slow for this kind of action and in my humble opinion being slow means to be dead very soon." They stayed in the bunker until a few other lads were able to help them down the hill after the firing had paused.

Later in the day I wrapped the dead man in a blanket, secured him with his belt and then lifted the head end to pull him down to the receiving station. On the way back I carried more med supplies up the hill on a stretcher that I drug along.

The gooks fired the first shot about an hour after dark. The exchange had started again. Their troops started to invade our hill. We fought back with machine and rifle fire.

The Scots had a bagpiper, who blew up his bag and started playing a variety of songs, which some of the troops sang the lyrics to. He used their stately march back and forth along the line right behind all the firing in a small depression. Bagpipes have a rather high pitch and also make a lower sound. The gooks hated the combination of that sound. I think their singing might be added to that mix. It seemed to take quite a bit away from the gooks' drive to fight. The piper did not get hit. However, one of his pipes did get a nick.

The Scots suffered some wounds but none were serious enough to leave the line. They stayed in position while they got patched up. I saved a ton of bleeding by using a lot of Yunnan. I made several rounds to administer eye drops and again tried to encourage them to drink water. They were much more receptive to my requests than any group had been before.

We were there two days. We ate K and C rations. I retained control of my bowels. Cannon fire continued all throughout the day, lots of it was very close. We all slept in very short nod-off naps interrupted by startling wake ups often caused by being hit by flying debris.

At the receiving stations I had developed a routine of sorts and had a dependable supply line of black market Yunnan. That was an out of pocket expense for me, as the supply center only honored requests written in Korean. The Aussies went for what would work and I had proven Yunnan's worth to Dr. Green. Still he thought I was half a bubble off center.

Chapter Thirty-Two

———◈———

"MAMA"

Next I was again with a British unit at a western location with lower hills and flatter lands. Here there was hard dirt and solid rock that was close to a foot below the surface. I saw some tank tracks that hardly made an impression where they went over foxholes. Tanks and artillery were hard at work.

Many chest wounds had large exit holes. It was very hard to get the bleeding to stop as bright red frothy blood flowed out in large amounts. They needed blood and water that was at MASH units. A man with that type of a wound would have to live to get to one.

There was a higher willingness to promptly move the seriously wounded off the field. On some chest wounds we used cauterization. Do you think I would just watch the blood spurt? I kept a lit cigarillo hanging from the side of my mouth much of the time because they were firmer and smaller than a cigarette with a hotter tip. They could go deeper into a wound than cigarettes. They worked well by puffing and blowing on them. I didn't care for their taste and the smoke was obnoxious. However, they were easy to get, smaller and more portable than clamps.

Some seriously wounded were calling "Mama" just like what I had heard a few days ago. All too often there was little I could do to stop the bleeding. For me it was hard to cope with. I felt like I was failing.

I finally took some positive action for those guys who could be dead in a minute. I told them, "I may not be able to save you. I will try!

Ask God to forgive you of your sins while I try." I got frequent nods of understanding. A few waved me along to others who I might be able to save. I felt very guilty doing that. I was turning my back on them. It was very exasperating and emotionally draining. That would stick with me.

A second medic, Walter, arrived with a reinforcing unit. He was also a Warrant Officer and a very pleasant chap to be around and to work with. He had a great attitude. You can't beat that.

I was out on a foxhole call to attend a severely hurt chap. There was a lot of hot lead flying in the air right then and the ground behind him was higher and getting pelted with it. We had to stay where we were for a while and my patient had lost quite a bit of blood. I had a bottle of water on my belt that I wanted to start. His rifle had its bayonet fixed so I worked it securely into the ground and placed the gun butt broadside to the gooks to protect this bottle of water. Still the shaking ground caused the bottle to slide to one side and was shattered by flying lead. Walter was close by and he had a bottle of water, which he offered. I removed the rifle off the bayonet then taped that bottle around the rifle's butt quite tightly. Then I replaced it on the bayonet. That worked better, but water was pouring out too fast. That was not good. I wanted to slow the water's flow. By habit and training I reached up near the neck of that bottle to make the adjustment. A shell landed close. I slowed a piece of something flying by with my left arm just below my bicep. That got my attention! I winced with the pain. It was a shallow wound, but it stung like a thousand wasps all biting at the same place at the same time! I put Yunnan on my wound and that added to the sting. It took quite some effort to keep my mouth shut.

This time I reached down low behind the bayonet and turned the patient's water flow down with my right. That too could have waited. In several minutes there was a lull in the firing. We were still not willing to rise up very high. Walter was fairly close to me. He was finishing patching a wound up. He took one look at my screwed up face and asked, "What happened to ya mate? Yer making quite an ugly face and tis a wee bit damp."

"I slowed a bit of something passing by on the fly. It took a bit of a bite out of my arm."

"Give me a look at it. - Right mate! Ya, got yerself a nice bite all right. I see ya put that gook stuff on it. That does it up quite right! All ya need now is a wrap on it. Does it hurt at all?"

"Aye a tad. Me nerves are working quite well thank you."

"Let me give you a bit of this stuff." He gave me a half shot of morphine. He had a tube of bright red lipstick. He put MS on my forehead, and then playfully took a swipe at my face. I woke up to what was coming and was able to dodge the last part of the swipe but still he got one side of my mouth and chin and a little up the other side. It made a red smile. "Aha, mate! I got yer kisser with it." He wrapped my arm.

I laid back, took a few breaths and got myself back in order in a few minutes. There were no new patients waiting our attention. They were fairly well cared for on the field. We were able to get the men we were attending back to the bunker and write up our notes.

After that they were carried down the hill to our med center. The South Korean civilian volunteers seemed to be quite close to us a lot of the time and they knew where to go. They trotted with the wounded. They did that with great concern. I thought it was the best ride for the patients. For the many small units and urgent patients, using the locals was far faster than calling for a chopper. I give all those local volunteers great credit and a hearty, **"Very Well done."**

When reinforcements came I was returned. Sometimes I got to clean up, eat and have a night's sleep before they sent me out to another receiving station. Hey, I'm a spare tire that was often needed.

Next time it was to the Aussies. For me it was a different world. There they wanted me to use what worked. I was able to put Yunnan into every wound and water bottles were quickly hooked up to patients if we had them. Here I was able to keep most of them alive at least for as long as I had them.

My Yunnan vendor seemed to know where I was and when my supplies were low. I'm fairly sure that the South Korean nurses passed the word along. When I was with them I just signed a chit for Yunnan and water and continued to work on patients. A nurse usually wrote up the patient reports and I signed them.

Why not choppers? First there were not enough choppers to cover the whole line and they were new toys. Then they had to find us, as we were not on their frequent go to list. There were no firm addresses or coordinates to punch into some modern device and fly to. The pilots had a chart that was usually on their knee. They had to find the spot and flew with one eye and the other eye and a finger on that chart. Oh, don't forget the number and name changes of our hills and other places. I'm sure that didn't help them much. It was not easy and each step did take some time. It was not like calling a taxi at home. I think that the choppers served the MASH and Med units for the most part. Both were new and few in number. Both were proving their worth in Korea and had their problems convincing the decision makers. I did not hear any at night so I don't think they flew at night.

Imagine being a patient on one. You are strapped to a litter, tied down to a shaking machine outside in the breeze, alone and cold too. Maybe you are covered. "How do you feel?" Is that a little like being in a coffin? That sure needed improvement! It would take another decade to develop something that could carry a few patients and a working medic inside.

Chapter Thirty-Three

DOCTOR WALKS

One hour after my return to our base camp Captain Bass asked for me again. "You impressed Dr. Blu and he has requested your service. Are you willing to serve with the South Korean forces?"

"Yes, of course!" Straight off I was sent to a small Korean med center much further east. It took a day to get there. Sure there were delays and detours because local crews were fixing up one of the North's favorite targets, the roads.

For the first few hours I assisted an American doctor and a Korean nurse while they finished up the night's causalities. It was nothing all that unusual and we had finished our patients well before lunch was served. The doctor picked up a rag and wiped his hands, turned and departed. As he did I think he said, "You're it! I'm out of here. I can't stand this carnage and not having a damn thing to work with!" Neither the nurse nor I clearly heard what he said. He was talking as he was walking away from us. My ears had been ringing loudly. We had no idea where he went or for how long he was going to be away. He got in our Jeep and drove away. We thought he might just be off to get lunch, but we never saw him again. Since the departing doctor took the jeep we were left afoot.

Later I sent a messenger to ask when the doctor was returning. The Korean Command Center's reply was that they didn't know where he was and that they could not send a replacement because there were none. "You are to do everything you possibly can for the injured." I

276

sent the messenger back with a large order of Yunnan and water. He was very happy to do that.

Korean food was very highly spiced. On that first evening I got a glob of whatever it was in my soup. It was not fully dissolved. It was horrid! It made me gag. I had to hustle outside to barf it up. From that day on that particular spice and smell would be extremely offensive.

Cannon were firing at dusk with great intensity from both sides and litters with wounded patients started to come in, most with shrapnel wounds. We stood there and treated everyone who appeared as well as we could. First, I poured Yunnan on their open wounds to stop the bleeding. At the same time the nurse started a bottle of water. Next we would clean and repair the wounds, and then sprinkled it with more Yunnan. All the Korean nurses liked me to do that. I closed the wound most often with tape and sutured the larger wounds.

This tent had a folding screen with a canvas and blankets over it set at an angle in front of the entry. That kept our lantern light from shining out and allowed litters to be brought in and out with ease. I didn't have to hold a pencil flashlight in my mouth all the time to see what I was doing. When questions arose we had to go to another unit and use their radio because they didn't have a doctor either. Our unit was thought to be too small for a radio, which was another scarce item at small med units. Yeah, that's another problem created by the political financial cutback that cost us a lot of time, effort, and lives. I can't treat patients if I have to walk two miles to ask a question. We wrote notes about any questions and had the patient carried to a hospital. That usually took five or six people and an hour or two one-way. We did that any number of times everyday. *Thank God for the local volunteers!*

We were almost out of Yunnan and were very low on intravenous water. The vendor Dr. Blu had referred me to appeared at our station. I could buy all the water and Yunnan I could use. My wallet quickly came out. After that he made arrangements where I would sign a chit and it would go thorough the accounting process.

I was working outside as much as possible where the light and air was better. I didn't know about it, but we were being observed and filmed. The filming continued while patients were brought in and we were working. I became aware of the filming by seeing a flash of light from a lens. I went over to them and invited them to get close up shots of what we were doing. Up close they would have a better truer story. They took several dramatic shots of the Yunnan stopping scalp bleeding on contact. Now that was clearly demonstrated and was on film.

A few days later after the sun was well up a patient was carried in from far away. His carriers were quite tired. My nurse said, "They say they have been trotting quite a distance." His bandage was leaking badly and he had lost a lot of blood. I tied off the bleeders and used Yunnan on his wounds and sutured them. He was yawning a lot. His vital signs were low. He was clearly in shock. He had clammy skin, which was turning bluish, and he had sullen eyes. His breath was shallow and rapid.

My nurse said, "I know this person very well. He is smart, cheerful and a hard worker! I am afraid we are losing him. He needs blood."

I think my nurse is correct! I wanted a doctor's opinion, a green light to go ahead. I was sure that this was definitely beyond my authority to just do it. There was a bicycle at this unit. I hopped on it and raced to the closest receiving station, about two miles away. There was a medic working in it also. He said, "Oh! Just do it."

I was doubtful. His opinion would have the same weight as mine. The next unit was another few miles down the road and had a doctor. I gave him the symptoms.

The doctor said, "Why in hell are you racing all over God's Green Earth asking a simple question? Go back, roll up your sleeve or someone with type O and do it, if he is still alive when you get there. Time is important!'

It was a fast ride back. I hailed the medic next to us and hollered to him as I sped by him. "I got the doctor's okay!"

"I told you so!"

When I arrived at our station I told the nurse, "I got an okay to do it. How is he?"

"Worse! He is barely hanging on."

"I am a type O." Promptly she snipped line from a used water bottle to use as a direct blood transfer line with two needles. After my blood had reached the other needle the nurse inserted the other needle into his water line. It took perhaps fifteen minutes before he showed any signs of improvement. The first thing I noticed was that his yawning had stopped. His pulse was improving, as was his breathing. I didn't know which was first. I stayed there another few minutes.

Several new patients were carried to us, so I quit the transfer, took a few gulps of water, and then patched up the new patients. All of them were sent to the hospital by an ambulance, which had just brought us more patients. That was the start of many more days to follow.

When we were scheduled to be relieved only the nurses came. There was no doctor. The senior nurse said, "You are to continue at this post. There are no replacements and our command is very happy with what you are doing."

I would sleep when there were lulls in the fighting. The Korean nurses took notes of what was done to the patients. They signed most of them. They also started writing in Korean and signing orders for Yunnan and water. I was using a lot of both. Surely I was not making enough to ever pay for all that I was using. Every few days I was able to ride that bicycle or walk to another outpost a few miles east and get an American meal.

The units at this med center would be changed at least five or six times. I lost track of that too, but it was always a Korean unit that did not have decent meals, in my opinion, or any doctors. I was not talking much either and noticed a fading energy level.

The belly wounds that came in were sent directly to a hospital. Without exception the intestines had many injuries that needed time and expert attention. I may have done many in the morgue but I did not have the time or stuff to do that here. I felt guilty about doing that. I had a lot of serious bleeding to stop and that was the highest priority. Shells burst and stuff constantly flies all around far and wide. You didn't have to be doing anything to get wounded. This is a war.

There was a village a little ways from our station. The North had pounded it with artillery causing great devastation to the place and the people. I treated their injuries. I noticed that they were quite undernourished; actually starving and so were some of the troops.

The villagers were not in on the supply distribution. My black market supplier agreed to bring rice and K rations for them. I asked in return that I get a daily bowl of rice that was just rice with no spices added into it at all. That was agreeable. I signed that chit and paid for it. I had a chilling thought. *Can I afford all this?*

Hey self, you prayed to serve and where can you spend any money here? You can't even buy a beer here.

That solved part of that problem. It would take me quite a while to realize that perhaps no one had filled out a requisition form for that village. I asked for one and it took almost week for the form to arrive. That really was the help they needed but broke our agreement of no spices in my rice, but that is the way I like it.

It is a hot humid summer with daily temperatures of one hundred degrees or more and the night not much cooler. Spices oozed out of everyone's sweat. I found the body odor a little offensive, but I mentally put all that stuff to one side and did my work, which took up all of every night and most of every day. We were working twenty hour days or more. They brought me wrapped food that I could eat and put in my mouth as I worked. When I sat down I went to sleep. They tapped my foot when patients were brought in. I was getting a tad groggy and a wee bit slower. I was so very afraid I would do something wrong. I concentrated hard on patients and did my level best for them. I was still not able to shake the feeling that I was inadequate. I tried hard not to do any harm.

Late one hot and muggy afternoon a Korean doctor and four nurses relieved me. They had a message for me to go to the Australian headquarters.

"Doctor Green wants to talk to you." *There must be a big problem, as I have not been called in before.* I was mentally preparing for trouble of some kind, mulling over what it could be. *Perhaps I had a reversal of a transfusion. Maybe I had over stepped my bounds.*

I climbed in the jeep they came in and was driven to our command post. It took the better part of two days with lots of detours. As usual it was because the roadway was in ruins. That concern didn't last long as I fell asleep at every stop and that was often.

When I arrived, Dr. Green was all smiles and said, "Well lad, it looks like you have lost a few pounds."

"I'm not all that fond of the Korean food."

"Neither am I. There are two reasons we called you in. We have a few papers for you to sign. The US Army could not process your request and sent it to Washington DC and back through the Navy who now want comment from us about your service and such."

"I will have to practice writing. I have done very little of that lately."

"It's too late to do that this evening as the staff has left. We can do all that tomorrow. The second reason concerns your performance."

My God now what? Don't they always save the worst for last?

"You are turning out rather well. I particularly like your use of Yunnan. That film up close was quite good at showing how fast you are stopping the bleeding. You are attending to your casualties decently. I'm giving you a promotion to First Warrant Officer."

"Thank you sir! Really, it is the liberal use of Yunnan and water. I have had some excellent Korean nurses. A few have been able to speak and write in English. They wrote up most of the patient notes. Also the local volunteers have been especially helpful. They trot with patients. That was a huge help. There have been some close calls. I guess it was several weeks ago, maybe longer by now that I had to ride the local bicycle a few miles to ask a question."

"You don't say? You didn't have a radio or a Jeep?"

"No sir, we had neither."

"What was the problem?"

"The assigned doctor walked off and took the jeep. Then a few days later I didn't know if I should give a patient blood or not."

"Tell me now, where would you get blood? Only the Army's Mobile Surgical Hospitals have that. No ice or refrigeration don't you know?"

"Out of my arm."

"I see. What type are you?"

"Type O"

"That would work." Doctor Green nodded his understanding.

"Was I authorized to do that?"

Then he looked at me as if he was surprised. He wanted to know the patient's condition and the circumstances. Then he said, "Now you have the rank to make more command decisions. Trust your judgment, as you seem to be on the right track. When in doubt do ask questions. I have them. Oh, by the way, we are taking care of those chits you are signing. Say, may I ask why did you buy all that rice and such?"

"A village is starving and so was I. We made an agreement that I get a bowl of rice a day without any spices and they get the rest of a five-pound bag. Eventually, I thought of the word requisition and then asked for a form that I filled out for them. They got a whole lot more than I offered and that broke our agreement."

I was able to shave, shower, and eat a few good meals before I was sent back to do the same thing and again at another Korean outpost further to the west. This time I had a hand held radio if I needed help or had questions, and a jeep. So, now every few days I was able to drive the jeep several miles to an American unit for a mid day meal. Most of the time it was to an Army unit. The cooks were mostly African-Americans. They treated me so very well.

"Hey man, let me fix ya something. Why don't ya come in more often?"

"They keep me busy day and night."

"Ah the women I'll bet."

"Aye, they keep waking me up, but only to treat a patient or two or more. It has had nothing to do with them personally. Anyway, I am too tired and stressed to be of service to them."

When I was late the cooks always went out of their way to fix something up for me. I was so impressed with them! They do good work!

Gasoline for the jeep was scarce. I ran out of gas several times. It would take days for them to refuel it. This assignment would last for quite some time. I had lost track of time again. We had little relief, not much rest, and very little water. That simply meant I didn't bathe, shave or wash my teeth. I was stinky, so what. So was everyone else. Also we didn't bathe every day in the 1950's. The nurses thought I looked better with a beard. They said, "You look distinguished."

WAR WOUNDS

I'm sure I spent most of my paycheck on Yunnan and bottles of water. I was able to get 'K' rations and I gave them to my patients, many of whom were greatly under nourished. I did a few more blood transfers. I must have been fairly popular. Everyday the wounded, including villagers, came in. I had a steady flow all night long and until late afternoon. I was just working injuries as fast as I could. I did no medical problems. They all went to a hospital further behind the lines.

During this time I learned that the North Koreans often just walked away from their wounded. Some of them made it to our receiving stations and were treated like anyone else. I could not tell the difference. I was told that most of those patients joined the South and fought the North. *Hey, I had prayed to be of service, so no squawks.*

I also learned that tens of thousands of South Koreans were starving. The US had given a Korean general several million to feed them. He didn't. He kept the money. The US Army went to the rescue by taking food in on rail cars, cooking and serving it to them. **Good show!**

Chapter Thirty-Four

---◆---

RETURN TO SHIP

When I was relieved from the Korean med station there were orders to go to the Aussie command base that was far to the west and south some. When I arrived Captain Bass told me, "You must pick up your recertification papers at a base where you filed them. You will be in a new Ford four-door sedan with four others. Dr. Green is assigned to a med station not far from this Command Post. Two others will be going to a spot about half way along the road and one in the party is going to your destination much further along."

"That sounds great. I will have someone to talk to."

A new olive green Ford four-door sedan that had a large white star painted on its side arrived with three people. Since they arrived in time for lunch, I was invited to have lunch with them. This party had Dr. Green and the new people were a US Navy Lieutenant Commander, Dr. Grey who was doing med duty before reporting to sea duty along with two women. An Army nurse, Lieutenant Hazel Hollister who only said, "Hello." Then there was tall thin, chatty and proper speaking British Army Nurse, Lieutenant Maxine Dover.

While serving with the Koreans I didn't have a whole lot to say. I just did my work. Now that I'm back with an English-speaking unit I found that I was having some difficulty speaking. I was not able to get words out. My lips were not working very well. The usual getting acquainted questions were going around the table. I was stumbling with the words a bit. I had some problem asking for the pepper. It came out as, "Paf fa feffer." After serving at the Med Center, Dr. Gray was reporting to my ship as the Chief Medical Officer. I mentioned that was my ship too, that came out, "ma sif foo." He said that the ship was going to Hong Kong for a public relations trip next month. He thought we might miss the trip because they so often hold medics over.

Maxine was quick to pick up on my bit of fumbling, as she was a speech therapist. Instantly I became her patient. Dr. Green and I sandwiched Maxine between us in the back seat. I really liked the smell of Maxine's breath. It was her toothpaste and she wore a light perfume. With a full belly and having been up all night I was asleep in short order. Dr. Green got out at a South Korean receiving center in about an hour. Dr. Gray drove the remainder of the trip to his and Hazel's new duty station. Maxine and I would drive another fifty or sixty miles. Our road would be the roughest and slowest part of the trip. It had been raining harder in the east.

We took turns driving. I liked the new Ford. It had a gearshift on the wheel post and it still smelled new. It had a hard time on these rutty and muddy roads and became high centered. A tractor had to tow us back to where we were able to get a jeep. After that delay the remainder of the trip in a jeep took several days.

Maxine took the opportunity to constantly drill me. She had me doing A's and O's to get my lips to work. She had me practicing lines like, "Rubber baby buggy bumpers" and the phrase, "The sun shines on shop signs." By the time we arrived at our base my mouth muscles were sore.

Maxine and I stopped at the Red Cross office so I could sign my papers. A witness was needed. Maxine volunteered to sign as a witness. Also, she arranged for my overnight stay on base as I had my Australian identification. We had a few drinks before dinner to loosen up my facial muscles. Wouldn't you know she wanted to talk more? I was forced to talk well into the night. I was able to put the drinks on my former tab I had set up during my last visit to this base. We got along quite well.

It was late August, or was it September now, the rainiest season in Korea and it was raining hard much of the time. There were mudslides nearby which closed the road. It took two days before the road was open.

My tour with the Aussies was completed and I started processing out. I asked about the recent bills incurred those past few days. The mustering out officer said he would attend to those while I was in a rest center for a few days. They didn't want me to be returned too terribly beat up.

On mustering out of the Australian unit both Dr. Green and Captain Bass thanked me for my service. It was nice to hear that I had a good survival record and had made a decent impression. I was invited to stay on and I could return any time I wanted to. That also was very nice to hear.

In a few days I was flown to Japan and took the fast train to the base. I arrived on the day my ship departed for Hong Kong.

I continued with the med study that I had missed. I finished all the exams that had been taken by the others. I passed all sections except pharmacology.

I had lost over twenty pounds and was very much out of shape. I wasn't able to charge up more than a few deck levels before I was winded. I started a stiff workout program of stretches, rope climbing, weight lifting, and jogging around the flight deck when it was clear. I ate, worked out and slept a lot on the few days of the ship's passage to Hong Kong.

When we anchored in the Hong Kong harbor there were small boats all around us. Many had divers who would dive for coins we tossed in the water. That was soon stopped because the water was so polluted the divers could become ill. We were prohibited from swimming.

We were told not to go to Kowloon, just across the bay from Hong Kong, as it was off-limits for some reason. They said, but I don't remember. I went ashore in Hong Kong with several shipmates and took a ride on a trolley. We rode from one end of the city to the other, and then toured the Tiger Balm Gardens that had lots of interesting displays. My impression was they were of Chinese dreams and nightmares in a local setting. The group broke up when some of us were being enticed away by some very beautiful girls.

John, a religious zealot, provided us with one of his many lectures concerning the seven sins and our inclinations. His finger was wagging directly at guilty me much of the time. I was communicating nonverbally with my two girls.

The following day four of us wanted to go up to the city's highest restaurant. A taxi ride up to it would cost as much as a very fancy meal. We had all afternoon and decided to hike up. That was a regular grind for me.

The restaurant overlooked the whole city and was above the smog and haze with a marvelous view. We could see the airport on a spit out in the bay. Its main runway had approach and departures over water. All the planes we could see had four huge engines. They were DC 6's and Connie's.

We arrived just as the owner was opening the door. He said, "You are first US Navy patrons to ever climb hill. I make you drink."

"I'll have a Navy Grog." We wandered around the balcony and took photos. Shortly we were given the best view window in the house. We thoroughly enjoyed the lush setting. The table had white lace tablecloth and sterling silverware. We were way over our heads in class. I gave the guys instruction in the use of the several spoons, forks and knives. Mum was a cook for several wealthy families so I had learned all that at an early age.

I ordered a house specialty that the waiter highly recommended. The other guys ordered other specialties. It was a bit pricey, but wasn't this a celebration? Hey, we walked all the way up here! A separate waiter served each of us. They just wanted to be doing something, as it was early. They were so happy that we chose to walk all the way up. Several photos were taken of us with the waiters.

My waiter cracked the eggshell for me, and then he carved off the top of the shell from my order while he made several remarks on how great it was. Gooey stinky stuff started oozing out of that cracked shell. The specialty was inside. Surprise! It was an embryo chick! Two guys barfed. I got a tad nauseated myself. Mainly, it was the surprise and stink of those guys barfing right on the table. No manners! I don't remember what they ordered but I know each of us had something different. Our orders were well beyond our ability to consume. We promptly paid for our uneaten meal, gave them a good tip and all staggered down the hill. The two guys who barfed returned to ship.

A fellow shipmate I had come aboard with, and I found a men's only type of a place. The Chinese girls there were very dressed up and looked quite nice. Most had Mandarin collars and button down blouses. *They would be fun to unbutton.* We watched a stage show. I think it was the Chinese version of a strip tease. The gals had long thin colorful flags they waved and rolled. We enjoyed the show along with something we knew was good to eat and to drink. No more house specialties.

Next day after I was sober, which was a bit late, I found another rum house with street and water views. A good number of my shipmates were also in there. I ordered another Navy Grog. It was so nice to watch the gals walk up and down the steep hills! They had very well developed derrieres and legs. Good gawking! By this time I was nearly out of money.

Before I finished my first drink a truck came through town with loud speakers ordering all military personnel to return to ship or base immediately. Liberty was canceled. Shore Patrolmen herded us back to the ship like we were wayward sheep. There had been an incident of some kind. Many rumors were flying.

Our ship departed Hong Kong that night for the Philippine Islands where we provided carrier landings for several squadrons serving on the islands. We did not go ashore.

When we were cruising in the Philippine Sea area I was assigned to lifeboat duty as its medic. While in that area our ship held several drills including man overboard. On our return to our base in Japan we were told that there was a gonorrhea epidemic. All hands were ordered not to patronize the bars or women ashore. If we got that disease we would get a court martial.

Dr. Gray called me into his shipboard office. There was a Personnel Officer there also. I was given a choice of what I wanted to do. I had invitations to serve with the Aussies who offered me an increase in pay if I were to return, or our Marines who were short several medics. I could fill in until reserves arrived. I thought I should help our Marines. *I had rested up this past week, but I was not in good physical condition yet.*

As the yeoman reached over to give Dr. Gray a form to sign a page slipped off the lap of the yeoman. I reached down to pick it up to hand it to him. I got a glance of it and I saw that it had Anderson and I listed as choices to send over. I felt honored, as there were many to select from.

The personnel guy had a piece of information for both of us. Bulletproof vests were to be worn by all personnel on or near a combat line. No exceptions! That was protective but they would be a hot item to wear on a summer day. I'm sure I would find out very soon!

Dr. Gray and I were off ship within the hour. I was clad in my field uniform and I carried my gray Navy helmet with its white patches and red crosses and a med kit. Our ship's helicopter took us to a receiving center well inland.

The receiving center had patients lined up because they were so short of help. I spent the reminder of the day and night assisting Dr. Gray. He gave me a bench to work from as so many injured were coming in. He didn't want the wounded to wait any longer than necessary. He had heard about my work with the Aussies from Dr. Green. He was there for any questions or issues I might have. That didn't take long. I got an abdominal injury with a piece of metal that could be close to arteries and the spine. I did not want to move anything. I called Dr. Gray over.

"I don't like this! We need more light and equipment including blood on standby for this guy."

He looked the patient over and immediately sent this patient to the rear. We had many wounded and that was where my attention was directed. A few patients later I got Dr. Gray's consent to use Yunnan on it.

"Dr. Green said, "The South Koreans were impressed with what you did. They wanted results and I do too. What did you do?"

"I used Yunnan and water."

"What's Yunnan?"

"It's a Chinese product that stops bleeding on contact so I was able to close very fast. Also it promotes healing by normalizing the tissue.

In that process it lessens scar tissue. From my view it is the right stuff. We use pressure, which collapses the blood vessels, but does it promote healing? I don't think so but it heals eventually."

"From what I hear I think that stuff merits a look. Where do you get it?"

"I buy it on the black market from the papa sans who take it off the Chinese dead."

"With whose money?"

"Mine."

"How much does it cost?"

"It varies from place to place and time to time. I haggle with them a little. The South Koreans see it as a way to profit from the war. I usually pay about fifteen to twenty dollars for a bag this size." I held up my cloth bag of Yunnan. One thing you may be interested in is that the Chinese keep secret everything about Yunnan, what is in it, how and where it is made."

Dr. Gray nodded his understanding saying, "We would never approve a secret process as we insist on knowing all the details. Also it seems to be quite expensive. Why it's a car payment!"

"It's very effective!"

In a few minutes he had a deep scalp injury and looked like he was having difficulty stopping the scalp from bleeding. I stepped over with a packet of Yunnan in hand.

"Would you like to see if Yunnan would be of any help?"

"Okay, let's try it. This one wants to keep bleeding."

I sprinkled a packet of Yunnan in the wound. Bleeding was stopped on contact.

"I'll be damned! Now that's impressive! I notice you use a lot of tape to close with. Dr. Green told me that you lost very few if any patients. How did you do that?"

"I put Yunnan in every wound and started intravenous water on arrival. It's important that both bleeding and shock are arrested. I guess I had better tell you that I was buying a lot of my water on the black market too."

"This line is getting too long. Show me what you did."

WAR WOUNDS

We removed the field applied pressure dressings and used Yunnan on the wounds and also started intravenous water on all of them on arrival. We caught up and would be working several more hours before we were relieved.

At mid day we were relieved and a peddler came forward who had been standing to one side. He stood by watching and waiting for our patient load to finish. He then stepped up, "I am Kala Ku, looking for the Australian Doctor Scott."

"I'm Scott. I've served with the Aussies as a technician. I'm not a doctor."

"Aha so! You are the one! I did not recognize you without a beard. Everyone in all of Korea knows of your work. Secrets and whispers travel very fast and far, yes? Do you remember me?" He moved directly in front of me. "I brought you Yunnan several weeks ago. I have much more."

"Of course I remember." *Oh boy, he is really putting the comments on thick. The price must be very high.*

Dr. Gray came over closer to get in on the conversation. He chimed in with, "Actually, doctors have the right to bestow their title to their students. Dr. Green told me that he placed you in a field med station on independent duty without any problems."

"Whoa! We are Americans and everybody and everything has to be certified, and have a stamp of approval from testing and so forth. Sorry, but one man's opinion would never fly in the American system."

Kala Ku said, "You must need more Yunnan by now. They told me you had left Australia. Happy to find you here."

"Yes, I returned to my ship. I was just serving with the Australian Army as a temporary technician."

"Happy to see you here, so few of you return."

I am being buttered up! I am down to my last few bags of Yunnan and somehow he knows that. I didn't have much cash either. My last payday was that of a seaman aboard ship. Also, I had sent some money home to mom. I keep my wallet like the Scots, draped over my shorts. I resisted the urge to look in my wallet. *I am haggling without knowing how much money I have. I'm trapped!*

He had three brightly decorated handbags each containing various sized bags of Yunnan. We bartered. Finally, we agreed on the middle bag. *I wonder how much money I have?*

I pulled my wallet out and held it open and facing me. There was one twenty-dollar bill in American money showing. I knew there was a ten under a flap in the wallet. I offered the twenty.

Cha Ku hesitated, reached his hand out. He was smiling. He then turned to Dr. Gray with a huge smile and bright eyes, "Would you like to buy some of our miracle Yunnan?"

"Whoa! I'm sorry but he is an American Medical Doctor. He will not be able to use it! You see, I am not a doctor! That is one reason I can use it. Also I was with the Aussies who allowed its use after I offered positive proof of its value."

"Ah So!" Cha Ku turned to Dr. Gray with his big dazzling smile. "Then perhaps for your personal use and personal patients. I have a complete pamphlet on all its uses." He held it out.

I took the pamphlet and quickly looked at the pages. "Is this in Chinese? He won't be able to read it."

A Korean nurse said, "Perhaps I can help translate." She looked at some of the pages. "No!" She quickly handed it back as if she had been handed a frog or something yucky, saying, "So, sorry, I don't know many of these signs." She then stepped back her head lowering.

"Perhaps an introductory sample for Dr. Gray?"

Dr. Gray spoke up, "I will only be here until noon the day after tomorrow. Then I am scheduled to be in Seoul for a few days so I will not have use for a lot. How much is it for a sample?"

"I will give you ten packs if you go to this address in Seoul. The person there will have a complete English translation. Your promise is to give Yunnan an open mind. To us this is what penicillin is to you. It is a true treasure."

"Thank you, I will do that."

Kala Ku reached out for the twenty, saying and waving the bill, "I know you are hiding money in your wallet's hidden pocket."

I was caught! How did I fail to hide that ten? "Hey, I need some money! I have an uncertain future and may need some cash."

"Yes, I understand. This is a little gift for you." He handed my twenty back. This is so very small. He bowed as he said that and presented all his bags. "It is because of the many good things you have done for my people and yours. You deserve a much larger reward." He paused, "I have enjoyed our conversation this morning." Kala Ku bowed low as he departed.

Chapter Thirty-Five

A MAIN EVENT

I was sent up to the line before Dr. Grey departed to go on his rounds. I was issued a bulletproof vest. They kept my grey helmet at the med center. My new helmet had a cloth covering the metal like all the others. I was handed a med bag with no markings and there was very little in it. Now I looked like anyone else with an extra bag and without a rifle. I saw that the big red crosses remained on the ambulances.

My ride was a vehicle that had tracks called a Weasel. I was perched on top of some ammunition, which was badly needed on the line. The Weasel was used to carry ammunition uphill and some patients down. The ride was very rough. I had to hang on tightly. The Weasel did not appeal to me as a good way to transport our wounded. Here the terrain was very rough and rocky. The driver proved this vehicle could climb over a two-foot high obstacle and up a very steep grade. No other vehicle could do that. It had tracks, which helped.

As soon as I arrived I was sent to the trench. I had patients to attend to as the gooks were sending a lot of lead up this hill and several had been hit. I was able to quickly and completely stop the bleeding with Yunnan. In a short while I got a patient with a chest wound. This patient had taken his new uncomfortable, heavy, stiff and hot bulletproof jacket off during a lull and took that opportunity to relieve himself. A shell hit near by and he received a good bit of shrapnel in his chest. One incision was several inches long. I did a little debridement and found more in there and it was quite deep. I didn't like that. I talked to the Corpsman in charge. He had me write up the required med record, strap him onto a stretcher and then we found a marine to help carry the other end down the hill. There I found an ambulance to take him to a hospital several miles away.

I don't know why but it took over an hour before I was put on a Weasel going back up to the outpost. This time there were three Weasels going up to the outpost all loaded with ammunition. This hill was not suited for chopper service as it was very barren and exposed to much flying lead. When I arrived I found that the line units had changed. A Lieutenant at the top told me, "I have a certified First Class United States Marine Corps Hospital Corpsman in the bunker and your main job newbie is to carry patients to him." *Now I'm really back to being a trainee!*

A few moments later a Sergeant told me to go down to the point man and bring him back. I would get cover over the open places from a Marine who would watch the gooks and me. I was told to stay low. I did the Australian ground crawl. Lots of lead was flying only an inch or less above my helmet and me. Once at the point I pushed some sand bags further over to one side to get to the point man. Those sand bags were very valuable as they received quite a bit of lead as I removed him from that hole. It was no small job getting him out. He was dead. I wanted so much to stand up and pull him up and out. I crawled into that hole with him. Then I pulled up on his belt and inched him along until he went over the edge. That ditch was not wide enough for both of us to be side by side. I would have to pull him along by crawling backwards. *I don't remember doing that in our training. How do I do this? I can't just turn around in the ditch, as it is too narrow and shallow. I would pick up lead.* I stuck my head in the hole and wiggled backwards up and over the edge. I got some good fire cover while crawling over the edge. I'm sure I rose up far enough to get hit if I didn't have that great cover. It was quite a struggle to wiggle going backwards uphill inch by inch. I did most of it by rocking back and forth and side to side. It took a long time to get back close to the trench at the top. I thanked the Marine for the fire coverage.

A little later, a machine gunner that was waiting for more ammo was holding his hands up, as they were hurting. I saw him. He made no call for aid. I nodded and crawled to him as soon as I could. He had bleeding hands from firing nearly constantly. The gun shook and it pounded his hands nearly to a pulp. I knew that I had some new bandage material in the bag, so I put it to use. It was round gauze and could be pulled tight around any appendage. It was quite expandable. I bandaged both his thumbs and all fingers and taped him up. I made a glove out of the bandages. Weeks later I would learn that I could have pulled that material much tighter. The machine gunner went right back to work firing as soon as his ammo was brought up. I helped bring some of that up to him.

My next task was to do the fireman's carry for another injured marine downhill to the med receiving center. I walked back up the hill. It became a regular grind.

My new boss had the med bunker in control. There was quite a lot of phosphorus and sulfur in the air, some of it causing burns. I asked him, "Should I make rounds to put salve on burns and drops in their eyes?"

"Yeah, that is a good idea."

My sleeved pen flashlight was very useful. Both sides must have exchanged several hundred rounds of artillery fire that night at this outpost. The noise level was extremely high. The ground shook all night long. Humans are not used to the firm ground shaking. It shakes us to the very core of our being. It is extremely upsetting mentally and physically. The exchange of rifle fire was very heavy. This was another night that seemed to be endless. *Would we live to see the light of day?* Finally daylight was increasing. I could see where the sun lit a high hilltop way off to the east.

I was ordered to the trench and given a handful of bandages. I went to a place were the trench was about chin high if you were to stand straight up. It was probably made for shorter people.

We were nearly out of ammunition. The order to fix bayonets was sent down the trench line. Faces were grim and jaws set. It is one thing to shoot someone and quite another to stuff a bayonet into a live human. In Boot Camp we had trained on gunnysacks.

The artillery exchange continued. Shrapnel hit one guy hard on his shoulder. I applied a pressure bandage. Another guy got a chunk of shrapnel in his right arm. I applied a bandage on that.

A third Marine called, "Hey, Doc! I don't want to expose my ass. Can you fix me up here?"

"Sure." It was pretty bad. I removed the fragment and pressed on a bleeder and then I dusted that wound with Yunnan, which stopped the bleeding and then taped a compress on his wounded arm.

A bugle sounded and a huge gook charge was on. They rushed the hill their guns bayoneted, teeth bared, their dirty ugly faces belching forth their foul garlic breath. One gook suddenly appeared right over my head. I grabbed a rifle from the side of the trench with its bayonet fixed. He had something in his hand as he jumped over the trench. I thrust the gun up. I had to push hard to stab him in the middle of his belly. Then I heaved him up over onto the backside of our trench. His momentum helped. He landed on his side. I jerked the bayonet out. The thing in his hand was a grenade. He dropped it into our trench. I rolled him off the trench ridge by pulling one leg over the other. He rolled over face up on top of the grenade. An instant before he hit the trench bottom the grenade went off. He rose up a bit then settled down. From that blast my last patient got a hit of shrapnel in his right calf. I dumped Yunnan on it.

A second gook appeared above me at the same place the first had a moment go. I thrust that same rifle's bayonet up into his neck. The bayonet entered at a point under his jaw. I continued pushing on the rifle butt. That push caused him to fall back down the hill. He fell against several others who were close behind him and coming up the steep hill. Now there were more gook faces glaring at us.

A marine with a portable flamethrower came up behind us. It was like a dragon belching huge flames. It roared flames out a long way toward a row of gooks ready to jump into our trench. Those flames took all the oxygen out of the air. It was difficult to get a breath of air for a moment. He waved a huge tongue of fire back and forth.

Their contorted faces seemed to melt like they were made of wax. He followed with another flaming sweep further out. Those flames took out about six-dozen gooks. The stench of burning human flesh has its own horrible smell. The air was full of it. The smoke and stench was overwhelming! I gagged then puked. It was a horrific thing to watch! It was a scene and stench that would linger all my life.

A gook bugle blew and the charge immediately ceased.

I slid back into the trench and took a few breaths. I removed the debris from the fresh grenade wound, then confiscated a bag of Yunnan from the grenade carrier and poured what was left of it into my patient's cut calf. I finished bandaging and taping his latest wound.

The Lieutenant appeared bellowing, "What are you doing? Who puked?"

I was still a bit shaky from the event but I spoke up, "I did. I'm just finishing a bandage."

With sarcasm, "You're no fucking good shipboard newbie! You can't stand to see an open wound or blood can you? I can sure fix that! Okay, you guys drop your shit in this trench, get the fuck out of here and police the area." He was glowering and bellowing as he was pointing at me, "You newbie! Get your fucking ass in gear and clean up your fucking puke and shovel all the rest of the shit out of all these trenches. Then you alone take all those fucking dead gook bodies down this fucking hill! That will give you a lesson you badly need!" With that he stalked off.

The guys slowly climbed up and out of the trench with a few expected grumbles. Policing meant they picked up shell casings and trash. Later the papa sans would carry the casings away and sell them back to us. I scooped up all the puke, blood and other waste and carried it to the latrine, then covered it with dirt. It was done one small trench shovel full at a time. That took a while.

The lieutenant stomped over to me growling, "Hey, newbie! I told you to move all those fucking dead gook bodies off this fucking hill down to that path before you leave this fucking hill." He was pointing to a path at the bottom of the hill. "The Koreans will carry them off to some place from there. Get your fucking ass on it now and finish before you leave! Our relief will be here about noon. If you are not finished, fuck you! We're leaving! Find your own fucking way back!"

I started pulling bodies from the bottom to the left, as that is where most were. The hill slope was steep and high. The sun was blazing directly overhead. The dirt became hot very quickly. I pulled and drug the bodies down hill. They felt like they were made of concrete. Many were grotesque, as a lot of them had been burned to death. Much of their flesh was burned away and was very charred. After a long time several Korean men came to remove the bodies from the ledge. First they removed any gold tooth fillings they could find.

I had another dozen or more bodies to pull down. The last gook was head down in our lookout hole I had been in earlier. It had a ledge useful to get in and out of on its north side. I hadn't seen that in the dark. On it was a pack of Camel cigarettes and a lighter. I was almost done and I needed a rest. I sat on a rock, picked up the pack and lighter; then lit one. I took a few drags, and then pulled those last bodies down to the ledge.

I put the cigarette pack in my shirt pocket. I sat on a rock for a few minutes. I was hot but I seemed to have stopped sweating and was no longer so thirsty.

I started staggering up the narrow path to the top. A young girl appeared suddenly. She spoke very good English with a British like accent, "They have gone away now. Come with me. I take you. There is an easy way to go back." She pulled on my reluctant hand.

I liked the thought of an easy way back, "Okay."

We soon came to an intersection of trails. At that place three North Korean officers were standing by the trail under the shade of a large bush by the side of the pathway. They had side arms.

The young girl said they wanted me to give them a smoke. I did not hesitate to tap the pack and three cigarettes slid out. I held them out so each officer could take one. The girl said, "They need a light too." I held up a finger to show one moment. I had a lighter in my pants pocket. I plucked it out then picked up my med bag, swung it over my shoulder, and then lit their cigarettes and mine. As I was lighting mine a bullet narrowly missed my nose, hand and cigarette. It hit one of the enemy officers on the outside of his chest. As the missile hit him he was turned and fell back onto the ground.

I turned to cuss the guy out. I grabbed my kit. It had no clamps. I put my knee on his chest for pressure, and took my lit cigarette to cauterize bleeders. I had to use several cigarettes on several large bleeders, and then I put his Yunnan on the wound. I asked for Yunnan from the officers and used those. I put a bandage in place and taped him up. I asked the girl to get a stretcher. She already had one standing by. "You are a very good girl!" They lifted him onto the stretcher and they trotted off. The other two officers put their hands together and bowed.

The girl said, "They are thankful for what you have done. You bow back now." I did. She took me by the hand. We pressed against some brush and in a few steps we were on a well-trodden path. The girl said with desperation, "We must hurry! You skip?"

"I'm too tired."

"Want to get shot?"

"No."

She called back sharply, "Skip!" as she went swinging and skipping along. "Skip!" She called back over her shoulder.

I was so tired I could hardly move but I forced myself to do it. It was difficult at first, but I did it. A skip was indeed a faster way to move and it felt good to swing along. We went along for a few minutes. I became a little light headed. *It must be the gaiety of the skipping!* It seemed like I had been struck in my face. Everything suddenly went black.

I woke up in a tent at a receiving med center on a cot with an empty water bottle attached to my arm. After awhile a medic came in and removed the needle and helped me to stand up. I was light headed.

There was a washbasin and a cloth. I used the damp cloth to clean my face and hands up for the evening chow call. I went for a very short stroll after dinner. It was only around the mess tent. I had turned the wrong way coming out. I wasn't any too sharp or steady. I was seen wandering around and was led back to the correct tent. I was told that Dr. Gray was relieved and there was a change of command. I saw that my new line gear, vest and helmet had been removed and replaced with my shipboard gear on the back of a chair. I drank as much water that evening as I could. I just was not able to drink or do much of anything. I was numb and just sat there. *"Thank you God for allowing me to live. I know I must still have more to do."*

The following morning I felt worse. Right after morning chow I was summoned by the now Commanding Officer of this Med Unit. I don't remember who he was or was with. The following is a summary of what I remember from his long and profane discourse.

I am now charged with disobedience of orders, practicing medicine without a license, and using an unauthorized medical treatment, some kind of a strange oriental powder, which was not approved by the American Medical Association, or any civilized country. I would get a court martial for all of that. He would make an example out of me. This report would appear in my permanent file. I was ordered to get off of his base immediately!

I departed feeling incredibly low. I was very lightheaded and extremely tired. I shuffled along towards a train station a full four or five miles to the east where a med train would leave that evening. I felt terrible, but had all day to get there and stopped many times. After several hours I came to a rise and a hairpin turn. I stopped to look at the train tracks shining in the sun. I would have to walk back along this ridge and around to the tracks. The short bushy way looked inviting. *Nope, I'm not up to such a steep grade right now. I have plenty of time to take the longer easier way.*

I saw and then in a moment heard a silver Soviet jet plane with swept wings moving at a very high speed in a nearly straight up climb. It rolled and turned to the north. Two others followed it closely. I was impressed by their speed. They were quickly out of sight, and then I heard several rumbles in the distance to the west. I was too tired and drug down to make anything of the airplanes or the sounds.

It was still quite some distance to the train station. It was all I could do to shuffle along.

Chapter Thirty-Six

SOME DIFFICULTIES

When I got to the train station there were boards nailed to cover its windows and door. It was a tacky small building with a low wooden platform with a single board wood bench.

It was hot and I was very sweaty and thirsty. I looked around for water and found none. I went to the shady side and lay down on the ground and went to sleep. I was awakened by a small steam engine pushing a medical car. It had a huge white patch with a large red cross in its middle. The car was far less than half the size of any that I had seen being used in the states. It was made of wood. I looked it over. It was hot and stuffy inside. In the front there was a small closet with a very small corner wash sink, a bucket, mop and some cleaning things. Beside the closet was a toilet, which had a semi circle draw curtain. The car had a few rows of wooden benches with room for two people on each side. There was a small desk at the end of the seats with large rolls of dust under them. Some of the racks had been removed and were stacked at the end of the car. I opened a spigot on the basin and sucked up some water. The water container looked to be rather small, maybe two gallons or so.

I got off the rail car and left the door open to air it out and continued to wait on the platform in the shade. In a while I went back to the rail car and took a second larger drink of water. I was not feeling well at all.

About an hour later the sun was casting longer shadows when an Army private appeared. He had a leg wound and a serious limp. We chatted for a while. He was being sent to Japan and an Army hospital. He took out a harmonica and started playing several tunes. Harmonicas have a rather lonesome pleasant sound. It brought up thoughts of home and the things I missed, like looking into the refrigerator and feeling its cool air. The smell of frying bacon also came to mind.

As the sun was setting an Army truck arrived with a very fat nurse and a few wounded ambulatory soldiers who slowly limped to the rail car. A Corporal wandered over to me and asked, "Who are you and where are you going?"

"Scott, Zakary Scott US Navy. I'm going to Japan."

He was trying to find my name. I was not on his roster. He seemed befuddled. "You're Navy?"

"Yeah." He seemed to be surprised I was Navy. He finally looked at me and saw my old grey helmet sitting by my side.

"You're off a ship?"

"Yeah."

He shrugged, and then he wrote my name and rank onto his list. "There will be plenty of room. Only half of the beds or benches will be filled on this trip."

Later a vehicle arrived with a few more wounded; most had arm or leg injuries. A small steam engine was backing up with some boxcars behind it and hitched up to the med car. Ours would be the last car of the train. The other cars looked to be open empty boxcars. It started moving a few minutes later.

The nurse received the roster and checked it. She pointed me out and loudly announced, "We have a hitchhiker, an able bodied Navy Seaman, the same rank as a Private First Class with us." The nurse quickly put me to work swabbing under the benches and the deck saying, "Isn't that what the Navy is good at, swabbing decks?"

I was immediately the target of what was to be hours of Army chiding Navy. I made some effort at first to counter some comments. That was only fodder for them and made for more snide comments.

The swabbing was badly needed and I was the most able bodied person other than that fat nurse. Dehydration doesn't show up like a bleeding wound. All of the other men were bandaged. Well, I was not all that well, but I was far better off than any of them. I kept my mouth shut. The good thing was that I got to drink several more paper cups of water. I almost drained that small tank.

After what seemed to be an eternity the train stopped on a slight slope. It was dark but there was a little more than half a moon peeking through breaks in the clouds. I got off and emptied the mop pail and then put the pail back on a step. There was a stream running under the tracks behind our car. I carried the mop several steps behind our railcar over to the bridge's railing and dunked it in the running water swirling it to loosen the grimy dirt. I pulled it out and gave it a wring, and then I looked around and saw that the train had silently rolled away. There were no whistles, bells, rattling of cars starting to move, or a cry of, "All aboard." I called out, "Hey, I'm here," but the car was too far away to be heard. It was difficult enough for me to stagger along, let alone to run after the train. It stopped, but for only a second when it passed an intersection over sixty yards or more from where I was standing. I was barely able to see it. I took a few staggering steps towards the train as it quickly and quietly rolled away. I stood alone beside the rails, watched the stream flowing rocks and faintly heard the sound of rushing water. There was the smell of rain in the air. It would rain hard later.

I was light headed. I steadied myself against the bridge railing. It was a few minutes before my eyes became accustomed to the dimming light. There was starlight and the moon shone when the clouds parted. I walked slowly down the track.

The stream followed at an angle. I climbed down to the stream where I scooped up a handful of water to smell and taste. I needed water. It was okay, so I continued to scoop the water and slurp it up.

The clouds parted and light shone all around. I could make out a lean-to on the other side. I wobbled over some stones and entered the darkness and carefully felt around. I found a mat of reeds. I sniffed and it did not stink, so I lay down on it and was soon asleep. I awoke to a clear bright morning. The sun had risen a little while ago. I was in a shadow.

I felt terrible, very beat up, quite stiff and achy, and was not moving well at all. I stretched some and then wandered to the stream where I watched the water flow over a rock. It beckoned. I knelt down on my hands and knees. My hands were both in the water. I lowered my face in the cool water and sucked it up. I rose up for a breath then bent lower for another mouthful. My hand slowly slid, my arms separated widely, and I landed face first into the stream. It felt good so I let myself drift downstream to a pool that was just around a bend. I took off my clothes and rubbed them on the sand in the cool water. Surface dirt was washed but the bloodstains remained. I washed myself all over. It took quite some rubbing to remove a little dried blood left from the trench and the outpost. I left the clothing in the stream hoping that the blood would just vanish. I sun dried and was a little warmer when I pulled my clothes out of the water and wrung them out, then stretched them out on brush in the full warming sun. I drank my fill of water while I was waiting for an eastbound train. It would take hours before I heard an engine far to the west.

My clothes were still damp. As quickly as I could, I pulled my clothing on and my wet boots. My body still did not want to move. I struggled down the track and around a rail switch well over a hundred yards away. Up line from the switch I leaned against a large rock behind a small bush to be partly hidden. The train's engine passed and squeaked to a stop behind a rail switch some twenty yards down the track. Two cars up line there was a boxcar with open doors so I pulled myself inside. The ends of the empty boxcar were in deep shadows. I had been facing the sun, so I was unable to see clearly into the back of that boxcar.

"Anyone here?" There was no answer. The train slowly started to roll along. The boxcar was small, empty, and dusty. The train stopped for a moment and rolled along again. It was good to be moving toward civilization and possible comforts again.

I removed my damp clothing and buttoned it around the open door railing. My shirt was tied on one side and pants on the other. The moving air would dry me again and the clothing. I stood in the sun.

When my clothing was dry I put it on. My boots were still wet so I tied them to the door railing to catch more air and dry as the train rocked and rolled along. In a while it came to an open valley. I was standing in the open door while we were passing a field where a man and a woman were working. They straightened up, looked, smiled and waved. I was holding my gray Navy helmet in my left hand. I waved back. The woman blew me a kiss. I blew one back. *That was nice.*

Late in the day the train rattled into Pusan. I waited for the train to stop, then slid off. I put my helmet on, stuffed my shirt in my pants and wandered towards a building several tracks over to what looked like an entrance.

A boy was riding up towards me on a bicycle. He said, "Need help! Come quick. Old man fall down on tracks." He gave me his bicycle to ride, as my walk was slow. He ran alongside of me urging me to pump faster towards the entrance building. He pushed me along a bit. An elderly man was laying face down across a track. It was all I could do to move him off the tracks with the help of that boy and two old men off the platform who took hold of his legs. We were able to lift him and carry him a few steps to the platform. None of us were very strong. A few people on the platform gave us applause. About a minute later a train rolled by at a high speed on that track. It would have crushed the elder to his death. I nodded, put my hands together and bowed a little. I thanked the boy and asked him, "Which way to the airport." He pointed the way. He said something in Korean and a few people scurried past me. Local emergency personnel arrived for the elder. There was quite a bit of excitement. Someone got me a rickshaw and paid for my ride. I thanked them. I was so very tired I fell asleep in the rickshaw.

At the airport counter I was asked for my flight authorization. I had none. I was told where to wait. Very soon two Korean Military Police approached and ordered me to go with them to an officer who asked some questions. Something was wrong and I did not understand what it was. They took my fingerprints. I got a little irritated. Then I was taken to a hospital where I was examined. That irritated me. I was admitted to a ward for recovering patients. That also irritated me. The oriental food irritated me. *I feel like hell and I want to go home!*

The food was below standard, cool and pasty. I was not able to eat much. I guess my stomach had shrunk up during my Korean receiving station duty. There was a small store that had candy, papers and such.

I went for my wallet as I did have a few dollars in it. Not now. It was empty.

A few days later I was told that I was on the 'missing in action' list and I would be going nowhere until the Navy issued further orders for me. I think it was about a week before I was able to leave with an authorization to travel. At the airport I was ushered right through and onto a plane preparing to leave for Japan. When I landed I took the fast train to our base then to a holding barracks. I got there in time to clean up before chow. Real American food! Wow! Did that ever taste good! Still I was not able to eat all that much.

The following day I had to stand before a military judge, helmet in hand, to explain why I was there and my business. I had my identification and my travel order to this base. I was again sent to the hospital for an evaluation.

What's wrong? I feel terrible. So what! I have felt this bad before and wasn't put in a hospital!

The examining doctor was an older man. He gave me a good exam, and they drew some blood. In a long while he returned and said, "You're quite worn down." He asked me where I had been and what I was doing. I gave him the recent details. He wandered behind me and sharply struck a table with a wooden ruler. I jerked quite a bit.

"You have shell shock. It comes from being around shells exploding nearby and all the constant noise and the earth shaking. It scares us witless. It was very common in World War One. We are seeing a lot of the same thing here in the Korean War zone, although many think its another diagnosis, a 'stress problem' is the new term. I'm calling it 'shell shock!' You are not the only person with this either. You need restoration. I recommend rest, relaxation, warm baths, a high protein diet, and some light exercise. Find a woman to play cards with and exchange a few laughs. That will do you no harm. You will feel better in a few months."

"It will take a few months?"

"At least that long, it may take a lifetime. It is indeed quite a high price we all pay. Shell shock does not show. The worst part is that all the civilians at home have no clue as to what has happened to any of us and neither does the medical profession."

"You said we."

"Yes we. I was in the medical corps in Europe during World War One and I still jump out of my skin when there is a sudden sound, like when the wind blows and a door slams shut. We were as confined as you guys who have been stuck in a foxhole or a trench for very long periods of time. Getting rid of shell shock is not a snap of the finger thing. Getting it is far easier than getting rid of it." On the side he mentioned, "There is an 'E' club on base." He winked.

I thanked him. I was assigned to a recovery ward where I was told to go into the solarium. They had a few magazines and the latest edition of *Stars and Stripes*. It had news about how well we were doing on the line. They made it sound as if we were making advances when actually we were stuck in a hole in the ground. They used soft words and made our daily nightmare seem light and easy.

Newsweek and *Time* magazines were full of the election between Ike Eisenhower, a Republican and Adlai Stevenson, a Democrat. They each had articles about the police action and the conflict in Korea, and they often used words like, a 'mere conflict.' They further minimized it by saying that the truce talks were being stalled over small problems. They made it all sound so small, easy and very diminished.

I read all of those magazines from cover to cover. There was a *Life* Magazine that had a cover photo of Ernest Hemingway and a story about his latest book *"Old Man and the Sea."* I was just not up to speed. That book was in the library and it took me several weeks to read all of that. I was still not able to come up to speed, but then there was no reason to hurry.

This ward had thirty men. Each morning in this ward we stood muster and were told what our duty of the day was. We had to keep the barracks clean. We all had things to do in rotation. Each task had a checklist of what had to be done. There was no hurry to get it done, any time before noon was just fine. If we were unable to do a task then that was okay too. Someone would come in and do it.

WAR WOUNDS

All the patients were ambulatory so we all walked to mess hall for chow. We each had colored chits for special diets. Mine was red for more red meat. I had a fried steak for lunch with lots of potatoes and veggies. I felt bad because I was not able to eat it all. I wandered back to that nice clean comfortable hospital bed and slept an hour or so. Later I went to the gym and make a feeble attempt at a workout. I was only able to go through a few motions. I meandered around the hospital and later went with a few others to the 'E' Club for a few beers. I was only able to drink a part of one and I was drunk as a skunk. Later I chatted briefly with a few of the sailors. Most were from the fleet. I was just not with it.

A few weeks later I met a fellow who was working as an inspector of the Pan Pan girls, whores, during the present gonorrhea epidemic. That sounded much more interesting than swabbing decks and cleaning up messes. We had several beers. He thought I would have a good chance to join the inspection group after I got out of the hospital. There was an urgent request to the fleet for assistance. My being a medic trainee was what they wanted for that job. They had on-the-job training.

Several weeks passed before the ship returned. I was feeling some better, but I was still very underweight and was rather slow gaining physical strength. I was released from the hospital and returned to the ship on light duty.

As soon as I was back aboard ship Dr. Gray called me into his office, "Good to see you alive! I heard that the med center we were at had been wiped out. It seems quite strange that I was relieved a day early."

"I become dehydrated and was sent back early the next morning and have been recuperating in a hospital."

"You have been invited to attend a parade in Seoul. Dr. Green and the Koreans both want to give you a medal for your service."

"Thank you. I would like to attend."

I had lost a lot of weight so I went to the ship's tailor shop and had my dress blues trimmed down for the occasion. They did the alterations. They left the material in as they thought I would soon be back for another alteration. I bought the decorations that I was eligible to wear. They knew all about that and put them on in proper order. Also I bought a wristwatch from the ship's store.

I attended another debriefing. The Chief from personnel would ask for my records from the Aussies. "They will be of great value in the future for school references, promotions and such." He knew about my invitation to go to Seoul for awards. He said I could go at my own expense but I would be unable to wear any foreign awards on my uniform. He had the regulation to prove his point. Only the general levels and those involved high up in international relations were able to wear them. That regulation and the fact that I would have to pay all the expenses made the trip seem futile. Nonetheless, I did check out the expenses and soon found that I didn't have nearly enough money to take that trip.

In a few weeks again I was called into Dr. Gray's office. "Zak, can you fill in for the swimmer for a few weeks? I see that you volunteered to do that. Two of them have contacted gonorrhea, which they concealed. They are still in the hospital. It is certain that they will not be fit to fly or swim for several more weeks."

"I would be delighted! When do I start?"

"I am concerned about your physical condition. You are still quite run down."

"I was not able to eat much of the Korean food as they put so many spices in it! I was just not able to hold it down. It all came right back up. I think I will be all right in a few more days with some good Navy grub. I will be able to work out more aboard ship than the limited time that was available at the hospital." *This will give me something to work for.* "I may not be quite as good as I was before I left ship, but I should be passable as a swimmer!" *I really wanted to do that!*

"Very well, I will put you on a high protein diet and prescribe an exercise program." He outlined a workout program. I was to work out three times every day, rope skipping, rope climbing, weight training, calisthenics and flight deck jogging.

I thanked him and went to see Lt. Gardner.

Chapter Thirty-Seven

---◆---

REGULAR DUTY

I appeared at Lt. Gardner's office and was warmly received. We had made a few pick up trips together. I was introduced to the other two guys. They were new to the ship and were pleased that their on-call shift had been cut from twelve hours to eight. I was fitted for a flight suit and a new type of a life vest and shown how to use it. Our ship's helicopter, a dragonfly, generally flew fairly close to the ship's fantail on landings and its bow on takeoffs, but not so close to be an interference.

A few days later an injured pilot in a crippled plane came in a bit too slow and low. He got a wave off and failed to gain enough altitude. He tried to turn and the wing tip struck the port aft end of the flight deck. His plane cartwheeled into the water. He had popped his canopy as soon as he hit the water. We were close by. As soon as he unfastened his seat belt we were there to pick him up and had him aboard the chopper. The plane sank very quickly.

On another day a jet pilot was in trouble during the launch. The catapult did not have enough energy to get the needed air speed. We were right there to pick him up. The ship sailed right on past and very close to us. That is one reason the catapults are placed on both sides.

A week or so later an AD Sky-raider saw a target of opportunity and flew to it. He got a good hit on his fuel tank and was losing fuel fast. He didn't have enough gas to make it back to the ship. He was barely able to make a precautionary landing on a northern beach. We were on our way at his first radio call. We arrived soon after he had landed on the beach. On landing a gear had made contact with a deep puddle of water and there was a rock in that puddle. The gear was bent backward and up. The plane spun around. The nose went down and that caused the huge prop to contact the sand, which made the hot engine stop quickly bending a few things inside. The crewman, Sam and I were ordered by the pilot to stay and push the plane out further into the water. He turned and climbed aboard our chopper and they went back to our ship.

We saw some driftwood and found a log about twenty inches in diameter and three to four feet long. We moved it end over end a few times to the damp beach, and then rolled it under the plane's belly up by the engine. I reached in the cockpit and pulled the gear to the up position, which would slowly lower the plane onto the log and then I moved the trim tab to its full nose up position. That would allow the plane to glide further underwater and hopefully into a deep area. We used a limb and put that between the tail cone and hook, turned it more out to sea and pulled backwards to move the plane. The plane slowly rolled along the log and went further into the waves. The drop off was quite sharp. Water is a little like heavy air, so, the plane would move well out to sea in a slow bobbing manner.

A two-man gook patrol saw the plane land and came running to investigate. They came over a sand dune some fifty yards away, saw us and started firing. We hit the ground. Sam had a pistol. He plugged one and winged the other. That bullet swung the second gook around and he fell back over a small sand dune out of sight. In that process his rifle was dropped. That gook was yelling. There was desperation in his voice. I crawled up the north side of the dune and peeked from between some tall grass to see what he was doing. He was on his side and still hollering. I snuck up behind him, grabbed his weapon belt and tossed it over the dune. Sam came up and tossed his belt and rifle out seaward.

I stopped the commie's bleeding by using his Yunnan.

Our pickup chopper was arriving. It was a helicopter from another carrier. We climbed back over that small sand dune.

Sam asked, "Why in hell did you do that?"

"He is a human in need. He may well be a brother of a South Korean soldier."

He rolled his eyes in disbelief as he said, "I plugged him and you patch him up."

Chapter Thirty-Eight

A WALK BACK

Late one afternoon a P-51 was providing support for a ground unit. The pilot got both his fuel tank and his right leg shot up. He was able to make a landing in a northern meadow and get out of his plane. We responded to the call. Sam the crewman removed the instrument while I put a pressure bandage on the pilot's wound and then we helped him into the chopper. I was told to stay by the meadow's east edge until they came back for me in about thirty minutes or so. I waited at the pointed out place in the shade on the east side of the grassy clearing under a scrub tree patch close to a number of large rocks. I could plainly see the clearing and the landed plane.

In a little while a good number of gooks, roughly fifty or sixty had entered the valley on a dirt road over a low ridge to the northeast. They had a short mile to get to the wreckage. Many went to look at the plane. Almost all of them looked in the cockpit. Many of them sat down in the pilot's seat. Then they set up camp on the other side of the clearing.

While they were doing that a silver Navy Panther photo plane flew high over the area. If I were in the field I would be very visible to the gooks. A reflector flash would be seen by the gooks. I did move out from under the brush on the far side and turned on my flashlight. I held my hand to shield the light from the gooks and pointed it up.

In a few minutes I heard the sound of a chopper, then the sound receded. *Due to this unwelcome company I don't think a helicopter is going to land here for me very soon*. I would have to wait. While I was waiting I was able to see a well-trodden trail or road on the west side of the clearing. It ran the length of the clearing on that side and further south. I could follow it south down a shallow canyon that generally went towards the sea. The gooks were on that path. They were not in an immediate attack mode. I could smell their cooking. In a while they had dinner and I guess some sake or something. I could hear some of their louder sounds and some laughter. I was close enough that I could see them but could not tell one gook from another. They all looked alike from where I was. They appeared to be very willing to stay put for quite sometime.

In accessing my situation they were all carrying guns, I had none. I carried only a med bag and a vest that had signaling devices, flares, a mirror, a knife, a light, but no canteen. I was ready for a quick pickup. My comfort zone was not high. If I did move surely I would be discovered. The coast was a mile or two over the hill behind me. We had passed one ridgeline while flying in. I would be very visible on a beach. I wanted to run while there was still light. *I am surrounded by dry dense brush. Surely I would make some noise moving through that thick brittle brush. I would probably be heard, seen and shot. If I walked the edge of this field I would be visible. I better wait right here until it's dark.* That was still awhile, but the sun was getting low to the west. I saw a second silver Panther jet pass high overhead. That would be a photo plane. The sun was behind me. I used my signal mirror to put a flash on a hillside and move it around and up quite a way. Perhaps that would be seen on film.

Waiting was difficult. It was dark when I ventured out and quietly moved south around the field to that east side path. There was little brush to move around in the clear area so I was able to move quietly in a crouch to make a smaller target and to look more like an animal. The further I went the better I felt. I was quite a distance south of the gooks before I stood up to walk upright.

It was a fairly clear night providing some ambient light. A half moon came up after a few hours. This trail entered an east west dirt road. I walked quietly to the east. In a while it turned south. I walked south all night. I looked at the stars to verify direction and stopped every few minutes to listen.

It was an hour or so after sunrise when I hear a jet flying west of me and going from north to south. I took out my reflecting device, held it out, and moved it about. It was a silver Navy photo plane. I moved to the middle of the road, held up the mirror a bit to try for a reflection and I tried to flash out an SOS and my name. It turned and flew right overhead very high.

I found a stream. It appeared to be from those mountains to my west and seemed to be good. I drank all the water I could and continued along this road. In a while I heard a truck coming and hid in the brush. It was an old tan Chevy six wheel ton and a half. I walked south all day stopping from time to time. I was sweating a lot. About noon I found a small muddy stream. I took a handful and gave it a sniff. It smelled rancid so I dumped it.

By late afternoon my walk had slowed greatly. Clouds were getting thick fairly fast. My energy level was quite low as was the sun. In a few hours it started to rain lightly. In a while the rain had started in earnest and the sun was setting behind thick clouds.

I had skirted a village. I was approaching a building with smoke coming out. Three guys came stumbling out making a lot of noise. One fired a gun into the air. I sat quietly by the roadside behind a large bush about two hundred yards away. They clambered into a vehicle and rushed off to the east.

As I approached that building a young Korean gal, Bong-Ca, had seen me and came out to take me in. She held an umbrella. I was dripping wet. Once inside Bong-Ca brought me a towel and a robe. She recognized the flight suit and my med bag. She spoke some English. "Yor American?"

"Yes."

She pushed me behind a folding screen to undress. She took my wet clothing and draped it over a chair close to the fire. She gave me a blanket to wrap up in. Two other girls pulled the screen back and presented their personal attributes and points of interest in several poses and sexy movements. *Now I know what kind of an establishment I am in.* Maybe at another time they would have been attractive.

I said, "Thank you, but not right now."

Bong-Ca asked, "Yor medic?" I nodded yes. "Yor hangare?"

"Yes, I'm very hungry and thirsty!"

Bong-Ca held her hand up and made motion like using chopsticks. "Like rice?" She was so cute doing that.

"Rice would be nice. How much?"

"Fifty won."

"I only have American money. I have a twenty-dollar bill. Will that work?"

"My ask Mama-San."

Mama-San was a thin woman with graying hair. She came from another room. Bong-Ca chatted with Mama-San. Bong-Ca came back to me and said, "Mama-San said, "Money okay but you offer too much. Maybe we give much more beer or rice and peas. Maybe very much me too?"

"Oh, thank you so much." I bowed my head. "Maybe some beer, rice and peas. Please no spices." *I really need water and edible food!* Mama-San smiled, nodded assent and took the twenty. She sure looked me over as she returned to her room.

I was standing by the fire. I felt a cold draft. There was a window that had a good size round hole in it. Considerable cool air was being blown in by the storm. I volunteered to tape it up with the tape in my kit.

"I ask Mama-San" She went into her room and soon returned saying, "You nice guy, patching broken window!"

Out of my med bag came a roll of tape an inch wide. I picked up a rag, wiped the inside, and taped that. The rain had let up. I went outside, wiped around the hole and applied tape and taped up the splinters too making sure the sides had made contact. That may do the trick for tonight. I went in and stood by the fire again. All the draft had vanished. It would soon rain hard.

Bong-Ca gave me a hug then put her hand on my back, "Yo'r cool." She pushed me much closer to the fire. "Need to get all warm. We can do fuckey fuckey later, yes?"

"I think I may be too tired."

"Warm up, yes?"

"Yes." I nodded. Bong-Ca gave me a second blanket, and then she went to the kitchen. I moved a chair closer to the fire and fell asleep.

Bong-Ca woke me up. She did not use the military foot-tap. She chose a more central sensitive place to tickle. I awoke immediately somewhat surprised at where she was tickling. She sure got my attention! She had a huge bowl of rice, peas and peanuts. Steam was rising from them. She put the bowl right under my nose. She also had a big soupspoon.

"Thank you!" I gave her a nod and lost no time eating. She went for a bottle of beer to show me. "I like. You like?"

I shrugged, "I don't know. You are an excellent cook! I don't know about the beer but your food is sure good! I will try it." She opened the bottle with an opener device on a doorpost.

I paused and raised the bottle. *I give thanks for my good fortune and the fact that I was able to do what I had done today, and I asked for more help tomorrow.*

After dinner she led me to a warm tub. I washed. I crawled onto a mat. Bong-Ca cuddled up to me and pulled a blanket over us. I was soon asleep. In the morning Bong-Ca woke me up using the same methods she had used before. This time I was showing that I was feeling much better than last night. Some of my energy had returned.

Later, Grandpa-San woke me from another nap as he was replacing the broken window. "You make patch good."

"Yours is better. It is a permanent fix"

"No. No! I do this too often." He pointed to a stack of windowpanes. He laughed.

Bong-Ca had made breakfast. It was a roll that had a sprinkling of cinnamon, a hot wheat cereal and tea.

"This is very good! Maybe I should marry Bong-Ca and stay here!" They all laughed after she translated.

Right after I arrived and was undressing Bon-Ca had picked my pocket and given my name and whatever to Mama-San. She sent one of her girls into the village and asked for information about me. This girl was related to a nurse who was serving the South Korean Army. They both returned to this building and talked a lot. I was pointed out and was the topic of much chatter all in Korean. I could tell by their glances and movements like peeking around another gal.

Mama-San spoke and Bong-Ca translated, "The words that come back is that you are well known to Koreans North and South. The word is that you have saved the lives of many North Koreans by taking care of their wounds and feeding them. You do much to quiet fear and hate. One time you put a needle in your arm and the other end into our son. Your blood gave him life. He would have died otherwise. Now you are family! We hear that no American has ever done that for our people. We are so honored that you come to this humble place."

"Mama-San, Bong-Ca brought me in out of the rain and cold. I was exhausted, hungry and dirty. You treated me like a king, warmed me, fed me and bathed me. You did not know if I had money or not. That is charity! That is most honorable!" I nodded my head in assurance.

"No. No. I had Bong-Ca bring your wallet to me just after you came in the door! Ha, ha!" She was so delighted in her devious methods. She was rocking back and forth with joy.

Bong-Ca brought us more tea. We saluted each other. Its taste was slightly orange. Very soon I fell asleep and would stay that way for hours.

I awoke under a cover on a wagon and under some hay. The cover had an opening out the back. I wiggled and pushed to get out and I looked around. *I have been here before. I was at a familiar place!* It was outside a base. I would later climb into the back seat of a mail plane that would take me back to the ship.

Chapter Thirty-Nine

MAN OVERBOARD

The fleet had been plowing straight into a late October polar tempest with typhoon level winds for nearly two days. All aircraft were lashed to the flight and hangar decks with cables.

For the Medical Department that meant treating a very long line of seasick sailors. I worked with First Class Petty Officer Anderson, "Swede" during morning Sick Call that was open all hours. We had worked half of our alternating six-hour shift on this extended duty and the messes were cleaned up when I asked Swede, "Can I go up to the forward gun tub for some fresh air and take a few photos of the bow waves?"

"Sure! Take ten." He paused, "Hey, I may as well go too. It seems to have been a long morning, and it's only ten o'clock."

We took our cold weather jackets, our 35-millimeter cameras, and then went to a gear locker to check out safety belts with lines and snap hooks to keep us from being washed overboard. With that gear we could get to the port walkway that had a safety line to snap onto running fore to aft. When we got there our pants were snapping in the wind. Cold ocean spray stung our faces as it came off wave tops. We had to hang onto the cable lines to get a look of the ship plowing through the very heavy sea. Waves must have averaged forty to fifty feet high. They were awesome! The entire ship's bow was well buried in every swell. Solid water often pounded against forward compartments. Occasionally solid water went well onto the flight deck. Crewmen berthing in those quarters were moved aft. The galley was serving only 'K' rations and coffee in half cups in an effort to avoid spills. Announcements were issued every hour warning all hands to watch when stepping over flex plates which were working nearly to their fullest and the ship did shake and roll over hard from time to time.

A few minutes after our arrival at the forward gun tub a loudspeaker very close to us came on with an announcement, "All outboard decks are now off limits." We had to hang on hard so much of the time we had only been able to take a few photos of water pounding and splashing up over the flight deck. We immediately went to an inside passageway. We were soaked and had enough cold fresh air! We looked about for other shipmates before we entered. We were alone in this area. We saw some guys well aft near other doors getting off this deck. As the ship lurched a hatch door behind us slammed shut. I secured it by its 'dog-ears,' watertight fasteners. As we were descending a ladder to the hangar deck a chilling announcement was made.

"Man overboard, man the lifeboat! - Man overboard, man the lifeboat! - Man overboard man the lifeboat!" Immediately that was followed by another hollow sounding announcement. "The following boat crew personnel report to the emergency lifeboat immediately: Brown, Jones, Miller, and Scott."

"Hey that call is for you!"

"Yeah, I got checked out in it during our trip to the Philippines. I'm the lifeboat medic."

"I know! I recommended you." I gave Swede my camera and safety belt. He continued to go below decks and called back. "See ya later."

"Later."

I was some thirty yards and two ladders from the lifeboat. I was the first one to it. I tried to remove its cover but found that it was locked fast as our cold weather gear was inside. In a few seconds the Chief arrived and was surprised that I was the first one there.

"Usually our medics are the last to get here." He had the key. By the time he had it unlocked the other crewmen had arrived. We whipped the cover off the lifeboat. The wind was howling and spray was lashing at us!

Chief loudly said, "Men this is not a drill! Almost two minutes ago by now a man was seen falling over the fantail railing and was splashing in our wake. You guys need to find him and get this boat back in five minutes or less. He cannot survive any longer and you have the same time frame! Good hunting and good luck!"

As he was talking we had boarded the boat and were putting on our foul weather gear. Life vests were tied tight, belts snapped on and secured to safety lines attached beforehand to the boats gunnels and keel. Like every emergency vehicle world wide, everything had been laid out in advance ready for any event and fast action.

The lifeboat was quickly lowered into the water in the trough of a huge swell. Jones, the boatswain, unhooked the carrying ring as soon as the boat slammed into the water. Then he heaved the ring to the side. Topside a crewman instantly hauled it up as the ship rolled to starboard. We had swung very close to the carrier's port side.

Miller our coxswain pushed the tiller hard to starboard to turn away from the ship. At the same time Brown gunned the engine to full throttle to move us out from under the flight deck's overhang.

That roll of the ship gave us lots of clearance. It took just two quick snaps of cold fingers for us to clear the ship and we were able to make a turn to port in that first huge swell. With full power we were driven abeam the stern of our ship. The strong wind had blown over that first wave and dumped very cold water all over us. It filled the boat and rolled us hard to starboard.

In a few seconds we were in the ship's wake. We quickly moved downwind out of the wake's quiet area. It became rough and water was blowing off waves as we moved away from the ship. We were close to where the person was likely to be found. We were tossed about like a cork as we pitched and severely rolled. Waves peaked up and broke freezing water into our boat. When we pitched bow up water gushed aft and out over the aft gunwales. Pitch bow down, water gushed forward and out spilling over the forward gunnels tossing us greatly from one side, then over to the other. All that moving water pushed us around and made it very hard to stand and look for our target person.

No two swells are alike. They bulge and heave as they rise and fall. Wind whipped the crest and drove angry gray freezing water pounding into our faces at hurricane force. I thanked God that this boat was unsinkable and we were securely tied down fore, aft, port and starboard or all of us would have been washed into the sea. We were whipped and jerked hard every which way. We rose up and down quickly, harder than any carnival ride. *This is no fun!*

I felt sick and wanted to puke. Just as I opened my mouth a wave hit me square in the face with the force of a heavy weight boxer swinging from the floor up. What a punch! It nearly knocked me out. My mouth had filled with salt water, jammed it right down my throat and into my eyes with an intense sting. My white hat was washed off my head. Very cold water poured down my back and pulled and swirled around my feet. "Damn!"

When we were atop a swell I could take a quick look for our ship. It seemed to be very far away, but I knew that was due to the spray and the darkness of the grey sky.

Each of us had a scan area. Mine was port side. I looked for my man.

It seemed like an eternity before Boatswain mate Jones shouted, "There he is!" Pointing to starboard up high.

"I see him," Miller shouted back as he pushed the tiller hard to port to move us up under a cresting wave. We were in a trough and turned very fast.

My scan area was to port. As I turned my head to starboard I shouted, "Where?"

"There in the next swell." Jones was continuing his constant pointing so not to lose sight of our man. The heavy sea made that very hard to do. We had several yards to move up and over one more wave, our target wave. Our boat rolled hard gunnel under water, as we turned to reach him. As it righted I saw him thrashing in the upper part of the swell.

It was John, one of the guys who came aboard with me. He was a loner, and a very religious guy who lectured us about our sinful ways. I was often a target of his sermons and finger wagging.

Brown jammed the throttle up to full and we moved under John as he was swept up to the very top of a wave. He rose up right above us. While the wave was breaking he was pitched close enough to grab onto. After some wrestling he was in my arms. We were breaching hard! I held my breath, closed my arms tight and hung onto him as the wave crushed down over us. That wave and his weight nearly broke my back. It seemed like our boat rolled completely over as water was all around. As it righted I called out, "I have him!"

Jones was able to let his line out enough to come back to us. He edged along the port side close to me holding a life jacket and a slicker. He secured the life jacket while John was resisting our efforts. I was trying to help him into it by trying to hold his wildly thrashing arms. Jones got the life jacket tied on and wrapped the slicker around both of us. We were all slipping to and fro, being pulled this way and that. *I'm sure our guts will be badly bruised from this beating!*

"Wait a second! I have to check him out."

It only took a moment to see that John was stiff, his skin was very cold, and his lips were bluish. All I saw were symptoms that he was in a severe state of hypothermia. He had no obvious bleeding injuries. Jones was ready to tie us together.

"Done!"

John slurred, "Le me go. - Le me go -." I nodded to Jones to continue tying us up. He too was staggering from the effects of the cold-water wind and rough sea but somehow he secured the line.

I had to shout to John who had slumped in my arms, "John, do you know me? Where are you?"

"God called me." He slurred like a drunk and spoke slowly.

Miller had turned our lifeboat towards the ship. We were now going mostly into the swells and back to the ship. It looked to be some hundred and fifty yards out and thirty yards to starboard. More water poured into our boat. It lurched, severely raised, rolled and pitched. Water was coming well over the bow as we plowed into each swell. Our prop was out of the water on each swell, Brown was able to pull the power off at the top to keep the prop and engine from over running. He also was prompt to push power back up as we slammed down into the water to push us ahead. In spurts of high and low power we were making progress towards our ship.

Each lifeboat crewmember was shivering severely. We needed to get aboard ship very soon. John was babbling. I shook him trying to keep him awake. I spoke loudly to be heard over the howling wind. We were tied toes to toes, face-to-face and nose-to-nose.

"John! Do you know me? I'm Zak Scott. We boarded ship together. Do you remember?"

"Yeah," he slurred. He slowly continued, "God told me to jump."

"God told me to grab you just now."

"Nah?"

"He did John! We have more to do!"

He slurred, "Nah!"

"Yeah, I was told that when I took a glimpse up there a few months ago."

"John, do you think it would help if we prayed for a calmer sea?"

He brightened up, "Yeah!" He slurred that, but quickly, clearly and loudly said, "Oh God please give us a calmer sea and less wind. Provide us with a safe return, in Jesus name!"

Wow, he really perked up and with a straight thought and comment! What a surprise!

"Good go Mate! "I gave John three good solid pats on his back and tried to get John thinking of something. My thinking was also slow due to the cold. I gave him another good shake.

"John did you get your mother a Christmas present yet?"

"Nah." He slurred.

"We need to do that very soon so it will get there in time."

"All they have is cheap stuff."

"Nah! I found some good stuff."

"Yeah?"

"Yeah. It is downtown. I don't remember the name of the place, but I can take you down there."

"Yeah." He was looking at me with the glazed eyes of a drunk in a stupor.

"A tea set for Mum! A nice one."

"Blu?"

"No it is white with red roses."

"Why?"

"Mum is English, don't you know, eh?"

"Yeah." Came out slowly.

"Yeah, I did that. It is being shipped home by the store." I was trying to be enthusiastic, but I was still yelling over the wind and waves.

"Yeah." - John went limp.

"Sure John."

I shouted, "Hey! Brown, use the radio. We need to get off this boat!"

He shouted back, "I just did! It is backing down now!" It seemed that this was taking hours, but the ship was slowly getting larger. I shook uncontrollably very hard.

Later, I would learn that the ship had struck a log that was under the water and had damaged a propeller while backing down. The ship's aft section had jumped and quivered as the power was quickly applied to full reverse. Several crewmen were injured in the bucking motions.

Death was patiently waiting for us all. It would come in one minute or so for all of us with no exceptions. Suddenly the wind seemed to subside and the sea lessened. We forged ahead. The ship was turning to port some fifteen degrees. We were in its wind and storm shadow. It was listing to starboard. The elevator was lowering, as was the boat ring.

I passed out. We were all in severe hypothermia. I was jerked hard and awoke a moment later. John was out cold! He was limp but still in my arms and tied to me. We were beside the ship. Jones and Brown were flat on the boat's deck. Only Miller was standing at his tiller and he was swaying to and fro. Sailors were sliding down lines to us. I saw Swede standing on the port elevator his blond hair streaming in the wind. He held a stretcher in each hand and wore a white deck jumper over his jacket with a big red cross. Again everything went dark.

We were all promptly carried down to Sick Bay where we were stripped, dried, rolled in blankets and put in a warm room with a Corpsman to stand watch over us. We were cold enough to pass out. So, there could be some heart issues.

It took hours but Miller woke up first. I awoke several minutes later. A Corpsman was in the room. He gave us a quick check over:

temperature, pulse, respiration, and blood pressure. We all had a blood pressure cuff on. He looked into our eyes.

"How are you?"

"Rough. Just a small back pain, but thankful to be here."

Miller said, "We did it!"

The Corpsman said, "Chow time is nearly over. Y'all need to hustle and get some."

We washed, pulled on dry denims and hurried off to mess well down the passageway.

Very soon the other two lifeboat crewmen were up and following us to mess. A cook was standing by to serve us. We all thanked him.

The next day I heard that John was in poor shape and would soon be air lifted to a hospital in Japan. He would later be medically discharged.

It was announced that evening our whole fleet would sail right into Vladivostok so we could turn around in its protected bay. We thought that was very sporting of them. The ship's company was restricted from being on deck and all portholes were battened and no photos were to be taken. Now the outside temperature was in the minus degrees with extremely high winds. We felt like we were in a submarine.

Our ship's next stop was in Japan where there was a dry dock. On approaching the dry dock all the available prop planes were lined up on the flight deck facing inboard secured to the deck. Half were forward and the rest aft. This was called a pinwheel. The aircraft prop pull was used to provide guidance into the narrow dock slot. Mooring lines from both sides were sent overboard on the dock where perhaps each line had one hundred men pulling on them. Between all of them the ship inched into the dry dock berth. A sudden gust of wind arose and caused the ship to bash against the entrance to the berth. After much tugging she was properly placed.

Then all the aircraft were lifted off by crane and put on rail cars. All their wings were folded up for transport to a near by airport.

The pumps were started to empty the sealed dry dock.

Avast! The dry dock doors were leaking! They worked on the doors all-night and late into the next day, but to no avail.

The ship went back into the bay with the tide. She was pulled out by tugs and then pushed into a docking.

An official schedule had this ship departing the line in late November and returning to the line after an overhaul stateside. All sorts of rumors were being told.

Chapter Forty

EXTRA DUTY

On my first shore liberty after our returning to port I visited the china shop where I had bought the tea set for my Mom last spring.

The proprietor said, "So good to see you! You are much thinner. Your order has recently been made and can now be picked up. Can Mama-San and the children all go up to Tokyo with you? The box is fairly large and more hands make easy work. We can then ship it to your home in California."

"Yes, of course they can come. That will be delightful!" We checked the train schedule.

We will arrive in Tokyo a little before noon, have lunch, see a temple and pick up the tea set in a little more than three hours. I was able to get a midweek pass by taking a day of leave and I bought round trip tickets for all of us.

On that day we had lunch at a 'famous place' near the train station. The popular temple was a few short blocks away and a few more to the manufacturer's location. Mama-San had a fold up cart with small wheels to put the box on. She could pull the box along on it.

While we were either traveling or at lunch and unknown to me an official announcement was made: "Starting at 1200 hours today all of Honshu Island Japan is quarantined for the next forty days due to the epidemic of gonorrhea. All military passes and personal service work permits are revoked."

Mama-San reminded me, "You can not go into this factory as it is for Japanese only. I take you to a famous place where many military go. It is nearby." She didn't know what it was known for, just that it was known to be military centered. "I will return for you in less than an hour." The streets were jammed with people and moving through them was slow. It turned out to be a men's only establishment so they were not allowed to go inside.

"That's okay. I'll sit where I can see you. Just wave and I will come out. I'll be watching."

I was undecided as to what I wanted as I rarely drink before dinner, and then it was a beer on a hot day. This day was quite cool. It was cold enough that I had worn my pea coat. I was the only patron in the house. The bar had a special for the day advertised at the door entrance. It was a mixture of tropical fruit juices and some rum. That sounded better than a beer and it was the same price.

"I would like one of those," pointing to the sign. A waitress took me to a table in the back. "I am surprised that you speak English."

"We all speak English here. We have many military customers come to this place. It is very unusual for us to be this quiet. You sit here with a nice view of door and outside, so you see family."

"Yes I would like to be able to see Mama-San when she comes back to get me." *How nice!* After being seated the waitress brought me a cozy and my drink.

"Can I use the restroom?"

"Of course." She pointed it out, so off I went. When I got back she was sitting in the outside chair. That way I would be able to see Mama San when she came. *That was thoughtful.* The waitress had a tall glass of something, which was the color of whiskey. I took a nice long swig of my tasty drink. "This is good." I asked, "I hear that it is forecast to become very stormy later today. When it is expected to start raining?"

"The news by local authorities said a very big storm with typhoon like winds would be here later today. They cannot give a time because it is so big and strong. Maybe in a few hours."

"Would a large storm interfere with the trains?"

"No. Nothing ever stops them." She was called to a telephone by the bartender and departed.

Shortly things started to get hazy and a bit dim. *Perhaps it was the clouds gathering and they were getting thicker.* It got darker after another swig and then much darker after the next one. I was unaware of when I passed out.

Mama San came to fetch me. She looked around while she was standing outside. I was nowhere to be seen. She asked the bartender "Where is my sailor friend?"

"There are no patrons in here, just the help. He departed a little while ago."

Mama-San had to hurry to catch the train that we had tickets for. At the train station she told the Military Police that I was not where I was supposed to be and where that was. She thought that to be odd. They told her, "That place and several others had recently been placed 'off limits' to all military personnel and that fact was well publicized." She scurried to get on the train.

A little later, the Military Police found me passed out on a bench up the street and around a corner only a few doors from that bar entrance. My wallet was empty of money but my pass and identification was still in it. I was told, "All shore leave and passes have been cancelled as of noon today." I was poured into a holding cell until the following morning when I was cuffed and transported to my base where I was escorted back to the ship and dumped in the brig.

At my Captain's Mast I was advised, "As of noon yesterday after I left the ship all liberty had been cancelled over the entire main island for all military personnel due to the gonorrhea epidemic." Then I was admonished for being 'off limits'. I should have paid attention and seen that there were no other military around an area that had attractions for military men.

My plea was, "I was not at any place where I could become aware of that announcement, and there were no signs posted on that building or anywhere around. How was I to know about it being off limits? Further I was not familiar with Tokyo. Also my pass expired several hours after the time I was taken into custody and I did nothing intentionally wrong."

Not one of my arguments mattered. I was off limits and shore leave was terminated in less than a few hours after I departed the ship. Guilty!

Since this was not the first Captain's Mast I have had, this time I had to serve a sentence. Commander Baker issued the sentence: "During this sentence any shore leave is limited to Saturdays from 1700 to 2100 hours. You are temporarily transferred ashore to serve the interests of the Navy. Your sentence will last until the day before this ship leaves this port, unless the Navy has other duty to further its interest for you to perform."

I was told where to go and to whom I should speak. I was given a stamped wax sealed letter of introduction to be opened only by the addressee. The ship would receive a letter of commendation for responding to help resolve the announced crisis.

I went immediately to that location. There I asked for an interview with a Miss Wadsworth.

"Do you have an appointment?"

"Not unless the ship made one for me. I was just told to come and see Miss Wadsworth, and I was to waste no time in doing so."

"Miss Wadsworth is not available this afternoon."

"When will she be available for an appointment?"

"I can make one for nine o'clock Monday morning. Will that do?"

"That will be fine. I have this sealed envelope to give to her. Should I leave it here now?"

"Yes, I will give it to her. One more thing, you must appear in dress blues for this meeting." I was wearing a winter undress uniform that was usually worn on base.

"Thank you." I left for the ship. On the way back I passed by the library. After many steps I thought, *Hey! This is a Friday afternoon and I have nothing to do the rest of today or weekend for that matter. Perhaps I can find what Jane had mentioned about the details of the female anatomy in the morgue lesson where the young woman was split up the middle.* I wanted to see the drawings and descriptions that were in the books. Jane had said they were inaccurate and vague.

I returned to the library and checked with the desk person.

"Am I allowed to be in here?"

"Yes, come in. May I see your identification?"

"Sure." I presented my card.

"If you are off a ship you're allowed to look at anything you want in this building. You're not able to check anything out to take back to the ship. We can hold items for you here for a month."

"That will be fine. I would like to look at an anatomy book."

"Follow me." She pointed the row out. "Reading desks are by those windows."

"Thank you."

"Welcome."

I found a book and went to the index and the pages and started to examine the drawings and text. They were rather generalized. Jane had pointed out a lot more detail. I was sitting where the sun was shining on me and I was soon napping.

A very attractive nurse came into the library and had been wandering around looking for something. She drifted my way to see what I was looking at before I fell asleep. I smelled something nice and fresh. It woke me up for a moment. I saw her strike an alluring pose close by. I nodded off again. She tapped my foot with hers, the military way to wake a person up. She pulled a chair up very close to me and asked, "Are you interested in this?"

"In what ma'am?"

"You seem to be showing an interest in this subject." Her left hand was moving over a drawing.

"Why, yes I am. I have a special interest." My interest indicator was showing an increasing level of interest. That attracted her attention. Her right hand was on her thigh. She was pointing and waving at the interest indication. I was embarrassed.

"That is good." She tapped her left index finger on the open book. Her finger was tapping on a drawing. "I can teach you something about this perhaps by using the brail system?" She rose, "Follow me," beckoning for me to come along. I followed as she briskly left the library for her apartment. I held a magazine to conceal my embarrassment. We paused at her door to introduce ourselves. She was Ginger.

Over a drink and in a friendly way Ginger quizzed me on everything I had done lately. She asked about where I had been, done what and with whom. In the twenty first century those same questions are asked when you donate blood. I answered all her questions. I told her how the oriental spices and smells had turned me off. Also the body odors in recent months were a huge factor for causing what I thought was my lower than average libido. Ginger clapped her hands sharply. I reacted with a quick jerk. She said, "I think you have two kinds of shock, they are shell and smell shock. I know of a remedy for both! Let's start with your nose." It was simply the use of several of our Americans common clean odors. She started with the items she had on hand, a popular tooth paste, several scented soaps and some light perfumes. We both brushed our teeth with the same toothpaste. Shipboard toothpaste had no taste or odor. I really missed those tastes and odors.

Ginger was coaxing me along. She had several things for me to do which were completed to the best of my ability. *A part of me wanted to fade. I felt that I was not up to par.*

"You know the adage, 'use it or lose it,' all you need is practice."

"I do indeed!" We worked diligently on my special problems all weekend and I made considerable improvement. She was impressed enough to want to continue our 'treatments' while the ship was in port if there was any possible way.

"I was told that I am to be transferred to some place ashore soon." I did not mention my sentence.

Monday morning she went to her office and I went aboard ship and put on my recently tailored dress blues and then went to my interview.

I was very surprised that Ginger was my nine o'clock morning appointment! The secretary gave us a formal introduction.

"I'm pleased to meet you Miss Wadsworth."

"I'm pleased to meet you Seaman Scott."

Ginger had a specialty in women's health and was attached to a public health clinic. She mentioned the cancellation of shore leave for all units.

"I sure know about that! I got caught up in that when I went up to Tokyo for the afternoon. That is why I am here."

"Well, maybe we can make some things better. We are quite short of help. Maybe I can get you into that unit."

Temporary assistants were recruited mostly from Corpsmen in the fleet and trained on the job. My being a medic trainee was sufficient for openers. I would have to prove my worth. Personnel probed into every detail about what I did as a medic. From that they thought I could help with the examinations. I got the complete tour of the facility by the staff

A doctor took the time to show me what I was looking at, the good, the bad, and the indifferent. "There is no time to delay. See it, act on it. If there is any doubt whatsoever take a swab right away."

During this wide spread epidemic all prostitutes in Japan had their license revoked. Every medical center swabbed each prostitute as they all had to be cleared by lab test results and a physician's examination.

A word about the exam: The patients were seated and situated by local Japanese assistants. The exterior pelvic area was examined for any anomaly. We examined the outer labia for adhesion, growths, discharge, discoloration or edema. Next we inserted a lubed speculum vaginally, opened up the calipers and pressed down with the left hand to depress the bladder area. A light was beside the table. We used a head reflector to better see up the vaginal channel. We were looking for discharge that may be squeezed out or a sign of any abnormality. If anything appeared we took a swab sample and streaked a media plate, and then we gave it to one of the attendants. They labeled the plate and ran it to the lab. Those with infections had to be inspected by a medical doctor before a work permit was issued, and then a temporary work card could be issued. All the 'working girls' were inspected every three days. The examination room was arranged in a square of four examination tables. We all had chairs with rollers and went from one prepared girl to the next.

When the doctor felt I was competent to do the inspections I was appointed to the position of an inspection specialist. I would have to report every day to Miss Wadsworth. Since I was the newest person I was last to report. The place was in the lobby of a nurses' resident building, now nearly empty.

Ginger arranged for me to have a room in the back of that building. It was close to the examination center and all the medics doing the exams were also being quartered in that building. There was room enough for four occupants in each apartment. They were quite nice accommodations with a tub, desk and easy chairs. Also it was quite close to the E & O Clubs. They had television sets, which were quite an attraction!

There I met Wanda the nurse in charge of that building, which recently had been set aside for a proposed program for women who were suffering from various nervous conditions generated by being near the front lines.

We started early and worked late. By the end of forty days the gonorrhea epidemic was controlled enough to lift the shore leave ban.

Several months ago Ginger had put in a transfer request to serve stateside in the northeast. It came through before the end of my sixth week. Ginger, Wanda and I were taking a smoke break waiting for Ginger's transportation to arrive. Sometime before she left Ginger had told Wanda about some of the massage techniques I had used on her. Wanda was recruiting crew and supervising patients' needs of a new program where massages were part of the treatment program. I might be a crew candidate.

Wanda said, "We will have to have a talk sometime soon."

"Any time that suits you."

Ginger was replaced with a gynecology doctor. He was Dr. White, a by the book kind of a person. You would know where you stood at all times. I continued checking the women. Dr. White watched all of us do inspections very closely. We worked side by side for about a week. He had a few tricks of his own. With the epidemic controlled he wanted most of us who had this experience to continue doing inspections part-time along with other duties.

Wanda ran me down as I was washing up to go on my lunch break, "Zak can we have that talk over lunch?"

"Sure."

Wanda had a similar background as Ginger. Also she had some news about my ship.

"I had a few drinks with some of the officers from your ship yesterday evening. It is dockside. All the squadrons have departed and most of the crew are being used to replace the needs of the Pacific Command. They knew for sure that the ship would be in a dry dock somewhere for at least three or four months."

"Say Wanda, by chance do you know about getting into schools? I heard a few guys talking about how difficult it is now and that quite a few have been rejected because they had discipline actions in their records."

"I have heard something like that too and I should know about that since I am getting into this new program and will have to help in the crew selection. The whole program is slow now but will pick up very soon. Our patients will have to be referred."

We went to the Personnel Office right after lunch to ask about that possible problem. They told us, "As of the first of October one Captain's Mast is a total bar for applicants applying for all schools. We are swamped with applications for every school."

I do have two Captains Masts in my record. Now, I'm sunk!

We wandered back to our duty stations. "Zak, I am pleased that your Captain Mast has the clause; unless the Navy has other duty to further its interest for you to perform.' Would you be interested in learning enough massage to be of use in the medical research starting up here? Doctor White is in charge. Maybe if you help us we can help you."

"Yes, I am very interested!" *That may be just the right thing for me to do.*

Very soon, Dr. White, Wanda and I had a conference. We started with my Captain's Masts. Dr. White started, "I had a talk with Lt. Commander Mason, a Navy attorney formerly from your ship and now on this base. He said that he knew all about you and that the Captain could set aside that non-judicial punishment action since he made them in the first place. Zak, if you were to work in my program and do well I may be able to help get your record cleared up. Also your work here will be very valuable for your getting into a school of your choice and your being at sea for a year is assurance of a leadership position while there. Both would serve to better your chances to go to an advanced school and for a promotion."

"I am very interested and anxious to start. I will sure do my best!"

"My recommendation would have greater standing if the time period were six months or more. People in personnel generally feel that a few weeks is generally not enough time to access a person's worth and good work. We know for sure that your ship is going to her homeport stateside for a short stay, then return for another cruise."

"I am willing to participate in your program until the ship finishes its next tour. Will your program last that long?"

"I'm very sure it will last longer than the scheduled tour. We are thinking of a year."

Later that day I was working with Robin, a massage therapist part-time. Many patients in this group had low back pain and tightness in the shoulders. She started using the Swedish long strokes with thumb pressure for some deep knots. Oriental methods were also taught and applied. I told her about a massage like procedure that Jane had me use on her and Ingrid that had good results on them. She asked for several demonstrations to be sure I was consistent.

"It will fall in the massage category and I'm quite sure it will become a part of the treatment regime. I will tell Dr. White and Wanda about it." Wanda would require several demonstrations also.

Dr. White had recruited several other Corpsmen for this project. The program was not starting off very well. He thought it would take some more time for the project to get up to expected levels. Referrals were the source for getting patients in this program. In the meantime he took on the task of offering us some training in gynecology. He had us follow him around on his rounds and assist his patients in the wards. We were instructed in their nursing care. He had us attend and assist some birthing deliveries that he conducted. I was amazed at how tough the female body was and the great amount of pain they could endure! As a child I had been told that women were delicate, like chinaware. They are not!

Each week Wanda assigned each of us volunteers two or three companions. We were to take them to meals and treat them as if we were best friends. If they asked for something I made sure they got it promptly. Every morning I served them coffee in bed. They loved that! I was desperate to get a good recommendation, as it would be a huge help to my entire future. I took to every task with great energy and interest.

All the women in the program received massage, meditation, hypnosis, physiotherapy and several other specialized therapies. For the most part American women rejected meditation where European and Asian women thought highly of it. What we all used that had good results was conversation, personal attention and some entertainment including ballroom dancing. Also on Saturdays there was a very nice hotel that received recordings of the City Services Marching Band's weekly radio program. After that there was a dance to popular music. Both were well attended and were a good social connection for the women.

There were many different responses to the treatments, which would lead to a different diagnosis and treatment regime. We reported and discussed every detail of every patient.

A little after my term was up Dr. White would separate the all-inclusive diagnosis into several various treatments. That happened in July of 1953.

Chapter Forty-One

DISCIPLINE PROBLEMS

After the latest tour of duty for my ship was completed I was transferred back aboard and soon was called into the ship's Personnel Office. I had a talk with Chief Petty Officer, Karl Pitcher who had been reviewing and approving applications for naval specialty schools for several years in Washington D.C. His turn for sea duty had again arrived.

"The Navy has had very good recruiting results and is well staffed. What that means is that the requirements for career schools has increased. For you the most difficult part will be your personal record. I see that you have had two Captain's Masts. At this time one is a complete barrier to being allowed to enter any of the Navy's schools."

"Neither was the result of my intentional wrong doing but of happenstance. I have done several tasks to prove my earnest worth by taking tasks others shied from. Is there anything that can be done to put those aside and allow me to become eligible for school?"

"I can talk to the Captain and the Executive Officer and see if those can be excused. You did serve your sentence and assisted in other pursuits as requested by the Navy and they have written favorable recommendations. I personally think that is commendable as were your other duties ashore that are noted in this file. Zak, I will pull some strings for you."

"Thank you. I would appreciate that very much."

WAR WOUNDS

En route to its homeport, San Diego, the ship stopped in Hawaii a few days to off load most of the squadrons and their crew and we conducted carrier-landing qualifications for the pilots stationed there.

Mum had written that business was very slow because the locals were going to the larger town a dozen miles away to buy dry goods and she was having difficulty making ends meet. I mailed some money home and wrote a letter to her saying that I had asked for some leave time, however there was no guarantee I could get much if any time off. I might not qualify for a school because I had some glitches on my record. I was trying to do something to clear that up. In the meantime I was most likely to remain aboard ship until my records were cleared and that is likely to take quite some time. The ship was definitely leaving for an east coast port a few days after arriving in San Diego.

A day after leaving Hawaii I was called to Chief Pitcher's office. He had news for me. "The ship's Executive Office has agreed to excuse your discipline records and write a letter saying your service has been average. That will get you accepted to school. However, that will only add one more page to your monstrous personnel file which is thicker than most men who have served for thirty years!" He had my file on his desk. It had a big red and green label and was close to an inch thick. He held it up. "Zak this is another problem."

"How did it get so thick and why does mine have a red and green label?"

"The red means you have disciplinary and the green indicates good but unusual issues. Yours is the only one I have seen with both red and green. It's due to your being missing in action a few times and the loss of your ID in a combat zone added a lot of paper. All those records are in here. There is more. Your being a volunteer has added more pages, however meritorious. Honestly Zak, I don't think anyone is going to wade through all this and come up with an acceptance for you. I have gone through the whole thing and it was something of chore, granted an interesting one. The reviewers are in the habit of seeing smaller clearer files. Let me show you one." He had several in his out file box. They all had only about half a dozen pages and had no collared marks on their covers. "I discussed this with Commander Baker who referred

341

me to Commander Mason who said he is very aware of you and your situation. He has concerns about your volunteering for service with the Aussies without first getting orders or permission from the Navy. There is a possibility of a court martial on that matter. He said that it could get quite complicated. His recommendation was for us to completely expunge your file. That would eliminate nearly all files in your jacket including your recent recommendations and all your other service. It will only show your service aboard this ship. You can take a few days to decide if you like."

"Will that remove the colors on my file?"

"Definitely, there will be no need for them and your new record will have familiar files for the reviewers."

"Will I be competitive then?

"Very much so! Think of it like you will all be in the same correct uniform and you will be ahead because of your sea duty and the ribbons earned by being on the ship. That I can guarantee!"

I just can't blow my whole future for a few favorable comments! I really need to do this!

"I don't need several days to decide. Clear the record so I can go to school. Nothing is more important. I have a compulsion to do this! Anyway most of what has happened is happenstance and I don't need to be held down forever by all of that."

"That is a sound choice. I will pull the strings by telephoning some of my former associates as soon as we dock in San Diego. Your record will show only your service aboard this ship. There would be no mention of any other service. Agreed?"

"Agreed."

"Your decorations will be those earned while serving as a crew member aboard this ship."

"Very good. Thank you."

I was very thankful for not being shackled by happenstance and to have been given a chance to start over with a clean slate. Best of all, I had served decently and survived. Still I felt haunted with the thought; *your work is not done!*

Chapter Forty-Two

GOING HOME

Axiom: To ignore a person is to cause great personal harm.
Our ship was precisely on time entering San Diego Bay. All available hands were called up to the flight deck in dress uniform where we lined the entire flight deck's perimeter.

As the ship entered the bay it quietly slipped through a thick fog bank. From across the bay a political dignitary was making a speech. We heard a few words and a cheer. In a moment a few bars of music from a band playing a march faintly drifted across the water.

Our ship moved into her moorings. Gangways were attached. There were many bleachers on the tarmac now holding only five wives and three small children, all with coats pulled up close to ward off the coolness of the foggy breeze. All were nicely dressed with hats and shiny shoes. Only five cars were parked in the vast area behind the bleachers.

There was no crowd, no band, no photographers, and no news reporters. There was only silence. The huge thick fog bank followed us in and was streaming inside the ship's hangar deck through the large openings in the carrier's side. The fog flowed from starboard to port and had ghostliness about it. It was cold, damp, grey and deathly quiet.

I was having a déjà vu, a momentary premonition. I felt that I had been here, heard this, and seen this all before. I was in a line waiting to go ashore on the huge now empty hangar deck that was cold and gloomy. A Chief Petty officer was answering someone's question, "Why all the silence?"

"We have performed our duty well and upheld our national honor. It is not proper for us to cheer ourselves."

On docking I had a thirty-six hour pass. I would be able to drive up home and take my parents out to breakfast or lunch and then catch the express train back. I should arrive home in the early morning hours.

I was looking forward to a stop for a hamburger. I was in my dress blues with my service ribbons. I was not noticed by anyone. I sat at the counter in a diner. My waitress never looked at me. She asked, "What will you have?" She was intent on looking out the window and down the street. That hamburger and coke sure hit the spot! I had really missed that combination!

I arrived home at two in the morning. No one was at home. There was a note on the refrigerator door saying that mom and my stepdad would be back late Monday evening. They had gone to visit my stepfather's daughter in the valley. There was a list of things for me to eat on the refrigerator's door.

In the morning I washed my car and called the former classmate who had expressed an interest in my car a few years ago. He bought it and dashed off.

I had hopes of getting a ride to the express train station in a city some dozen miles away. I called and looked up a few friends. They all had moved away or were not available. In my dress blues I started to hitch hike the twelve miles to the train station where I could board the train.

A World War II Veteran, an Army Air Force Transport Crewman, picked me up. "Hi, I'm Sam. I served in the Pacific with the Army Air Force Transport in World War Two."

"Hi, I'm Zak a Navy Medical trainee, Korea."

"Were you on the line?"

"Yes."

"I'm pleased to meet someone who made it back!" We shook hands.

That would be the only acknowledgement of any kind I would get or hear about concerning the war in Korea for the next thirty years. My wife, then of twenty years finally asked after another restless night, "What happened over there?"

The End

Printed in the United States
By Bookmasters